Reception,
Appropriation,
Recollection

Religions and Discourse

Edited by James M. M. Francis

Volume 33

PETER LANG
Oxford · Bern · Berlin · Bruxelles · Frankfurt am Main · New York · Wien

W. R. Owens and Stuart Sim (eds)

Reception, Appropriation, Recollection

Bunyan's *Pilgrim's Progress*

PETER LANG
Oxford · Bern · Berlin · Bruxelles · Frankfurt am Main · New York · Wien

Bibliographic information published by Die Deutsche Bibliothek
Die Deutsche Bibliothek lists this publication in the Deutsche National-
bibliografie; detailed bibliographic data is available on the Internet at
‹http://dnb.ddb.de›.

British Library and Library of Congress Cataloguing-in-Publication Data:
A catalogue record for this book is available from *The British Library*,
Great Britain, and from *The Library of Congress*, USA

ISSN 1422-8998
ISBN 3-03910-720-8
US-ISBN 0-8204-7983-7

© Peter Lang AG, International Academic Publishers, Bern 2007
Hochfeldstrasse 32, Postfach 746, CH-3000 Bern 9, Switzerland
info@peterlang.com, www.peterlang.com, www.peterlang.net

All rights reserved.
All parts of this publication are protected by copyright.
Any utilisation outside the strict limits of the copyright law, without
the permission of the publisher, is forbidden and liable to prosecution.
This applies in particular to reproductions, translations, microfilming,
and storage and processing in electronic retrieval systems.

Printed in Germany

Contents

Acknowledgements	7
List of Contributors	9
Note on Text	13
Frontispiece to the third edition of *The Pilgrim's Progress*	14

W. R. OWENS AND STUART SIM
Introduction — 15

VINCENT NEWEY
1   Bunyan's Afterlives: Case Studies — 25

DAVID WALKER
2   Bunyan's Reception in the Romantic Period — 49

NORMAN VANCE
3   Pilgrims Abounding: Bunyan and the Victorian Novel — 69

NATHALIE COLLÉ-BAK
4   The Role of Illustrations in the Reception of
    The Pilgrim's Progress — 81

MARY HAMMOND
5   *The Pilgrim's Progress* and its Nineteenth-Century
    Publishers — 99

ISABEL HOFMEYR
6   Evangelical Realism: The Transnational Making of Genre
    in *The Pilgrim's Progress* — 119

	RICHARD DANSON BROWN	
7	Everyman's Progresses: Louis MacNeice's Dialogues with Bunyan	147
	JULIE CAMPBELL	
8	'A Mighty Maze of Walks': Bunyan's *The Pilgrim's Progress* and Beckett's *Molloy*	165
	MICHAEL DAVIES	
9	The Relevant Pilgrim: John Bunyan in *A Matter of Life and Death*	185
	STUART SIM	
10	Bunyan and his Fundamentalist Readers	213
Bibliography		229
Index		247

Acknowledgements

The essays included in this volume were first delivered as papers at the fourth triennial conference of the International John Bunyan Society held at Bedford, 1–5 September 2004. The conference was organised jointly by colleagues at the Open University and De Montfort University, and we are grateful to both institutions for their support. We are also grateful to Joanna Turner for her help in turning the manuscript into camera-ready copy, and to the International John Bunyan Society for a grant towards publication. Most of all, we wish to thank our contributors for their willingness to submit their essays for inclusion, and for agreeing to the various revisions necessary for publication in this volume.

W. R. Owens and *Stuart Sim*

List of Contributors

JULIE CAMPBELL is Lecturer in Literature and Drama at the University of Southampton. Her main area of research is the work of Samuel Beckett and she has published a number of articles and reviews on Beckett's prose fiction and drama.

NATHALIE COLLÉ-BAK is Maître de Conférence (Lecturer) at Université Nancy 2, France, where she teaches English literature and phonetics. Her doctoral thesis, defended in November 2002, was 'Illustrating a Classic: A Study of the Editorial and Iconographic Traditions of John Bunyan's *The Pilgrim's Progress* from 1678 to 1850'. Among her other research interests are book history, reading and reception, religious and popular iconography, and text-image relationships. She has given a dozen papers and published several articles on these subjects.

RICHARD DANSON BROWN is Lecturer in Literature at the Open University. He is the author of *The New Poet: Novelty and Tradition in Spenser's 'Complaints'* (1999), and is co-editor of *Shakespeare 1609: 'Cymbeline' and 'The Sonnets'* (2000), *A Shakespeare Reader: Sources and Criticism* (2000), and *Aestheticism and Modernism* (2005). His latest book, *Louis MacNeice and the Poetry of the 1930s,* is forthcoming.

MICHAEL DAVIES is Lecturer in English at the University of Liverpool. He is the author of *Graceful Reading: Theology and Narrative in the Works of John Bunyan* (2002), and has published essays on various subjects from Shakespeare to Bunyan and other Restoration writers.

MARY HAMMOND is Lecturer in Literature and Book History at the Open University. She is the author of *Reading, Publishing and the Formation of Literary Taste in England 1880–1914* (2006), and is editor, with Shafquat Towheed, of a volume of essays on *Publishing in the First World War* (forthcoming). Among her other publications are a number of articles on fiction and publishing in the nineteenth century, and she is currently working on the development at the Open University of the 'Reading Experience Database 1450–1945'.

ISABEL HOFMEYR is Professor of African Literature at the University of the Witwatersrand in Johannesburg, South Africa. She works in the field of postcolonial literary studies. Her books include *'We Spend Our Years as a Tale That Is Told': Oral Historical Storytelling in a South African Chiefdom* (1993), and *The Portable Bunyan: A Transnational History of 'The Pilgrim's Progress'* (2004).

VINCENT NEWEY is Professor of English at the University of Leicester. He is editor of *The Pilgrim's Progress: Critical and Historical Views* (1980) and has published extensively on Bunyan and other writers of the Puritan tradition. His books include *Cowper's Poetry: A Critical Study and Reassessment* (1982), *Centring the Self: Subjectivity, Society and Reading from Thomas Gray to Thomas Hardy* (1995), and *The Scriptures of Charles Dickens: Novels of Ideology, Novels of the Self* (2004). He is a Past President of the British Association for Romantic Studies, the field of other of his major publications and scholarly interests.

W. R. OWENS is Professor of English Literature at the Open University. His publications include two volumes in the Oxford *Miscellaneous Works of John Bunyan* (1994), editions of *Grace Abounding* (1987) and *The Pilgrim's Progress* (2003), and a co-edited collection of essays, *John Bunyan and his England, 1628–88* (1990). From 2001 to 2004 he was President of the International John Bunyan Society, and he is editor, with Stuart Sim, of the journal *Bunyan Studies*. He is also the author, with P. N. Furbank, of four books on Daniel Defoe, and they are joint General Editors of *The Works of Daniel Defoe* (44 vols, in progress).

STUART SIM is Professor of Critical Theory at the University of Sunderland. He has published widely on modern critical and cultural theory as well as on seventeenth- and eighteenth-century prose fiction. His books include *Negotiations with Paradox: Narrative Practice and Narrative Form in Bunyan and Defoe* (1990), *Bunyan and Authority* (2000, with David Walker), *Post-Marxism: An Intellectual History* (2000), *Fundamentalist World: The New Dark Age of Dogma* (2004), and *Empires of Belief: Why We Need More Scepticism and Doubt in the Twenty-First Century* (2006).

NORMAN VANCE is Professor of English at the University of Sussex. His publications include *The Sinews of the Spirit: The Ideal of Christian Manliness in Victorian Literature and Religious Thought* (1985), *Irish Literature, a Social History* (1990; 2nd edn 1999), *The Victorians and Ancient Rome* (1997) and *Irish Literature since 1800* (2002). He is currently working on a study of fiction and secularization.

DAVID WALKER is Senior Lecturer in English at the University of Northumbria at Newcastle. He is the author, with Stuart Sim, of *Bunyan and Authority: The Rhetoric of Dissent and the Legitimation Crisis in Seventeenth-Century England* (2000) and *The Discourse of Sovereignty from Hobbes to Fielding* (2003) and is the editor of volume 2 of the series *British Satire, 1785–1840* (2003). He is Book Reviews Editor of *Bunyan Studies*.

Note on Text

Throughout this volume, references to *The Pilgrim's Progress* are keyed to the following edition:

> *The Pilgrim's Progress*, ed. W. R. Owens, Oxford World's Classics edition (Oxford: Oxford University Press, 2003).

References are included in parentheses in the text, in the form: *PP*, followed by the page number.

Printed for Nat: Ponder in the Poultry.

W. R. OWENS AND STUART SIM

Introduction

Few authors have seen their reputations alter as much over the years as John Bunyan. Literary reputations traditionally go up and down, but Bunyan's has been the subject of a dramatic series of reappraisals over the last three centuries. Here is an author capable of being appropriated to the cause of groups as diverse in their goals as Evangelical preachers, Chartist revolutionaries, Christian missionaries, and Marxist intellectuals. Surveying the reception of *The Pilgrim's Progress* (1678, 1684), we find its author being regarded first as a religious enthusiast and prisoner of conscience who happened also to be an untutored natural genius, then as a literary craftsman who is among the founders of the English novel and a social and political commentator of penetrating psychological acuity. In this continuing process of reappraisal, Bunyan has made his way in from the margins to the very centre of Western culture, not least in the way the West has impressed its values on the rest of the world since his day, spreading *The Pilgrim's Progress* wherever the Bible went as a popular handbook for its belief system. Bunyan's most famous and enduring work has long since transcended mere national barriers to give us 'transnational' Bunyan, a figure received, appropriated and recollected by a succession of generations and cultural traditions right through into the twenty-first century.

Nowhere is the diversity of Bunyan's appeal more apparent than in our own day, where the author has become a subject of intense academic interest, with scholars eager to track down new evidence of his imprint on global culture from a variety of critical perspectives. The present volume of essays, drawn from the International John Bunyan Society's fourth triennial conference in Bedford in 2004, is testimony to the extent of Bunyan's legacy, and of his pilgrim's 'progress' into an impressively wide range of contexts. The Bunyan pictured in these pages is an author who has inspired readers across the ideological spectrum and right across the world, including colonizers and colonized alike. *The Pilgrim's Progress* has, in a variety of complex and sometimes unexpected ways influenced not only other writers, but religious leaders, political radicals, film-makers, and visual artists as well.[1] Bunyan has been a global success in religious, commercial, and aesthetic terms, at some points a cultural hero beyond criticism (as the Victorians tended to regard him), at others a figure of considerable controversy. To this day there is a notable divide in his readership between those who appreciate Bunyan primarily for his religious message (one suspects he will always be a hero to the more radical of Protestant believers), and those for whom his literary achievement is what matters most. That divide is present within the academic establishment itself, where some privilege the literary qualities of Bunyan's work, others highlight its theological and religious aspects, and others value it as having an essentially political significance. From at least the Romantic period onwards, *The Pilgrim's Progress* has been celebrated for its literary merits, but a growing number of studies have focused on its political significance. Political approaches have indeed probably dominated somewhat from the time of the appearance of Christopher Hill's influential Marxist readings of seventeenth-century British society, with Bunyan as a critical figure within these readings. Much of the earlier writing about Bunyan was from a religious perspective, and it is noticeable that in recent scholarship Bunyan's theological purposes have again been advanced as a central component of his vision and achievement, and this 'pro-theological' camp is becoming more assertive within Bunyan studies generally. International Bunyan conferences can be lively affairs when these various constituencies confront and interact with each other, but such controversy and intellectual engagement can only be to the good.

1   For studies of Bunyan's influence on visual artists, see Kathleen Powers Erickson, 'Pilgrims and Strangers: The Role of *The Pilgrim's Progress* and *The Imitation of Christ* in Shaping the Piety of Vincent van Gogh', *Bunyan Studies*, 4 (1991), 7–36; Glyn Hughes, 'Barry Burman's *Pilgrim's Progress*', *Bunyan Studies*, 9 (1999/2000), 69–76.

Looking back over the reception history of *The Pilgrim's Progress*, several clear trends of interpretation become apparent. Initially and no doubt predictably given the socio-political circumstances of Restoration England, it is the theological or evangelical aspect that is the main source of the work's appeal. The Preface to the first French edition of 1685 was kept short because, as the translator put it, 'we would rather present [the work] to you directly so that you can test by your own experience what is being provided for your Christian contemplation and judgment'.[2] Through the adventures of his pilgrim Christian, Bunyan, himself a martyr-like figure for his twelve-year imprisonment at the hands of the Restoration regime, articulates a nonconformist message full of hope for his persecuted brethren: they will ultimately prevail, unlike the Worldly-Wisemen from the town of Carnal-Policy or the great Lords of Vanity Fair who seem to be in control. The commitment to religious belief is the attraction here, a commitment maintained no matter what trials are placed in Christian's way, from the 'foul *Fiend*' Apollyon, through the show-trial at Vanity Fair, to imprisonment by Giant Despair.

Over the course of the eighteenth century, however, Bunyan's reputation subtly changes. Often somewhat grudgingly, his literary ability comes to be recognized, although it is not necessarily considered to be of the highest order. In David Hume's infamous judgement,

> Whoever would assert an equality of genius and eloquence between OGILBY and MILTON, or BUNYAN and ADDISON, would be thought to defend no less an extravagance, than if he had maintained a mole-hill to be as high as TENERIFFE, or a pond as extensive as the ocean.[3]

Hume's lofty strictures notwithstanding, during the eighteenth century Bunyan enters into his 'untutored genius' period, someone whose natural talent rises above the meanness of his social position, his

---

2 Cited in *The Pilgrim's Progress: A Selection of Critical Essays*, ed. Roger Sharrock (London and Basingstoke: Macmillan, 1976), p. 44.
3 David Hume, 'Of the Standard of Taste' (originally published in *Four Dissertations*, 1757), cited in ibid., p. 50. (John Ogilby (1600–1706) was the author of verse translations of Virgil and Homer.)

meagre learning, and the political turmoil of his time. The author of a Preface to a handsome edition of *The Pilgrim's Progress* published in 1728 paid generous tribute to Bunyan's skill in handling his allegory, but thought it extraordinary that 'a plain, simple Man, as Mr. *Bunyan* was, without the Assistance of any profound Learning or Erudition, should, notwithstanding, have composed so useful and admirable a Treatise'. Gradually, the claims for his literary ability become grander, until we find Samuel Johnson in 1773 placing *The Pilgrim's Progress* in some very heavyweight company indeed: 'It is remarkable, that it begins very much like the poem of Dante; yet there was no translation of Dante when Bunyan wrote. There is reason to think that he had read Spenser'.[4] Bunyan's literary stock is unmistakably rising.

Possibly the most famous verdict on Bunyan in the Romantic period comes from Coleridge, who declared that 'the Bunyan of Parnassus' is to be preferred to the 'the Bunyan of the Conventicle'.[5] Coleridge here neatly distinguishes between Bunyan the religious polemicist and Bunyan the literary artist, and the distinction is one that has had a profound (if in some ways also baneful) influence right up to our own day, as the description above of the current state of Bunyan studies in academic circles would indicate. Sir Walter Scott similarly sought to emphasize literary merit over theological intentions or political implications in Bunyan. It might have surprised Coleridge however to see just how widely the 'conventicle' aspect of Bunyan's work could be interpreted by later generations. It is that side that appeals to political radicals more than the strictly literary (hard though it is to separate these nowadays, in the view of most literary scholars). The Bunyan who advocates that we continue our pilgrimage towards our chosen goal, resisting the disruptive tactics of our enemies as best we can on our difficult and dangerous path through life, speaks to enthusiasts of all persuasions. Standing up for and even being prepared to suffer for your beliefs communicates a powerful message, as the Chartists were among the first specifically political movements to recognize in Bunyan. It is easy to identify with the heroic pilgrim figure struggling against the odds. John James Bezer, a Chartist leader

---

4   From James Boswell's *Life of Samuel Johnson* (1791), cited in ibid., p. 51.
5   Coleridge, in a note of 1830, cited in ibid., p. 53.

who re-read *The Pilgrim's Progress* while in prison for his political activities, found that this was the aspect of the book that spoke most immediately to him: 'Glorious Bunyan, you too were a "Rebel", and I love you *doubly* for *that*'.[6]

Yet the Victorians managed to transform this Bunyan into a much more broadly representative figure, one who exemplified all that was best in British culture, a culture which could be exported wherever Britain's influence extended. *The Pilgrim's Progress* was turned into a means of moral instruction, for British Sunday School children and colonized native peoples around the globe alike. It became a book that could be found just about anywhere on earth. Its specifically seventeenth-century nonconformist character was, predictably enough, severely diluted by this development, although it was never to go away entirely, as its impact on such figures as William Hale White ('Mark Rutherford' in his authorial guise) would demonstrate. More significantly, 'transnational Bunyan' was subjected to some very creative reinterpretation on the part of his readership within colonized communities. African Bunyan, Chinese Bunyan, or Japanese Bunyan is manifestly not White Anglo-Saxon Protestant Bunyan. His readers have never been slow in adapting Bunyan to their own cultural concerns. The sociology of Bunyan's transnational reception history is a fascinating topic in its own right, as scholars such as Isabel Hofmeyr have amply proved.[7]

Concurrently with this trend, however, Bunyan has continued to be admired and analysed for his literary skill, and as we pass into the twentieth century it is this that comes to predominate. Increasingly, Bunyan takes his place within the history of the novel, with *The Pilgrim's Progress* being held not just to prefigure the novel tradition in English, but to establish some of its major themes and preoccupations. According to Arnold Kettle's assessment, what makes *The*

---

6   Cited in *Testaments of Radicalism: Memoirs of Working Class Politicians 1790–1885*, ed. David Vincent (London: Europa, 1977), p. 167.

7   See Isabel Hofmeyr, *The Portable Bunyan: A Transnational History of 'The Pilgrim's Progress'* (Princeton, NJ: Princeton University Press, 2004). For 'Japanese' Bunyan, see Kazuko Nishimura, 'Bunyan's Reception in Japan', *Bunyan Studies*, 1:2 (1989), 49–62.

Pilgrim's Progress and *The Life and Death of Mr. Badman* a part of the tradition of the English novel is their 'realism': 'a concern with the actual, unimaginary problems of living besetting the average man and woman of the time'.[8] *Mr. Badman*'s realism may be the more obvious, with its non-allegorical setting in a seventeenth-century urban context, but at the very least we can say that *The Pilgrim's Progress* is a proto-novel, and critical to our understanding of how the novel subsequently developed. The clear link between Bunyan's 'Giant Despair' and Defoe's 'Island Despair' in *Robinson Crusoe* is there to see for anyone who cares to delve into the early history of the English novel, and Bunyan is now firmly part of the English literary canon in this respect.

The range of interpretations of Bunyan offered in contemporary literary criticism is impressively wide, with historicist, feminist, deconstructive, postcolonial and postmodernist readings, for example, all competing for our attention. Bunyan remains a source of considerable fascination within the academy, an author guaranteed to arouse critical controversy. This range of interpretations is extended in the present volume, which may claim, indeed, to be the first book entirely devoted to tracing some of the many ways *The Pilgrim's Progress* has been received, appropriated, and recollected from the author's day to our own.[9]

The keynote is sounded in the opening essay by Vincent Newey in a wide-ranging exploration of some of Bunyan's 'afterlives'. In 'case studies' of the influence of Bunyan on writers from the eighteenth and nineteenth centuries such as William Cowper, Charles

---

8   Arnold Kettle, *An Introduction to the English Novel*, 2 vols (second edn, London: Hutchinson, 1967), I, 40.

9   A number of valuable articles have discussed the reception of Bunyan and *The Pilgrim's Progress*. See Richard L. Greaves, 'Bunyan through the Centuries: Some Reflections', *English Studies*, 64 (1983), 113–21; N. H. Keeble, '"Of him thousands daily Sing and talk": Bunyan and his Reputation', in *John Bunyan: Conventicle and Parnassus*, ed. N. H. Keeble (Oxford: Clarendon Press, 1988), pp. 241–63; W. R. Owens, 'The Reception of *The Pilgrim's Progress* in England', and Jacques B. H. Alblas, 'The Reception of *The Pilgrim's Progress* in Holland during the Eighteenth and Nineteenth Centuries', in *Bunyan in England and Abroad*, eds M. van Os and G. J. Schutte (Amsterdam: VU University Press, 1990), pp. 91–104, 121–32.

Dickens, George Eliot and William Hale White ('Mark Rutherford'), as well as on a Hollywood movie and a twentieth-century novel by Peter Ackroyd, Newey finds *The Pilgrim's Progress* to be a significant precursor text – but not in any simple or straightforward sense. Rather, he finds 'appropriation for fresh purposes, a revised perspective, often a going against the grain'. This complex and sometimes paradoxical history of Bunyan's reception is a theme of all the essays that follow.

For David Walker, a defining moment in the reception of Bunyan comes with the publication in 1830 of Robert Southey's edition of *The Pilgrim's Progress*. His essay provides a detailed account of the famous and influential reviews of that edition by Scott and Macaulay, demonstrating how in each case the literary judgements of these critics were coloured and shaped by their widely divergent responses to the political developments of the seventeenth century. Whereas for Scott (and Southey, in his Introduction) Bunyan is a figure who rises above the religious and political turmoil and fanaticism of his age, Macaulay sees Bunyan's religious beliefs as charged with political significance, and as indivisible from their seventeenth-century context. Macaulay's approach, however, would not be picked up again until the twentieth century.

Norman Vance takes us further into the nineteenth century, showing in his essay how Bunyan became a significant influence on a wide range of novelists, even when – or perhaps particularly when – these later novelists were far from sharing or endorsing Bunyan's world-view. As he suggests, most Victorian writers would have read *The Pilgrim's Progress* in childhood – 'a time of extreme imaginative responsiveness' – and the effects of this early reading can been seen in the work of writers as diverse as Charles Kingsley, Thomas Hardy, and Mary Ward. One of the most frequently mentioned aspects of childhood experience of reading *The Pilgrim's Progress* in the nineteenth century was the part played by illustrations to the text. This is the theme of Nathalie Collé-Bak's essay, and what she demonstrates is how illustration came to assume a greater and greater prominence, to the point where there were even editions of *The Pilgrim's Progress* comprised *solely* of pictures, where the text was entirely absent. Her argument is that illustration has played a key role in shaping readers' experiences of *The Pilgrim's Progress*, and has been instrumental in the work's evolving and changing reception.

Mary Hammond's focus is also on the publishing history of *The Pilgrim's Progress* in the nineteenth century. Her research demonstrates not only that there were many different 'markets' for this famous book, to which publishers responded, but that an analysis of these various editions can reveal much about the larger shift from a predominantly religious culture in the Victorian period to the much more secular culture that developed in the later nineteenth century and into the twentieth. She finds this large shift mirrored in the transition from heavily didactic, expository editions, where the religious themes of *The Pilgrim's Progress* are prominent, to editions presenting Bunyan's work as a 'literary classic'.

With Isabel Hofmeyr's essay we turn to the transnational significance of *The Pilgrim's Progress*, and how in undergoing an international circulation the work was transformed and redefined generically. The particular focus of her essay is on how *The Pilgrim's Progress* has been read in different ways by different groups of readers, first as an evangelical and didactic work, later as a work of literary 'realism'. In exploring the tensions between these two reading strategies, she shows how, when the work came to be translated into African languages for evangelical purposes, there was also an effort to naturalize or indigenize the text, including the provision of indigenized illustrations, a process which, in turn, led to a perception of the work by its African readers as 'realistic'.

The following three essays consider the impact of Bunyan on two twentieth-century writers, and on one of the most popular British films of the Second World War. Louis MacNeice greatly admired Bunyan, and Richard Brown, in a close reading of a number of MacNeice's works, traces some of the complex psychological, spiritual and literary issues at stake in the poet's repeated appropriations and re-readings of *The Pilgrim's Progress*. MacNeice, as we know, was the son of a bishop in the Church of Ireland, and it may not be entirely without significance that Samuel Beckett, another writer from an Irish Protestant background, also alludes to *The Pilgrim's Progress* in his writings. Julie Campbell brings out in convincing detail some of the ways in which Bunyan's allegory features in Beckett's novel *Molloy*, and relates the concerns of both works to Jungian theories about the unconscious and how religion and art can have psychotherapeutic effects. Michael Davies tells the fascinating story of how Bunyan came to make a brief appearance in Michael Powell and Emeric Pressburger's classic film *A Matter of Life and Death* (1946; released in the USA in 1947 as *Stairway to Heaven*). His essay explores the question of why Bunyan should have been chosen for a walk-on part in this film. As he shows, this brief on-screen appearance by Bunyan is significant as an indication of the continuing cultural charge associated with his name and reputation in a film that is concerned with the re-examination and re-establishment of English national identity and values just after the Second World War. Bunyan's appearance in the film had an important contemporary political relevance, Davies argues, in that the heroic seventeenth-century Dissenter works as a 'visual epigraph' to represent the film's wider promotion of political liberty and individual rights in the face of tyranny and oppression.

Finally, in a challenging and provocative essay, Stuart Sim opens up the question of what Bunyan and *The Pilgrim's Progress* mean today. Noting that some of Bunyan's strongest admirers have been 'fundamentalists' – including political radicals and twentieth-century Marxists as well as religious Protestant fundamentalists – Sim argues that this is because there are ways in which Bunyan and his writings can be seen as 'fundamentalist' in temperament and outlook: 'intolerant, repressive, authoritarian, and biblically literalist'. Sim is aware of the danger of historical anachronism in applying this later term to a writer from the seventeenth century, and of the need to recognize the particular context of state repression in which Bunyan was writing. Nevertheless, he suggests that the legacy of Bunyan in the early twenty-first century, where fundamentalism seems to be everywhere on the rise, may be a more complex and troubling one than some of his admirers may want to believe.

The clear message from the essays in this volume is that *The Pilgrim's Progress* has always had the power to generate varying responses and animated debate, and that this power remains undimmed. Christian's journey continues to inspire the imagination of readers into the twenty-first century.

VINCENT NEWEY

1 Bunyan's Afterlives: Case Studies

Seconds

There appeared in 1966 a Hollywood movie entitled *Seconds*, directed by John Frankenheimer. It is a discourse on the theme of salvation. Arthur Hamilton, a world-weary banker (played by John Randolph) is lured into hiring the services of a secretive business company which offers its clients new lives. After a physical reconstruction (at which point Rock Hudson takes over) the protagonist, renamed Antiochus Wilson, is given a fresh identity as an artist living in California, while his disappearance is accounted for by a faked death in a hotel fire. Those like him are known by insiders as 'reborns'.

The narrative abounds with motifs from Puritan tradition. Hamilton is called by voices on a crowded railway station, and is summoned by a text (a piece of paper with the direction '34 Lafayette Street'). The language of spiritual crisis and conversion then becomes more distinctly evident when the evangelistic founder of the company (played by Will Geer) steps in to remind his wavering supplicant (or in sales jargon 'mark') that 'rebirth is painful' and that 'There never was a struggle in the soul of a good man that wasn't hard' – reminding us of one of Christian's supports in his distress at the River of Death where Hopeful recollects that it is the wicked who *'are not troubled'* (*PP*, p. 148). Similarly, the accompanying encouragement that it is 'easier to go forward when you know you can't go back' is one Christian had leaned upon in the Valley of the Shadow of Death when reflecting that 'the danger of going back might be much more, than for to go forward' (*PP*, p. 63).

There is, however, deep irony in this reiteration of a religious idiom. In the scene just cited, our suspicions of the duplicity of the organization are intensified when Hamilton is blackmailed with shots that have been fabricated of him apparently raping a young woman: his putative liberators are actually his captors. More generally, *Seconds* is throughout an allegory of the emptiness of the American dream, which is understood as a hollow inversion of spiritual idealism. Our 'reborn' finds no more fulfilment second time around than he had the first. His new life repeats the futility of the old, merely adding a pointless hedonism to a materialistic existence where, he subsequently laments, the guiding aspiration is the possession of 'Things'. He has exchanged a drab Vanity Fair for a flashy one. Dispirited and confused, Wilson returns incognito to his former home in search of his bearings. Conversation (with his 'widow') and reflection on the personal past, staples of Puritan self-help and reorientation, fail him. He discovers hardly a trace of himself, even in the memory of Mrs Hamilton, who recalls mostly his 'silences'. He leaves the house bearing all that is left of him there – an ornamental statuette commemorating the vainglory of a sporting triumph.

Seconds has no real hope for the future in terms either of individual or collective regeneration, though it does have affirmations. One of these is belief in the importance of human relationships, which is expressed not only negatively by way of the lovelessness of Hamilton's marriage but also through the suggestions of a repressed, or renounced, homoerotic bonding between him and his 'old buddy' Charlie Evans, the tennis partner for whom he had once scratched the inscription 'Fidelis ETERNUS' – 'faithful unto death' – with his belt buckle on the underside of their college doubles trophy when they were together in the locker-room after the match. Wilson's upbeat realization, at the nadir of his disillusionment, that what he really wants is 'choice' – to make his own decisions rather than to be or do what was 'supposed' of him – is by no means out of keeping with this seeming scenario of forbidden love, although his awakening has more general reference to the desire for freedom of action.

But freedom is exactly what he can never have, as we learn in stunning fashion in the final segment of *Seconds*, which is called 'The Next Stage'. Returning to the company in the expectation that he will be able to 'begin again' on a sounder footing, he ends up as the cadaver in the next of its ventures. Before the horrifying conclusion, where the surgeons put the hammers into the side of the head to stage a traffic accident, he is visited again by the firm's founding father, who now plainly doubles as Chief Executive and Uncle Sam, explaining that he had set out with the intention of battling against 'human misery' – helping people 'find yer dream come true' – but that the 'profit' motive had taken over among the younger executives, producing (as is implied in what he says) a ruthless and impersonal system where once there had been an ideal. In 'The Next Stage' the indictment of a capitalist America that has commandeered the Pilgrim Fathers' promised land, is thus pressed home. The socio-economic web for which (in the terminology of Louis Althusser[1]) Hamilton was snatched from birth has its extension, not an escape route, in the 'dream' for which he is later recruited, and to which, though his eyes are at last opened, he cannot resist being a sacrifice.

The penultimate sequence of *Seconds*, which follows this interview, interestingly points to a lack of cohesion and reduction to formality in the religious aspect of the present. Wilson bound down by two men in white coats and being wheeled along a corridor to a doorway, is accompanied by a cleric who claims ordination in three faiths, as priest, rabbi and minister, and recites the service for the burial of the dead in a tangled mix of the Protestant, Catholic and Jewish versions. The Protestant centre no longer holds; yet, this strange hybrid officiator does say that Wilson's belonging to the Protestant religion offers a certain 'definition', which, though an enigmatic statement in itself underlines the particular mythos on which the scene of his destruction rests. No one who knows *The Pilgrim's Progress* can fail to make a connection between Wilson's fate and the end of Part One:

> So they told the King, but he would not come down to see him; but commanded the two Shining Ones [...] to go out and take *Ignorance* and bind him hand and foot, and have him away. Then they took him up, and carried him through the air to the door that I saw in the side of the Hill, and put him in there. Then I saw

---

[1] See Althusser's account of the insertion of the individual – or 'subject' – into the prevailing ideology of the social framework: Louis Althusser, 'Ideology and Ideological State Apparatuses', in *Lenin and Philosophy, and Other Essays*, trans. B. Brewster (London: New Left Books, 1971), pp. 127–86.

that there was a way to Hell, even from the Gates of Heaven, as well as from the City of *Destruction*. (*PP*, p. 154)

Among its evocations of Puritan tradition, it is the drama of the damnation of Ignorance that *Seconds* finally settles for in its depiction of the anguish of modernity. The dark side of the Calvinist scheme persists in, and has helped to determine, the imagining and grasp of a latter-day condition of false hopes and helpless subjection. But this closing movement of the film at the same time casts a deconstructive light, or shadow, back upon the original dispensation, making of it an oppressive ideology. The man who in *Seconds* is responsible for the whole set-up – our Chief Executive and Uncle Sam – trebles as God, a Creator whose good intentions have gone awry but cannot be modified or gainsaid. We are asked to view the universal plan as a tyranny. At least one substantial book on Calvinism has been written along these lines – John Stachniewski's *The Persecutory Imagination*.[2] As we shall see, however, this effect of *Seconds* is by no means an isolated example of what we may call backwards refusal or subversion.

Seconds shows that Puritanism remains deeply embedded in modern consciousness and imagination. It also illustrates the relations between host and precursor texts, which are of course never a case of straight perpetuation. With retrieval and continuity come inevitably distance and change – appropriation for fresh purposes, a revised perspective, often a going against the grain. The process most regularly reflected in works that recollect Bunyan is that of secularization, whether as loss, as with *Seconds* inasmuch as it deplores the hegemony of acquisitive materialism, or as opportunity, as with the missionary humanism of George Eliot. We are all – critics, scholars and readers no less than creative writers – exponents of Bunyan's afterlife. About two decades ago, I too ended a piece with Ignorance, bringing this character in from the cold margins of an unrelenting creed to the centre of sympathetic attention, celebrating Bunyan's rendering of the pathos of his predicament, which I saw above all in

---

2   John Stachniewski, *The Persecutory Imagination: English Puritanism and the Literature of Religious Despair* (Oxford: Clarendon Press, 1991).

the picture of him 'fumbling for his roll and in that silence [...] which speaks volumes about his vulnerability':[3]

> Then they asked him for his Certificate, that they might go in and show it to the King. So he fumbled in his bosom for one, and found none. Then said they, Have you none? But the man answered never a word. (*PP*, p. 154)

For this I was much chastised from some quarters: how could one claim that Bunyan shows concern for a reprobate. My point was – and remains – that Bunyan's vision comes out as ineluctably double, proceeding on the one hand by the dictates of faith, which cast Ignorance as one worthy to be damned and on the other by the light of nature, which situates him as a moving spectacle of exclusion and dereliction. What is in focus here at one level is the intrinsic quality of Bunyan's imaginative genius, which reaches beyond the doctrine to which he both rationally and emotionally subscribed. Yet history – that is, the rise of liberal humanism which has been a concomitant of mass deconversion – has also tipped the balance against the Calvinist verdict and in Ignorance's favour. To understand Bunyan's theological commitment, his promotion of 'grace-ful' reading, does not explain why his work has lasted or why generally it has been found significant.[4] There was, as we shall now see, an eighteenth-century admirer of Bunyan who, in his own spiritual autobiography, paradoxically sounded a secularizing chord even while insisting upon his credentials as an orthodox believer.

---

3   'Bunyan and the Confines of the Mind', in *The Pilgrim's Progress: Critical and Historical Views*, ed. Vincent Newey (Liverpool: Liverpool University Press, 1980), pp. 21–48 (p. 44).

4   For a straight, though rich, theological approach, see Michael Davies, *Graceful Reading: Theology and Narrative in the Works of John Bunyan* (Oxford: Oxford University Press, 2002).

William Cowper

Ignorance's consignment to the pit stuck in the mind of a recluse who on 2 September 1788 wrote from the Lodge at Weston Underwood in Buckinghamshire to his confidant, the vicar of St Mary Woolnoth in London, on the shape of his spiritual life:

> When I have thought myself falling into the abyss I have been caught up again; when I have thought myself on the threshold of a happy eternity, I have been thrust down to Hell. [...] I have no expectation but of sad vicissitude, and ever believe that the last shock of all will be fatal.[5]

William Cowper knew *The Pilgrim's Progress* well. He shows an easy familiarity with its detail when playfully upbraiding a correspondent, Samuel Rose, by means of a metaphor Christian applies to Hopeful, Rose being 'like one that has the egg-shell still upon his head'.[6] We should note, however, that the relevant moment in *The Pilgrim's Progress* – Hopeful is told that he talks 'like one, upon whose head is the Shell to this very day' – introduces Christian's disquisition upon the unpardonable sin of 'selling' Christ, the rejection of the Saviour whereby the sinner 'sells his *Birth-right*, and his Soul and all, and that to the Devil of Hell' (*PP*, pp. 123–4). Unlike Bunyan, who recounts in *Grace Abounding* his slow release from a harrowing sense of having committed this irrevocable transgression, Cowper never could overcome the conviction that he was guilty of, as he phrases it in his autobiographical *Memoir*, the 'sin against the Holy Ghost'.[7] Cowper sold Christ and found a Hell on earth:

---

[5] *The Letters and Prose Writings of William Cowper*, eds James King and Charles Ryskamp, 5 vols (Oxford: Clarendon Press, 1979–86), III, 209.

[6] 5 April 1792: *Letters and Prose Writings*, IV, 46.

[7] *Memoir of the Early Life of William Cowper, Esq. Written by Himself* (London: R. Edwards, 1816), ed. Maurice J. Quinlan, *Proceedings of the American Philosophical Society*, 97 (1953), 359–82 (p. 376). All references are to this edition, and are included in parentheses in the text.

> Damn'd below Judas; more abhorr'd than he was,
> Who, for a few pence, sold his holy master.
> Twice betray'd, Jesus me, the last delinquent,
> > Deems the profanest.
> > > ('Hatred and Vengeance', ?1774, 5–8)[8]

The 'vicissitude' he speaks of in the letter to John Newton has its counterpart in Cowper's poetry in widespread oscillation between tragic self-consciousness, of which these verses are an extreme expression, and therapeutic engagement with the external world, especially the exercise of a capacity to be renovated in the presence of nature.

These two aspects of Cowper, the intense subjectivity and the well-being of a 'natural faith', signal and had powerful impact upon processes of literary and cultural re-formation. Cowper's (pre)romanticism and (pre)modernity cannot on this occasion be my topic, however.[9] Rather, there is a comparison to be drawn between Cowper's *Memoir* (written in 1766, though published posthumously in 1816) and *Grace Abounding*.

In the latter, the theme of religious faith and doubt is indivisible from the drama of psychical events. One good example is Bunyan's emergence from his obsessive struggle with the idea that he had perpetrated the unpardonable sin, a period of soul-trouble which had consisted of visitations from opposing scriptures, the one about Esau selling his birthright and finding no place of repentance and the encouragement of 'My grace is sufficient':

> I had a longing mind that they might come both together upon me; yea I desired of God they might.
>
> Well, about two or three dayes after, so they did indeed; they boulted both upon me at a time, and did work and struggle strangely in me for a while; at

---

[8] *The Poems of William Cowper*, eds John D. Baird and Charles Ryskamp, 3 vols (Oxford: Clarendon Press, 1980–95), I, 210.

[9] See my *Cowper's Poetry: A Critical Study and Reassessment* (Liverpool: Liverpool University Press, 1982).

last, that about *Esaus* birthright began to wax weak, and withdraw, and vanish; and this about the sufficiency of Grace prevailed, with peace and joy.[10]

Bunyan's recovery is driven by his own intercession in willing an end to the conflict within him, and eventually he brings even the Esau sentence over from the debit to the profit side, working out that it describes not a 'hasty thought', as his had been, but one of 'deliberation'.[11] The resolution, however, no less than the foregoing turmoil, involves an instinctive assumption of the potency of the texts themselves, their force as the divine Word; the protagonist at last enlists their efficacy in the service of his recuperation.

With the *Memoir* it is otherwise. Though the work is conceived as a conversion narrative, its religion is a borrowed language, something incidental rather than integral to the inner life. Thus Cowper writes of his protracted attempts at suicide when he was a young lawyer in the Inner Temple, which were the prelude to his sojourn from 1762 to 1765 at Dr Nathaniel Cotton's asylum at St Albans where he first encountered Evangelicalism:

> I drew up the shutters, once more had recourse to the laudanum, and determined to drink it off directly; *but God had otherwise ordained*. A conflict that shook me to pieces suddenly took place. [...] Distracted between the desire of death and the dread of it, twenty times I had the phial to my mouth and as often received an irresistible check; and even at the time it seemed to me that an invisible hand swayed the bottle downwards as often as I set it against my lips. [...] Still, indeed, I could have made shift with both hands, dead and lifeless as they were, to have raised the basin to my mouth, for my arms were not at all affected: but this new difficulty struck me with wonder; *it had the air of a divine interposition*. (p. 373: italics mine)

The references to providential care and intervention appear as formulaic afterthoughts, a postscript to the proceedings themselves.

Where poison had failed Cowper turned to the garter, trying to hang himself on the bedroom door; but, after prolonged unconsciousness and sensations of 'flashes' all over his body, the instrument, by

---

10 John Bunyan, *Grace Abounding to the Chief of Sinners*, ed. Roger Sharrock (Oxford: Clarendon Press, 1962), p. 67.
11 Ibid., p. 71.

'the blessed providence of God', snapped (p. 374). Looking back, Cowper imagines an eerie scene where one of the servants must have passed right by his suspended corpse without noticing it:

> Soon after I got into bed I was surprised to hear a noise in the dining-room, where the laundress was lighting a fire; she had found the door unbolted, notwithstanding my design to fasten it, and must have passed the bed-chamber door while I was hanging on it and yet never perceived me. She heard me fall and presently came to ask if I was well, adding she feared I had been in a fit. (p. 375)

What strikes us about this is the clash between quotidian routine – the laundress going about her chores – and the private anguish of Cowper's derangement, by which the latter is made at once more terrible in itself and, within the larger scheme of things, appallingly inconsequential. What Cowper chooses to underline, however, is his slip in not locking the door of his chambers, which he presents as evidence of God's extra-special interest in his preservation, a divinely-ordered fail-safe device 'to keep open every way of deliverance that nothing might be left to hazard' (p. 374). That Cowper never entertains the possibility that his mistake was an unconscious cry for help is in perfect keeping with his refusal to embrace the psychological implications of the scenario he paints, where, in another occurrence of the metaphor of oscillation by which he characteristically defined his troubled existence, the details of action and counter-action – hands being raised and pressed downwards – signify, as he momentarily seems to comprehend, the dynamics of a split within himself, 'the desire of death and the dread of it' (p. 373). Cowper was disturbed that, under the influence of 'Satan and [his] own wicked heart', he had misread as the healing effects of pleasant surroundings God's elective visitation during his convalescence near Southampton following an early mental breakdown (p. 368). The misrecognition truly lay in his taking an inward resistance to collapse as numinous design.

The flatness of the religious content of the *Memoir* can be attributed to Cowper's desperate personal need to take up an available framework of ideas by which he could make sense of his unruly life, but it is nonetheless indicative of a wider climate of faint or fading belief. The living testament of the seventeenth-century adherent, John

Bunyan, becomes with the eighteenth-century convert, William Cowper, a lifeline, a belated or post-mortem document. In Cowper's *Memoir* the centre of creative energy has shifted decisively to the sphere of universal psychology. The matter-of-factness with which he details his ordeals guarantees their authenticity yet increases their nightmarish texture, making him, as often in his poetry, the exponent of surreal happenstance. There is, moreover, an interesting overall movement in the text: whereas Bunyan had progressed to maturity of spirit, and to the public role of preacher, Cowper chronicles a return to the security and state of dependency he had enjoyed before being left an orphan on his mother's death during his sixth year. He calls the asylum at St Albans, which he was reluctant to leave, 'the place of my second nativity' (p. 380), suggesting not so much a spiritual rebirth (though he is on the surface talking of one) as a repetition of the paradise of 'the nursery and the immediate care of a most indulgent mother' (p. 366) from which he had been so early expelled, of which yet another version is found, as the end of the *Memoir* records, in the form of the Unwin family, in whose 'society' he took shelter after St Albans.

I cannot here go into the complexities of Cowper's search for stability and place of repose; but it is clear that, to quote George MacLennan, 'in considering the *Memoir* we seem to stand on the threshold of a psychoanalytic culture' in which the home is a primary site of ontological difficulty and resource.[12] That Cowper's first bout of madness was triggered by anxiety over having to undergo an examination at the Bar of the House of Lords as to his fitness for appointment to the post of Clerkship of the Journals writes large an attendant historic shift, involving, as Richard Sennett and Lawrence Stone have shown, the problematization of adult male life in terms of potential alienation from the public sphere consequent upon the dramatic increase in the late eighteenth century of the mother's direct

---

12 George MacLennan, *Lucid Interval: Subjective Writing and Madness in History* (Leicester: Leicester University Press, 1992), pp. 78–95 (p. 94). McLennan's chapter is the best account we have of the psychology and cultural significance of Cowper's *Memoir*. I am indebted to it on several points.

input into child-rearing.[13] Cowper's flight to the bosom of the Unwin household, and above all to the loving attention of Mrs Unwin, his surrogate mother, marks a retreat from what he termed the 'mortal poison' of 'public examination' (p. 370).

Charles Dickens and George Eliot

Among nineteenth-century authors, Charles Dickens is the one most variously in touch with Bunyan. In *The Old Curiosity Shop*, for example, Nell likens herself and her grandfather to Bunyan's 'Pilgrim', and their journey through the Midlands, with its factories of 'a hundred strange unearthly noises' and men 'moving like demons among the flame and smoke', is based upon Christian's experience of the Valley of the Shadow of Death.[14] In a more sustained way, *A Christmas Carol* is an adaptation of Puritan conversion narrative in the service of an enlightened capitalist ideology where wealth and consumption dominate but people are also made to matter – an *ab initio* polarity to the mordant disenchantment of *Seconds*.[15] There are the slight yet telling echoes such as the turnabout of the Wicket Gate

---

13 See MacLennan, pp. 82–3, quoting both Sennett and Stone. In his *The Fall of Public Man* (London: Faber & Faber, 1986), Sennett discusses the increased emphasis in eighteenth-century bourgeois culture on the division of adulthood and childhood into separate spheres: 'the gradual concern with the special state of childhood marked off certain limits to public expression […] by 1750 a father would be embarrassed to dress up his son's dolls' (p. 94). Stone describes a 'liberation of maternal love': 'Childhood came to be regarded as the best years of one's life, instead of the grim purgatory it had been in the seventeenth century'; see his *The Family, Sex and Marriage in England 1500–1800* (Harmondsworth: Penguin Books, 1982), p. 285.
14 Charles Dickens, *The Old Curiosity Shop* (1841), ed. Angus Easson (Harmondsworth: Penguin Books, 1985), ch. 43, p. 417.
15 See my *Scriptures of Charles Dickens: Novels of Ideology, Novels of the Self* (Aldershot: Ashgate, 2004), ch. 2 for an account of *A Christmas Carol* in this light, and *passim* for a range of other connections between Dickens and Bunyan or Puritan genres.

and 'yonder shining light' (*PP*, p. 11) that fix Christian's course on the road to the Celestial City when, in *Our Mutual Friend*, Bradley Headstone, a murderer, approaches the Lock House – 'He mended his pace, keeping his eyes upon the light with a strange intensity, as if he were taking aim at it' – that is the starting point of his last few strides to self-destruction.[16]

Headstone's death is a grim affair not only because there is no redemption but because there is no damnation either, only two bodies, the schoolmaster's and that of his enemy, sunk in the ooze of the Lock. There is nothing in Dickens of the everlasting torment that awaits Ignorance; no place for an eternity either transcendently bright or abysmally dark. He does, however, insist upon one kind of afterlife, which is that of a reputation for good works or ill, as the unregenerate Scrooge bears witness when, shown the future, he is confronted with the contrast between his own standing as anathema and that of the 'loved, revered, and honoured head' with 'good deeds springing from the ground, to sow the world with life immortal'.[17] This is Dickens as champion of the Religion of Humanity, the creed most conspicuously theorized by Ludwig Feuerbach in *The Essence of Christianity* (1841), which argued that humankind was mature enough to cast off the supernatural forms in which it had projected its own deepest needs and potentialities and to take the step from the principle of 'God is Love' to that of 'Love – for one's fellow men and women – is God'. Observing that 'from a traditional theological point of view, Dickens is a very long way from the Christian perspective', Barry Qualls, in *The Secular Pilgrims of Victorian Fiction*, comments that his 'good "Christian"' often comes speaking the language of – guess who – Ignorance:[18]

---

16 *Our Mutual Friend* (1864–65), ed. Stephen Gill (Harmondsworth: Penguin Books, 1985), bk 4, ch. 15, p. 868.
17 *A Christmas Carol* (1843), ed. Michael Slater (Harmondsworth: Penguin Books, 1985), stave 4, p. 118.
18 Barry Qualls, *The Secular Pilgrims of Victorian Fiction* (Cambridge: Cambridge University Press, 1982), p. 136.

> *Christian. [...] The Word of God saith of persons in a natural condition [...] every imagination of the heart of man is only evil, and that continually. [...]*
> *Ignorance. I will never believe that my heart is thus bad. (PP, p. 138)*

Though the creator of Daniel Quilp's motiveless malignity or Headstone's insane repressed passion can hardly be said to have 'taught that man was perfectible', as an early reviewer would have it when associating Dickens with the Germans who 'made humanity their God',[19] he certainly set essential store by goodness of heart and a sense of responsibility for the welfare of others.

One place where he does so is at the outset of Nell's journey through her Valley of the Shadow:

> The child herself was sensible of a new feeling within her, which elevated her nature, and inspired her with an energy and confidence she had never known. There was no divided responsibility now; the whole burden of their two lives had fallen upon her, and henceforth she must think and act for both. 'I have saved him,' she thought. 'In all dangers and distresses, I will remember that.' (ch. 43, p. 406)

This is a salient passage partly because the word 'saved' and the emphasis on the fortifying agency of memory exhibit a definite link with Puritan confession and partly because it is echoed by a later writer who, with even greater zeal than Dickens, espoused the Religion of Humanity:

> And what sort of crisis might not this be in three lives whose contact with hers laid an obligation on her as if they had been suppliants bearing the sacred branch? [...] She yearned towards the perfect Right, that it might make a throne within her, and rule her errant will. 'What should I do – how should I act now, this very day if I could clutch my own pain, and compel it to silence, and think of those three!'
>
> It had taken her long to come to that question, and there was light piercing into the room. She opened her curtains, and looked out towards the bit of road that lay in view, with fields beyond, outside the entrance-gates. On the road there was a man with a bundle on his back and a woman carrying her baby; in the field she could see figures moving – perhaps the shepherd with his dog. Far off in the bending sky was the pearly light; and she felt the largeness of the world and the manifold wakings of men to labour and endurance. She was part

---

19   *Rambler*, January 1862; quoted in Qualls, p. 136.

of that involuntary, palpitating life, and could neither look out on it from her luxurious shelter as a mere spectator, nor hide her eyes in selfish complaining.[20]

Thus Dorothea Brooke, in George Eliot's *Middlemarch* (1871-2), enters at dawn into 'a new condition', recognizing her obligation to help the three people with whose lives her own is intertwined – Ladislaw whom she loves and thinks (mistakenly) is having an affair with Rosamond Lydgate, Rosamond herself, and Lydgate the husband. The recollections of Bunyan are specific but also distinctively remodelled. God is displaced by 'the perfect Right' of duty towards others. Dorothea's question is not '*What shall I do to be saved?*' or to gain 'Eternal Life' (*PP*, pp. 11, 13) but how to 'act now' under the influence of 'the vivid sympathetic experience' of the troubles of those around her. Whereas Christian shuts his ears to the wife and children that 'cry after him to return' (*PP*, p. 13), Eliot's burdened traveller, accompanied by a woman with her baby, signifies the demands of family ties. What is revealed to Dorothea in the flash of her enlightenment is the sacred claims of humankind: the far-off 'pearly light', though redolent of the Celestial City 'builded of Pearls' (*PP*, p. 146), is no unearthly realm but a setting for discovery of 'the largeness of the world' and for 'the palpitating life' in which the individual must actively participate and find fulfilment. When Dorothea then symbolically changes her raiment – as Christian and Hopeful do at the Celestial City – it is to go forth to redeem Rosamond from her egotism, as she herself has been redeemed.

It is possible to view Eliot's relation to Bunyan in a positive light. By holding fast to elements of a spiritual ontology she raises Dorothea's experience and the insights to which it gives rise to the level of a holy call, making them matter immensely. She preserves the 'special sense of dignity in ourselves' which W. H. Mallock, in his attack on the Positivists entitled *Is Life Worth Living?* (1880), feared would be lost with the exclusive worship of this-worldly goals and

---

20 George Eliot, *Middlemarch* (1871-2), ed. W. J. Harvey (Harmondsworth: Penguin Books, 1985), ch. 80, p. 846. For more detailed scrutiny of the connections between chapter 80 of *Middlemarch* and *The Pilgrim's Progress*, see my 'Dorothea's Awakening: The Recall of Bunyan in *Middlemarch*', *Notes and Queries*, 229 (1984), 297-9. My present conclusions are different.

happiness.[21] At the same time, it is also true that she uses *The Pilgrim's Progress* ruthlessly against its own interests as a religious text, absorbing it into the scripture of her own secular humanism. She practises a termination. Yet Bunyan's work is not so easily taken over or laid to rest. It has found a life in several traditions, one of which is inadvertently implied by Eliot's own description of life outside Dorothea's window. The man with a bundle, the woman, the shepherd in the field, the trials of 'labour' and 'endurance', prompt thoughts of *The Pilgrim's Progress* as, in the words of the Chartist Thomas Cooper, the 'book of books' of the working class, a function chronicled by Cooper himself, by E. P. Thompson, and by the recent historian of the rise of the English novel, Michael McKeon, where Christian's exploits make all men potential heroes capable of victories over oppression and of coming into their own.[22] Eliot's picturesque images – the window is also a frame – occlude the realities of the lower end of the social scale and generalize the idea of sympathy in strictly middle-class hierarchical terms, but they raise the simulacrum of a position politically distinct from her own. It is not with the socialist Bunyan, however, that I wish to end up.

William Hale White

In the church rolls of the Old Meeting in Bedford Bunyan is listed as number 27 to be admitted to membership. William Hale White, who lived from 1831 to 1913, is number 1936.[23] Hale White was another of

---

21 W. H. Mallock, *Is Life Worth Living?* (London: Chatto & Windus, 1879), p. 136.
22 Cooper's phrase is quoted by E. P. Thompson in *The Making of the English Working Class* (1963; rev. edn Harmondsworth: Penguin Books, 1972), p. 34. For Michael McKeon's Marxist reading of *The Pilgrim's Progress*, see his 'Bunyan and the Literalization of Allegory', *The Origins of the English Novel 1600–1740* (Baltimore: Johns Hopkins University Press, 1987), pp. 295–337.
23 Catherine Macdonald Maclean, *Mark Rutherford: A Biography of William Hale White* (London: Macdonald & Co., 1955), p. 54n.

the Victorians who lost their faith, an 'honest doubter', but he remained in some ways deeply attached to the Nonconformist and Calvinist tradition in which he was fostered. He kept over it a watch that is sometimes nostalgic but characteristically serious and constructive. Of all Bunyan's hosts, Hale White is the one most interior to his world, and the one who most regularly defines his own milieu, concerns and direction in its terms or over against it.

In his book on *John Bunyan* (1905) Hale White develops the policy of letting Bunyan's texts speak for themselves: 'We will use for the most part Bunyan's own words, so that it may be seen how little translation they need.'[24] There is a considered motive at work in this approach. While conceding Bunyan's renown as a 'theological' writer, for two centuries the 'beloved interpreter of their religion to common folk', Hale White – in a move from which we can still learn – sees his appeal in the late nineteenth century as resting firmly upon his communication of the 'experience of life, with its hopes and fears, bright day and black night' (p. 2). *The Pilgrim's Progress* is accordingly described as 'almost entirely the story of the pilgrimage of man, not of Puritan man especially, but man in all ages' (p. 120). Bunyan's expression of the fundamentals of existence is paramount; no critic need, or should, come between the reader and the words. In a still-valuable chapter of alert exposition, the sermons – *Doctrine of the Law and Grace Unfolded* (1659), *The Barren Fig-tree* (1672), *The Heavenly Footman* (published posthumously in 1698) – are adduced to show that even the Calvinism of the Puritans was never 'mere speculation' but always a striving for 'a theory of the world and its government [...] by which we can live' (p. 76).

It emerges near the end of *John Bunyan* that Hale White had the conscious aim of rebutting Matthew Arnold's charge against Nonconformity – in *Culture and Anarchy* (1869, revised 1875) – of 'Philistinism', which Arnold distinguished from the 'sweetness and light' of the higher culture based upon a classical education and the less strenuous forms of Christianity. Hale White complains of

---

24 [William Hale White,] *John Bunyan, By the Author of 'Mark Rutherford'* (1905; London: Thomas Nelson, n.d.), ch. 3, pp. 120–1. Further page references are given in parentheses in the text.

Arnold's 'wild talk' and turns his own word, 'sweetness', against him, claiming of Puritanism that 'Whatever sweetness there may be in England at the present moment is largely due to it' (pp. 239, 246). This is a defence of the conduct that is rooted in principles of absolute right and wrong, of obedience to 'divine ordinance' (p. 241). Yet, in generally looking beyond morality, as well as doctrine or dogma, to intrinsic human relevance Hale White makes of Bunyan an Arnoldian 'criticism of life', a secular scripture. These are apt phrases to describe Hale White's own writings, many of which he produced under the pseudonym of 'Mark Rutherford'. His was a complex and original genius, but we can recognize Bunyan's presence in it, both on and beneath the surface. We may take examples from two texts, the novel *The Revolution in Tanner's Lane* (1887) and the semi-fictional *Autobiography of Mark Rutherford* (1881).

Hale White's principal theme is suffering. The episodes that he foregrounds and virtually anthologizes in his account of *The Pilgrim's Progress* in *John Bunyan* – the Slough of Despond, the struggle with Apollyon, the Valley of the Shadow of Death, Doubting Castle, and the River of Death – bring repeatedly into focus the combination of infinite vulnerability and inexhaustible strength in the individual. In his own work this configuration of being-in-the-world is not only transferred to modern contexts but carried to the centre of ordinary emotional circumstance. The great trial of Zachariah Coleman in *The Revolution in Tanner's Lane* – the cross he must always bear – is his loveless marriage:

> There was to be no joy in his life? Then he would be satisfied if it were tolerable, and he strove to dismiss all his dreams and do his best with what lay before him. Oh, my hero! [...] The divinest heroism is not that of the man who, holding life cheap, puts his back against a wall, and is shot by Government soldiers, assured that he will live ever afterwards as a martyr and saint: a diviner heroism is that of the poor printer, who, in dingy, smoky Rosoman Street, Clerkenwell, with forty years before him, determined to live through them, as far as he could, without a murmur, although there was to be no pleasure in them. A diviner heroism is this, but divinest of all, is that of him who can in these days do what Zachariah did, and without Zachariah's faith.[25]

25   Mark Rutherford [William Hale White], *The Revolution in Tanner's Lane* (1887; London: Hogarth Press, 1984), ch. 1, p. 24.

There is a moment later when Zachariah, an unshakeable Calvinist, cannot resist questioning God's decree in subjecting him to his torment but curses himself for permitting the rebellious notion, believing it to be a sin. The narrator comments, 'Poor wretch! He thought he was struggling with his weakness; but he was in reality struggling against his own strength'.[26] For a space the text turns against the predestinarian rigour of Calvinism, commending the protest of Zachariah's heart and mind. Yet Hale White more commonly keeps imaginative faith with his heritage and its ways of comprehending humanity's weaknesses and resilience. When Zachariah, on the run in Manchester because of his radical politics, faces the 'infinite abyss' of despair not only is his predicament put in the form of the Valley of the Shadow of Death but Bunyan's 'immortal *Progress*' becomes an ingredient in his story, supplying him with two of the weapons in the armoury of the Puritan pilgrim, the consolations of memory and the support of the Word. As Christian had relied upon the Bible, so does Zachariah upon *The Pilgrim's Progress*:

> He remembered that quagmire [...] into which, if even a good man falls, he can find no bottom; he remembered that gloom so profound 'that oftentimes, when he lifted up his foot to set forward, he knew not where or upon what he should set it next'; he remembered the flame and smoke, the sparks and hideous noises, the things that cared not for Christian's sword [...]; he remembered the voice of a man going before, saying, '*Though I walk through the valley of the shadow of death I will fear none ill, for Thou art with me*'. Lastly, he remembered that by and by the day broke, and Christian cried, '*He hath turned the shadow of death into the morning*'.[27]

The fiends neither of Hell nor of hell-on-earth care for the *sword*, but *words* hold them off.

The Autobiography of Mark Rutherford reveals with particular force Hale White's distance from yet intimate residual contact with Bunyan's vision. It is a reverse replication of *Grace Abounding*. Where Bunyan traces his progress from sinfulness to a state of grace, the *Autobiography* relates a de-conversion, a history elaborating Hale White's own. In his exposition of *Grace Abounding* in *John Bunyan*,

---

26 Ibid., ch. 7, p. 91.
27 Ibid., ch. 9, p. 115.

Hale White lingers over the segment unfolding the psychomachia of the opposing texts, where that about Esau finding 'no place of repentance' and that about the 'arms of grace' being open had fought it out in his head. There is something of such terrifying monomania in the *Autobiography*: Rutherford, for instance, describes his obsession with the problem of futility arising from loss of belief in immortality ('Why this ceaseless struggle, if in a few short years I was to be asleep for ever?') as one of the 'ideas that would frequently lay hold of *me* with such relentless tenacity that I was passive in their grasp'.[28] Rutherford's brain becomes a place where pressing issues of an epoch of unsettlement and shock take root. Yet the seam of mind-debate running through the *Autobiography* takes more centrally another form, and one that looks back, rather, to *The Pilgrim's Progress*. Some of the characters of *The Pilgrim's Progress* are Christian's helpers (Help, Evangelist, Interpreter), some antagonists and seducers representing attitudes that he must fend off (Worldly-Wiseman, Talkative, Atheist). Edward Gibbon Mardon in the *Autobiography* is at once Rutherford's friend and his enemy. Rationalist and unbeliever, he is a projection of inclinations that Mark can neither acknowledge in himself nor altogether suppress. Names are indicators of character-type and function in Bunyan's allegory. Hale White often uses this device, but never more pointedly than with his seductive and troublesome double, whose first and middle names evoke traditions of scepticism in matters of religion (the reference is to the author of *The Decline and Fall of the Roman Empire*) while 'Mardon' itself both suggests the act of 'spoiling' ('to mar') and is an anagram of 'random', signifying the threat of disfigurement and chaos that he, or the ideas he epitomizes, pose to Rutherford's intellectual and emotional life. The motifs Rutherford employs to describe Mardon's effect upon him indicate various degrees of active assault. A notable instance is the 'sledge-hammer' of Mardon's criticism of Rutherford's attempt to hold on to the 'Christ-idea' whether or not it was ever made flesh, which

---

28 [William Hale White], *The Autobiography of Mark Rutherford, Dissenting Minister* (1881), ed. William S. Peterson (Oxford: Oxford University Press, 1990), ch. 6, p. 90.

leaves Rutherford 'stunned, bewildered'.[29] More horrifying still than being bashed is the relentless 'process of excavation'[30] – a gradual hollowing-out from within – which is Rutherford's longer-term fate.

Mark reaches his lowest point when he runs for very life from the utter isolation he comes to experience when he takes a job at a small school after resigning his unbearably soulless ministry among the Unitarians. (Contrast the eponymous Heavenly Footman of Bunyan's sermon running for the prize of salvation.) Shut up in his attic bedroom, he looks out upon the metropolitan landscape:

> There were scattered lights here and there marking roads, but as they crossed one another, and now and then stopped where building had ceased, the effect they produced was that of bewilderment with no clue to it. Further off was the great light of London, like some unnatural dawn, or the illumination from a fire which could not itself be seen. I was overcome with the most dreadful sense of loneliness.[31]

There are echoes in this of Christian's sight of the Celestial City, and of Dorothea Brooke's awakening in the 'pearly light' of dawn to the 'palpitating life' beyond her little world. Rutherford's depression is the inverse of both Bunyan's understanding of spiritual triumph and George Eliot's secular displacement of it. The roads of the urban sprawl symbolically criss-cross, leading nowhere, mirroring the pattern of the bars of the prison house of the aimless or introverted self. For Rutherford there is no heaven, and the only hell is the 'bottomless abyss' of insanity, on the edge of which he presently trembles. So numbing is the ache of modernity in him that not only is he bereft of the old guiding language of religion, he cannot find words at all for his condition: it is a 'nameless dread'.[32]

In this text and its continuation, *Mark Rutherford's Deliverance* (1885), Hale White does identify routes beyond this seeming impasse – ways of carrying on and of enriching existence. Best known is his Spinozan and Wordsworthian pantheism, where the personal God is

---

29 Ibid., ch. 4, pp. 60–1.
30 Ibid., ch. 5, p. 65.
31 Ibid., ch. 8, pp. 133–4.
32 Ibid., ch. 8, p. 134.

exchanged for One resident in and spread through the universe. There is a trace of this philosophic stance in the passage with which the *Deliverance* concludes. Rutherford settles at last for a holiday in the country with his family:

> We beheld the plain spread all out before us, bounded by the heights of Sussex and Hampshire. It was veiled with the most tender blue, and above it was spread a sky which was white on the horizon and deepened by degrees in azure over our heads. Marie [...] wandered about looking for flowers and ferns, and was content. We were all completely happy. We strained our eyes to see the furthest point before us, and we tried to find it on the map we had brought with us. [...] Rather did summer dying in such fashion fill our hearts with repose, and even more than repose – with actual joy.[33]

Christian had set his course by 'yonder shining light' of faith, Providence, and the heavenly kingdom (*PP*, p. 11). On an altogether smaller spiritual scale, and with the map of a lesser salvation, Mark and his wife Ellen take a transient 'repose' and 'joy' from the seasonal beauties of nature. The more obvious recall in this episode, however, is of another Puritan writer: that is, of Milton's Adam and Eve, who, expelled from Eden in *Paradise Lost*, find the world 'all before them'.[34] The late-nineteenth-century descendants of our first parents and Marie their daughter (who reminds us of Eve gathering flowers) snatch a vestigial prelapsarian pleasure from beholding 'the plain all spread out before [them]', and from being together. The event comprises both a naturalization and domestication of the mythic imagination. The *Autobiography* and *Deliverance* end, not in grace or glory, but in mutuality and thankfulness for small mercies. But this seems an apt prescription for the times – a low-key but genuinely practical existentialism.

W. H. Mallock, the interpreter of Positivism we met earlier, observed that 'positive thought reduces all religions to ideals created by man; and [...] teaches us also that we in the future must construct new ideals for ourselves'.[35] Hale White did not in the long run rest

---

33   [William Hale White], *Mark Rutherford's Deliverance* (1885; Oxford: Oxford University Press, 1936), ch. 9, pp. 132–3.
34   *Paradise Lost*, XII, 646.
35   Mallock, *Is Life Worth Living?*, pp. 19–20.

with the frugal substitute idealism we have just witnessed. He never altogether relinquished the sense of life as a passionate spiritual drama, and in *Catharine Furze* (1893) made trial of the sphere of sexual experience – a mutuality reaching deeper and higher than that of familial oneness or accord – as a locus for the pursuit of salvation. The man who admired John Bunyan was also surprisingly the forerunner of D. H. Lawrence. But that is another story.[36]

Whose Music?

There was published in 1992 a novel about a boy with special powers who is transported to the inside of great books.[37] In the first of his adventures he finds himself on a plain, with a girl in a slightly flounced white dress running towards him and calling out 'Life, life, eternal life! How shall I grapple with the misery I must meet with in eternity!', and a man with a burden on his back lamenting 'Oh dear! Oh dear! I shall be too late!' (p. 27). He then encounters two men dressed identically in frock-coats and stove-pipe hats who introduce themselves with 'I am Obstinate. And this is Pliable. Or is it the other way around?' (p. 28). He comes across a Red Queen who plays word games, a figure named Giant Despair, and a Mad Hatter who claims the office of Interpreter. He rescues the girl, Alice, from the Slough of Despond: '"Just look at my lovely white dress," she said. "It's ruined. Shit!"' (p. 37).

The mixing up of *The Pilgrim's Progress* and Lewis Carroll's *Alice in Wonderland* and *Through the Looking-glass* reflects the fact

---

36 See my 'Mark Rutherford's Salvation and the Case of Catharine Furze', in *Mortal Pages, Literary Lives: Studies in Nineteenth-Century Autobiography*, eds Vincent Newey and Philip Shaw (Aldershot: Scolar Press, 1996), pp. 172–203 (pp. 182–99), which also supplies material for some of my present discussion of the *Autobiography* and the *Deliverance*.
37 Peter Ackroyd, *English Music* (London: Hamish Hamilton, 1992). All references are to ch. 2, and are given in parentheses in the text.

that the boy, Timothy, is dreaming, and also, as a White Rabbit points out to him, that these two stories are themselves 'both dreams' (p. 34). Bunyan cultivates the realm of the surreal, the oneiric dimension, which Carroll came to make his own. But there is something else in Peter Ackroyd's mind in this segment of his *English Music*, as there is in the critic John R. Knott Jr.'s earlier brief conjunction of Bunyan's and Carroll's texts. Knott compares the question-and-answer session between Alice and the Cheshire Cat, in which the Cat insists that getting 'somewhere' rests upon one's personal idea of where the goal lies, with the similar exchange between Christian and Hopeful and the shepherds of the Delectable Mountains in order to emphasize 'the subjectivity of the individual way of faith' in *The Pilgrim's Progress* – that no easy or certain directions can be laid down since progress is dependent upon the inward condition of each and every wayfarer.[38] Ackroyd, however, is concerned, more radically, with the elusiveness, instability and subjective nature of meaning itself. When Timothy scrutinizes the volume that Christian has dropped on the ground, he can make no sense of it: 'the words always swarmed to the margins of the page and left a white space at which he stared in bewilderment' (p. 28). The Red Queen's verbal games or misunderstandings ('morning'/'mourning', 'I scream'/'ice cream') are followed later by Timothy's wandering into the middle of a chaotic athletics competition where the running, leaping, swerving, even sleeping contestants are figures of speech or elements of prosody – Apostrophe, say, or a Tumbling Verse. Surveying the mélée, Timothy observes that 'there is no order here because there is no meaning', but then asks 'how can you decide to have a meaning in the first place?', and 'who decides what meaning you should have?' (p. 36).

Ackroyd's text gives no definitive answers to such questions, and indeed seems to suggest that true meaning is somehow always out of reach. What we assume to be the truth is untrustworthy because constructed: the Red Queen casts doubt on the horrors of the Valley of the Shadow of Death since they were reported to her by the White Queen, who 'makes up a great deal just to impress people' (p. 30). Of

---

38   John R. Knott Jr., *The Sword of the Spirit: Puritan Responses to the Bible* (Chicago: University of Chicago Press, 1980), pp. 141–2.

exegesis, even the biblical kind, it is similarly implied that it is but a projection of presuppositions, as the volume Christian let fall becomes a reflective surface, 'a looking-glass book': 'You're only meant to hold it and *look* as if you've read it. That is the meaning of criticism' (p. 31). At his House the Mad Hatter asserts that he 'can explain all the books that ever were invented' (p. 43), but proceeds to explain nothing at all, even of those, including something called 'Vanity Fair', of which he displays pictures.

Yet the Mad Hatter leads his visitors out of his disappointing 'significant room' into the garden, where a celebration takes place. Here the creative legacy is honoured. The end-point, the *telos*, of the journey of Timothy and his companions is not a Cross of Salvation or a Celestial City but a notation, an English Music. On this 'Ground' there are, beneath an oak with silver leaves and golden branches, a collection of musical instruments. Where there was Faith is now a shrine to the Literature of the nation (a tree suggests a sacred emblem, its species Englishness). We began with a modern text, *Seconds*, which exposed the corruption of a people's vision of social and personal fulfilment; we conclude with a contemporary obeisance to a literary heritage seen as an orchestration of dreams. In the distinction lurks a question parallel to that raised in the settled historical shift from religious/spiritual to secular/natural values: is life, though still worth living, a less serious, or a trivial, affair?

English Music prompts thoughts too of just what sense can nowadays be made of *The Pilgrim's Progress* itself. Is it destined to be, as on the evidence it is for Timothy, even for Peter Ackroyd, a beautiful but meaningless creation? Be this as it may, when the music plays it is ascribed specifically to the ambit of Timothy's making: '*He* made it up. It is his music, after all', insists Alice (pp. 45–6). Though Pilgrimage by inviolable rules to transcendent ends is no longer our proper sphere, we can rejoice in the open Adventure of Reading and Response – an adventure which we have seen exemplified by some prominent engagements with Bunyan but which has infinitely more possibilities in relation to this abiding author.

DAVID WALKER

2 Bunyan's Reception in the Romantic Period

The publication of Robert Southey's 1830 edition of *The Pilgrim's Progress, with a Life of John Bunyan* marks a significant point in Bunyan scholarship and also in the politics of reception of Bunyan's work in the Romantic period. Southey's edition is the subject of two fundamentally contrasting contemporary reviews that home in on the history of political events in the seventeenth century and conclude from those events a radically divergent view of the relationship between Bunyan's life and art. These reviews were written by Sir Walter Scott and Thomas Babington Macaulay and act within the context of this essay as a focal point for a more discursive consideration of the reception of *The Pilgrim's Progress* in the Romantic period.[1] As we shall see, the opinions of both Scott and Macaulay are formed, to a significant extent, by the influence of the historiography of the seventeenth century available to the Romantic reader, which is in turn formulated by Romantic opinion of the mid-seventeenth century civil wars.

Perhaps the most well known remark made by a Romantic critic on Bunyan's work was made by Coleridge when he stated his preference for the Bunyan of Parnassus rather than the conventicle. Coleridge's preference for Bunyan the literary genius as opposed to the Bunyan that went to prison for his faith is part and parcel of the older Coleridge's turn away from radicalism in the early years of the nineteenth century. This is a far cry, of course, from the views of the young Coleridge whose radicalism in the 1790s was pronounced. Coleridge's apostasy is well documented by contemporaries such as Byron and Shelley, amongst others. It is Hazlitt, however, who has left

1   Sir Walter Scott's review is in the *Quarterly Review*, 43, no. 86 (October 1830), 469–94. For Macaulay's review see the *Edinburgh Review*, 54, no. 108 (December 1831), 450–61.

us with the most compelling portrait. In his pen-portrait of Coleridge in *The Spirit of the Age* (1825), Hazlitt informs us that 'Liberty (the philosopher's and the poet's bride)' has been sacrificed in Coleridge's work and ideas 'to the murderous practices of the hag Legitimacy', and he 'at last turned on the pivot of a subtle casuistry to the *unclean side*'. Coleridge's only saving grace is that he has not disgraced himself by accepting government posts such as poet laureate (Southey) or stamp collector (Wordsworth).[2]

As Peter Kitson has argued in his article on the 'emplotting' of the English Revolution and its links with the French Revolution, Coleridge in the 1790s was one of many intellectuals to be intoxicated with the writings of the English Commonwealth men of the seventeenth century. Of this company, Milton, Harrington, Neville, and Algernon Sidney are merely the most well known names in a long and distinguished list.[3] Radical politics – and, of course, political reaction – are everywhere apparent in the Romantic period generally, with the 1790s in particular receiving the lion's share of critical and historical attention. The focal point of literary studies seeking to make connections between Romantic writers and the poetry, prose and politics

---

2   William Hazlitt, *The Spirit of the Age*, ed. E. D. Mackerness (London: Northcote House, 1991), p. 62.

3   Peter Kitson, '"Sages and patriots that being dead do yet speak to us": Readings of the English Revolution in the Late Eighteenth Century', in *Pamphlet Wars: Prose in the English Revolution*, ed. James Holstun (London: Frank Cassell, 1992), pp. 205–30 (pp. 206–7). See also Joseph Nicholes, 'Revolutions Compared: The English Civil War as Political Touchstone in Romantic Literature', in *Revolution and English Romanticism*, eds Keith Hanley and Raman Selden (Hemel Hempstead: Harvester Wheatsheaf, 1990), pp. 261–76 (pp. 263–4). For a more sustained treatment of Coleridge's radicalism in the 1790s see Nicholas Roe, *Wordsworth and Coleridge: The Radical Years* (Oxford: Clarendon Press, 1988). For an analysis of how the politics of the seventeenth century was perceived by a very wide range of writers and thinkers in the eighteenth and nineteenth centuries, see Blair Worden, *Roundhead Reputations: The English Civil Wars and the Passions of Posterity* (London: Penguin, 2002), and Peter Kitson, '"Not a reforming patriot": Representations of Cromwell and the English Republic in the late eighteenth and early nineteenth centuries', in *Radicalism in British Literary Culture, 1650–1830*, eds Timothy Morton and Nigel Smith (Cambridge: Cambridge University Press), pp. 183–200.

of the seventeenth century has tended to concentrate upon Milton. Coleridge's joint authorship with Southey of the tragedy *The Fall of Robespierre* (1794), as Nicholas Roe has pointed out, in its depiction of the eponymous hero as a fallen angel, owes more than a little to Milton's Satan from *Paradise Lost*. As he undoubtedly admired Robespierre, though with reservations, this speaks volumes for the distance politically that Coleridge travelled during the course of his life.[4] Oddly, as perhaps the greatest prose writer of the seventeenth century Bunyan has with few exceptions suffered critical neglect in such analyses. The reason for this lies perhaps in the manner in which Bunyan and *The Pilgrim's Progress* were interpreted by those writers in the Romantic period that have been most influential in the development of literary criticism in the academy.

N. H. Keeble has noted in his sketch of Bunyan's reputation from the seventeenth century down to our own times that

> throughout the eighteenth century Bunyan's reputation ran in two channels which rarely converged. While from one quarter there came dismissive and patronising comment, from another issued testimony of a very different order.[5]

As Keeble goes on to argue, the Romantic predilection for individual genius and imagination ensured that Bunyan was not only read for the didactic content of his masterpiece, much beloved by evangelicals, but also for his literary originality. Such a view of Bunyan is exemplified in the work of Sir Walter Scott who refers to Bunyan implicitly and explicitly throughout his *œuvre*, nowhere more apparently than in

---

4 Roe, *Wordsworth and Coleridge*, pp. 206–8. The most critically sophisticated recent study to demonstrate the influence of Milton's masterpiece on the writers and thinkers of the Romantic period is by Lucy Newlyn, *Paradise Lost and the Romantic Reader* (Oxford: Oxford University Press, 1993).

5 N. H. Keeble, "'Of him thousands daily sing and talk': Bunyan and his Reputation', in *John Bunyan: Conventicle and Parnassus, Tercentenary Essays*, ed. N. H. Keeble (Oxford: Clarendon Press, 1988), pp. 241–63 (p. 249). See also Richard L. Greaves, *Glimpses of Glory: John Bunyan and English Dissent* (Stanford: Stanford University Press, 2002), pp. 610–34.

Jeanie Deans' trip south to the court of Charles II in *The Heart of Midlothian*.[6]

Scott also demonstrates a wide and affectionate knowledge of *The Pilgrim's Progress* in his letters, using the text to gloss aspects of his mood to his correspondents. This is particularly – if a little obviously – the case when Scott writes of bearing or putting down enormous burdens. In a letter of 1809 to John B. Morritt, a classicist, renowned traveller, and close personal friend, explaining his relief at getting through a particularly onerous task, Scott writes: 'I have wrought my way hitherward and honest Christian in the pilgrim's progress never felt more relieved when his burthen dropped from him and rolled into the sepulchre'.[7] Elsewhere Scott makes repeated reference to being dragged from 'the slough of Despond' by the timely arrival of a letter that has revived his spirits.[8] And insofar as cultural affairs are concerned Scott also has recourse to Bunyan. In a letter to the American author Washington Irving dated 1 March 1820 Scott takes a pithy dig at booksellers whilst simultaneously celebrating their alleged loss of power.

> They have lost the art of altogether damning up the road between the author and the public, which they were once able to do as effectually as Diabolus, in John Bunyan's Holy War, closed up the windows of my Lord Understanding's mansion.[9]

And in a letter to Lady Louise Stuart, with reference to the completion of his life of Napoleon, Scott remarks: 'I positively felt last week like Christian when released from his burthen and could willingly have sung when I went on my way'.[10]

---

6   See Keeble, 'Bunyan and his Reputation', pp. 253–4; see also Douglas Gifford, 'Scott's Fiction and the Search for Mythic Regeneration', in *Scott and His Influence*, eds J. H. Alexander and David Hewitt (Aberdeen: Association for Scottish Literary Studies, 1983), pp. 180–8 (p. 184).
7   *The Letters of Sir Walter Scott*, ed. H. J. C. Grierson, 12 vols (London: Constable, 1932–37), I, 210.
8   Ibid., p. 54.
9   Ibid., VI, 142.
10 Ibid., X, 236.

The casual manner in which Scott refers positively to Bunyan in something as intimate as a letter to a friend speaks volumes about the affection in which he held his work. But it is not only in the area of the private sphere that Scott has recourse to Bunyan's works. Consider the following sentiments expressed in letter of 1814 to Miss Clephane, the daughter of a highland family with whom Scott was friendly:

> As for public news I begin to think of the last twenty years like honest John Bunyan [:] 'I awoke and behold it was a dream'[,] and were it not for certain feelings that hint to me [...] I would think there were little in public matters which would persuade me that I had outlived the Republic [...] and the no less formidable imperial dynasty of France and have seen that most extraordinary people set down where they were taken up after such seas of blood and mines of treasure as have been expended on these gigantic plans of ambition.[11]

The reference to Bunyan in relation to revolution in France and the twenty-year period following it naturally begs comparison with the mid-seventeenth-century revolution in England and its own republican moment. I will have more to say on this later when I consider Scott's review of Southey's edition and life. For the moment I am interested in Scott's perception of Bunyan's political and religious views and the point of contact between them and his fictional writing, chiefly as both Scott and Bunyan had lived through tumultuous times.

Coleridge's remarks on Bunyan and his obvious distaste for the 'fanaticism' of seventeenth-century sectarianism are of a piece with his attempted de-politicization of Milton's *Paradise Lost*. Wordsworth too sees in *The Pilgrim's Progress* a 'beautiful allegory' that transcends its time, a work that is not of its moment but for posterity.[12] That Blake saw Milton and Bunyan in an entirely different light from Coleridge has framed much of the history of the critical reception of both *Paradise Lost* and, to a lesser extent, *The Pilgrim's Progress*, down to our own times.[13] As far as Bunyan is concerned, much turns

---

11   Ibid., III, 446.
12   *The Prose Works of William Wordsworth*, eds W. J. B. Owen and Jane Worthington Smyser, 3 vols (Oxford: Clarendon Press, 1974), III, 315.
13   As has been well documented by critics, Milton's reputation in the Romantic period was huge. The classic study of Miltonic influence on Romantic poetry is

on Blake's analysis of the purpose of allegory as a literary device. Blake felt that allegory served a function beyond the expression of literary imaginative genius, and wrote in *Vision of the Last Judgement* that 'Allegory is seldom without some Vision. Pilgrim's Progress is full of it'.[14] As well as executing about thirty sketches to illustrate *The Pilgrim's Progress* in 1825 Blake, as becomes one brought up in a Dissenting tradition, demonstrates, like Scott, an easy familiarity with the text and drew upon it to illustrate his state of mind in letters to his friends.[15] In a letter to William Hayley dated 4 December 1804 he echoes Bunyan's masterpiece with reference to Christian in the Valley of the Shadow of Death:

> I have indeed fought through a Hell of terrors and horrors (which none could know but myself) in a divided existence; now no longer divided nor at war with myself, I shall travel on in the strength of the Lord God, as Poor Pilgrim says.[16]

Blake's visionary, apocalyptic poetry, mixed in the cauldron of eighteenth-century and Romantic Dissent, has a revolutionary edge that finds inspiration in the life and times of Bunyan's Christian. Nor is he the only nonconformist writer to draw on Bunyan in such a way. So too does William Hazlitt, the period's most notable critic and journalist. In an essay entitled 'The Letter-Bell' Hazlitt invokes the Shrewsbury countryside with its 'blue hills near the place where I was brought up', and the road he followed, 'by which I first set out on my journey through life'. It 'stares me in the face as plain, but from time and change not less visionary and mysterious, than the pictures in the *Pilgrim's Progress*'. In the very next sentence Hazlitt extends by association, journey, light, vision, mystery, and Bunyan's masterwork into a eulogy for the French Revolution: 'I should notice, that at this

---

      by Harold Bloom, *The Anxiety of Influence* (Oxford: Oxford University Press, 1973). See also Newlyn, *Paradise Lost and the Romantic Reader*.

14   *William Blake's Writings*, ed. G. E. Bentley, 3 vols (Oxford: Oxford University Press, 1978), II, 1008.

15   See G. E. Bentley, *The Stranger from Paradise: A Biography of William Blake* (New Haven and London: Yale University Press, 2001), pp. 429–30, and E. P. Thompson, *Witness Against the Beast: William Blake and the Moral Law* (Cambridge: Cambridge University Press, 1993).

16   *William Blake's Writings*, ed. Bentley, II, 1616.

time the light of the French Revolution circled my head like a glory, though dabbled with drops of crimson gore: I walked comfortable and cheerful by its side'.[17]

Scott's review of Southey's edition of *The Pilgrim's Progress* in the *Quarterly Review* explicitly engages with the politics of nonconformity and Dissent in the seventeenth century and in the process tries to whitewash the radicalism that many have read into the allegory. The years between the publication of *The Heart of Midlothian* in 1818 and the appearance of Scott's review in 1830 were turbulent ones in terms of religion, though less so as far as political radicalism is concerned. Yet the ghosts of their union were still in the machine. The question of religious toleration, and the related issues of anti-Catholicism and protestant evangelicalism – or what some saw as nonconformist fanaticism – are framed by Scott in the review of Southey's edition in the context of Bunyan's religious experience in the seventeenth century. This of course is also the case in relation to *The Heart of Midlothian* where the Deans family patriarch is a committed Presbyterian, a doctrine that is more or less followed by his deeply pious daughter Jeanie. Even here, however, as John Sutherland has noted in his recently published *Life*, Scott offers a view of nonconformity in *The Heart of Midlothian* that is altogether more benign than that which is presented to the reader in, say, *Old Mortality* (1816). Old Davie Deans is representative of 'the domestic and virtuous aspect of the Cameronian faith', and lives out his days as having been 'adopted' along with his daughter Jeanie by the Duke of Argyll, and put to work as estate managers on his highland property.[18]

Although Scott was anything but a friend to political radicalism, his Toryism was not of a bigoted and intolerant kind. He went against the so-called 'Protestant' faction in a party that sought to safeguard the hegemony of the Anglican Church. He supported the repeal of the Test and Corporation Acts in 1828 and also supported the bill for Catholic Emancipation in the following year. In this respect, at least in regard

---

17 Cited in Tom Paulin, *The Day Star of Liberty: William Hazlitt's Radical Style* (London: Faber, 1998), p. 218.
18 John Sutherland, *The Life of Sir Walter Scott* (Oxford: Oxford University Press, 1995), pp. 211, 212.

to equality for nonconformists, Scott is in sympathy with the spirit of later seventeenth-century ideas about toleration. He demonstrates a haughty disdain for religious intolerance, based perhaps on his role as enlightened Tory and public intellectual. He was a 'Scottish Addison', and one who seems not to have put much importance on the mere forms of religious devotion.[19] Perhaps Scott's softening towards Presbyterianism and tolerance towards religious pluralism was accelerated in the 1820s by the retreat of the perceived threat from political radicalism in the lower orders of society. Such a shift has been noted by modern commentators from across a wide ideological divide, including E. P. Thompson and particularly and most recently, Ian McCalman and Jonathan Clark. McCalman writes that:

> This quiescence is attributed to the draconian anti-radical repression of 1819–22, to the improvement in economic conditions in the early and middle portions of the decade, to the more liberal reforming disposition of the Tory government and to the widespread popular diffusion of the values of respectability and self-improvement.[20]

According to Jonathan Clark, the speed of 'economic recovery in the 1820s produced the dramatic withering away of both the rural and urban clamour for Reform, as its opponents predicted it would'.[21]

Such equanimity towards religious diversity was by no means ubiquitous in the Romantic period, however, and does not extend apparently to those further down the social pecking order, where *The Pilgrim's Progress* also takes its place in the religious dogma and working class politics of the early nineteenth century. As the historian Norman Gash informs us:

---

19 Ibid., p. 72.
20 Ian McCalman, *Radical Underworld: Prophets, Revolutionaries and Pornographers in London, 1795–1840* (Oxford: Oxford University Press, 1998; first published by Cambridge University Press in 1988). See also E. P. Thompson, *The Making of the English Working Class* (Harmondsworth: Penguin, 1963), pp. 781–915.
21 J. C. D. Clark, *English Society 1660–1832* (Cambridge: Cambridge University Press, 2000), p. 521.

Lower down the [social] scale, in a society where a worn volume of Foxe's *Book of Martyrs* was often a treasured possession in the cottages of the poor along with the Bible and *Pilgrim's Progress*, the historic anti-Roman prejudice was still alive.[22]

If radical reformers were relatively quiet, then religious reformers were not. According to commentators such as Sutherland, Scott by the 1820s appears not to have seen any correlation in his own time between sectarian and political radicalism. The two appear as distinctively different issues in England in the 1820s. In the decades before the 1820s, however, the situation was markedly different. E. P. Thompson long since recognized this connection, arguing that Bunyan stands alongside Paine, Cobbett, and Owen as representative of artisan radicalism. Thompson flatly states that '*Pilgrim's Progress* is, with *Rights of Man*, one of the two foundation texts of the English working-class movement'.[23] It is from this tainted alignment between unrestricted religious freedom, political radicalism and republicanism that Scott in his review is eager to free Bunyan and *The Pilgrim's Progress*.

The important factor to bear in mind here then is not Scott's so-called enlightened view of religious toleration in the 1820s, but his concern that nonconformist religious beliefs should be kept entirely separate from political ideology. In *The Pilgrim's Progress* Christian's journey into grace and the problems that he must endure in order to reach that state of grace, is the controlling metaphor of the text. In Scott's fiction a variation on the same rule applies. *Old Mortality* and *The Heart of Midlothian* are texts that, according to Sutherland, book-end Scott's own journey from bigotry to enlightenment, insofar as religious toleration is concerned. This, in line with recent historiography of the 1820s, is itself indicative of a general feeling of economic well-being and the perception amongst contemporaries that political radicalism is on the wane. Christian's journey, with its by-ways and false dawns, and its encounter with false prophets and mistaken ideals – social, political, and religious – is mirrored in what James Chandler

---

22 Norman Gash, *Aristocracy and People: Britain 1815–1865* (London: Edward Arnold, 1979), p. 139.
23 Thompson, *Making of the English Working Class*, p. 34.

refers to as Henry Morton's 'movement back and forth across apparent ideological borders' in *Old Mortality*.[24] As Chandler goes on to suggest, since Lukács's seminal work on the historical novel, we are conditioned critically to view Scott's heroes in novels such as *Old Mortality* and *Waverley* as 'figures in the middle, passive mediocrities between active extremities in conflict, not world-historical in themselves but shaped by world-historical struggle'.[25] Morton's movement across the ideological borders of Anglo-Scottish relations and internal Scottish conflict sees him continuously searching for the right road towards a state of contentment. His involvement with armed conflict is central to this process.

In a throwaway line in his review in the *Quarterly* Scott says: 'Of John Bunyan's politics we know nothing, except that for a time he was enrolled in the Parliamentary army'.[26] For many literary critics and some historians this has proved enough to provide at least a starting point for a further investigation of Bunyan's politics. Christopher Hill, for one has drawn attention to the possibility that Bunyan as a private soldier might well have been radicalized by the Civil War, in the same manner that soldiers were after the First and Second World Wars. The spread of sects and the militancy of some army chaplains such as Paul Hobson allied politics to religious fervour and encouraged radicalism in both fields. Similarly, Richard Greaves has drawn attention to the presence in Newport Pagnell of the radical preachers Paul Hobson and William Erberry, and to the growing atmosphere of antinomianism and the spread of sects.[27] The New Model Army was a highly politicized organization suffused with radical independency and was consistently the most authoritative power bloc in the nation from the

---

24 Chandler, *England in 1819: The Politics of Literary Culture and the Case of Romantic Historicism* (Chicago and London: Chicago University Press, 1998), p. 213.
25 Ibid.
26 Scott in *The Quarterly Review*, p. 471.
27 Christopher Hill, *A Turbulent, Seditious, and Factious People: John Bunyan and his Church* (Oxford: Oxford University Press, 1988), chapter 5. Greaves, *Glimpses of Glory*, pp. 22–3.

regicide of Charles I in 1649 – in which it was a significant player – to the restoration of Charles II in 1660.[28]

In *Old Mortality* Scott is alive to the radicalism of life in the army in the 1640s when he has Morton defend the actions of a radicalized soldiery:

> the violence of their zeal expended itself in their exhortations and sermons, without bringing divisions into their counsels, or cruelty to their conduct. I have often heard my father say so, and protest that he wondered at nothing so much as the contrast between the extravagance of their religious tenets, and the wisdom and moderation with which they conducted their civil and military affairs.[29]

It follows from this that Scott was far from ignorant about the alliance between religious fervour and political radicalism in the army in which Bunyan served. Morton, however, is keen to emphasize that there was a separation between the zeal that 'expended itself' in 'exhortations and sermons', and the 'wisdom and moderation' that defined political and military action. Given Scott's knowledge of the period this seems wilful blindness unless the explanation lies in the moment of Scott's writing, in his determination not to hold up to the radicals of the present the political theology of the revolutionaries of the past.

Scott, like Coleridge, prefers the Bunyan of Parnassus and seems fully to endorse Southey's view of sectarian politics in the mid-seventeenth century, which he quotes approvingly:

> 'In an evil hour were the doctrines of the Gospel sophisticated with questions which should have been left in the schools. [...] Many are the poor creatures whom such questions have driven to despair and madness, and suicide; and no one ever more narrowly escaped such a catastrophe than Bunyan'.[30]

---

28 See Austin Woolrych, *Soldiers and Statesmen: The General Council of the Army and its Debates, 1647–1648* (Oxford: Clarendon Press, 1987). See also Woolrych's 'Historical Introduction' in *The Complete Prose Works of John Milton*, gen. ed. Don M. Wolfe, 8 vols (New Haven and London: Yale University Press, 1953–82), VII, 1–228.

29 Sir Walter Scott, *Old Mortality*, ed. Angus Calder (Harmondsworth: Penguin, 1985), p. 275.

30 Scott, in *The Quarterly Review*, p. 472.

The implicit suggestion here is that such questions of theology and eschatology should be left to those with the education and social standing best fitted to address them. Too much dabbling in affairs that is above them by the uneducated leads naturally to a psychological crisis at best, and self-violence at worst. Scott undoubtedly concurs. At the beginning of the review Scott describes Bunyan's education as 'clownish and vulgar'.[31] Similarly, he is entirely dismissive of individual inspiration: 'So strong is the power of the human imagination, that he who seriously expects to see miracles, does not long expect them in vain'.[32] There is an echo here of David Hume's *Enquiry Concerning Human Understanding* and that philosopher's remark that 'the mind invents or imagines some event, which it ascribes to the object as its effect, and it is plain that this invention must be entirely arbitrary'.[33] Hume, however, is dismissive of Bunyan as a writer, comparing him very unfavourably with Addison:

> Though there may be found persons, who give the preference [to Bunyan over Addison,] no one pays attention to such a taste; and we pronounce without scruple the sentiment of these pretended critics to be absurd and ridiculous.[34]

Posterity, of course, has begged to differ.

Scott is clearly at odds with Hume's opinion of what constitutes the literary; this is not the case, however, in relation to seventeenth-century dissent. In his scorn and contempt for visionary religion and religious independency, millenarianism and antinomianism, Scott demonstrates further similarities here with the views of Hume. In his hugely popular *History of England* Hume shows little respect for the achievements of the Rump Parliament and the Protectorate of Oliver Cromwell. In sentiments that echo Hobbes, Hume declares that all of

---

31 Ibid., p. 469.
32 Ibid., p. 473.
33 Cited by Patricia Harkin, 'Romance and Real History: The Historical Novel as Literary Innovation', in *Scott and His Influence*, eds J. H. Alexander and David Hewitt (Aberdeen: Association for Scottish Literary Studies, 1983), pp. 157–68 (p. 162).
34 David Hume, 'Of the Standard of Taste', in *Essays Moral, Political, and Literary*, ed. Eugene F. Miller (Indianapolis: Liberty Fund, rev. edn, 1985), p. 231.

those stepping outside the circle of religious conformity contributed to a state of imminent anarchy: 'The bands of society were every where loosened; and the irregular passions of men were encouraged by speculative principles, still more unsocial and irregular'. He goes on to argue, in terms that would influence Scott and Southey, that

> excepting their principles of toleration, the maxims, by which the republicans regulated ecclesiastical affairs, no more prognosticated any durable settlement, than those by which they conducted their civil affairs.[35]

Both Southey and Scott argue that there is no real understanding of Bunyan or of *The Pilgrim's Progress* without a similar understanding of '"the stage of burning enthusiasm through which he passed"'.[36] They understand it, however, in extremely negative terms, and it is at this point that their conservative politics are at their most pronounced. *The Pilgrim's Progress* is the product of enthusiasm experienced and then denied. Had Bunyan not denied it then he would undoubtedly have gone the way of Ranting libertines such as Lawrence Clarkson, whose *The Lost Sheep Found* (1660) is condemned by Scott as a debauched and obscene text.[37] Scott goes on to develop this line of argument with a voyeuristic concentration on Clarkson's alleged sexual excesses. Clarkson's particular brand of self-indulgence – his antinomianism – results in behaviour that is in marked contrast to that of Bunyan, whose 'religious despair' is benign in comparison, saved as he was from 'profligacy and atheism [and] by his constant course of scriptural study'.[38] This not only misunderstands Clarkson's position in religious terms, but also mistakes Bunyan's scriptural literalism as a vehicle of politically quiet reflection.

Bunyan's innate decency, it seems, allied to his moderate interpretation of Scripture, kept him from the wilder shores of seventeenth-century enthusiasm. This is a view that Scott extends to the Quakers,

---

35 Hume, *The History of England*, 6 vols (Indianapolis: Liberty Fund, rev. edn, 1983), VI, 4, 40.
36 Scott, in *The Quarterly Review*, p. 475.
37 Ibid., p. 476.
38 Ibid., p. 478.

once 'frantic [...] who thanks to time and toleration have now settled down into the gentlest and mildest of religionists'.[39] Persecution of nonconformists following the restoration of the Stuart monarchy, according to Scott, was not unexpected, and indeed 'not unnatural'. Prison, it appears, did Bunyan no harm at all. In fact 'The fruit of his submission to the will of God was probably a state of peace of mind and contentment, such as in his lifetime he had not hitherto enjoyed'.[40] In this extraordinary statement Scott is apparently arguing that Bunyan's imprisonment is an extension of the will of God and that the Great Persecution of the later seventeenth century is somehow divinely sanctioned. On the leniency and freedom on parole that Bunyan occasionally enjoyed during his twelve years of imprisonment Scott follows Southey, and quotes him to that effect: '"the fever of his enthusiasm had spent itself; the asperity of his opinions had softened as his mind enlarged"'.[41] More recent scholarship has been vigorous in its defence of Bunyan's consistent anti-authoritarian position in the Restoration period.[42]

In a twenty-five page review Scott devotes roughly half of it to absolving Bunyan from the pernicious charge of fanaticism. His innocence in this regard – and here Scott and Southey are once again in complete agreement – is what makes the high art of *The Pilgrim's Progress* possible. All of this is markedly different from the rather trenchant reading of Southey's edition rendered in the *Edinburgh Review* in 1831 by the great Whig historian Thomas Babington

---

[39] Ibid., p. 479.
[40] Ibid.
[41] Ibid., p. 480.
[42] Stuart Sim and David Walker, *Bunyan and Authority: The Rhetoric of Dissent and the Legitimation Crisis in Seventeenth-Century England* (Bern: Peter Lang, 2000); Stuart Sim, *Negotiations with Paradox: Narrative Practice and Narrative Form in Bunyan and Defoe* (Hemel Hempstead: Harvester Wheatsheaf, 1990); Thomas Luxon, *Literal Figures: Puritan Allegory and the Reformation Crisis in Representation* (Chicago and London: Chicago University Press, 1995); Tamsin Spargo, *The Writing of John Bunyan* (Aldershot: Ashgate, 1997); Greaves, *Glimpses of Glory*; Hill, *A Turbulent and Seditious People*. For a view that emphasizes theology and faith rather than politics see Michael Davies, *Graceful Reading: Theology and Narrative in the Works of John Bunyan* (Oxford: Oxford University Press, 2002).

Macaulay. Yet in the first instance at least we can be forgiven for thinking that Macaulay is showing uncharacteristic critical restraint. He begins by praising Southey's scholarship and the very high production values of the edition. And other than stating his 'dissent' from Southey's political opinions Macaulay confines himself for the first half of the review to a mild chastisement: 'His attempts to excuse the odious persecution to which Bunyan was subjected, have sometimes moved our indignation'.[43] By mid-point in the review, however, Macaulay's indignation has got the better of him and the tone and tenor of his language becomes more strident and much less forgiving.

> In whatever age Bunyan had lived, the history of his feelings would, in all probability, have been very curious. But the time in which his lot was cast, was the time of a great stirring of the human mind. A tremendous burst of public feeling, produced by the tyranny of the hierarchy, menaced the old ecclesiastical institutions with destruction. To the gloomy irregularity of one intolerant Church had succeeded the licence of innumerable sects, drunk with the sweet and heavy must of their new liberty. Fanaticism, engendered by persecution, and destined to engender fresh persecution in turn spread rapidly through society. Even the strongest and most commanding minds were not proof against this strange taint. Any time might have produced George Fox and James Naylor. But to one time alone belong the frantic delusions of such a statesman as Vane, and the hysterical tears of such a soldier as Cromwell.[44]

The most striking aspect of this quotation is the manner in which Macaulay forces his reading of Bunyan back into the history of England's most tumultuous political events and in the process lays the blame for fanaticism, not on the heads of those who practised it, but those who instead tried to force religious uniformity on a recalcitrant and significant minority. We are very far indeed here from the view of Scott and Southey that the literary output of Bunyan's imaginative genius occurred despite and not because of the times in which he lived.

In line with a strain of aristocratic anticlericalism that has its roots in seventeenth- and eighteenth-century Whig republican thought, Macaulay's view of the seventeenth-century established church is also

---

43 Macaulay, in the *Edinburgh Review*, p. 450.
44 Ibid., p. 456.

dismissive and contemptuous. Sects, on the other hand, are not so much soaked in fanaticism as 'drunk', that is, intoxicated 'with the sweet and heavy must of their new *liberty*' (emphasis mine), a word which is itself soaked in the Whig rhetoric of 1688 and beyond. As the review develops Macaulay does not shirk the question of guessing where Bunyan's political loyalties lay. Whereas Scott finds it impossible to determine Bunyan's political allegiances from the text, or indeed from his life, Macaulay states unequivocally that no true understanding of *The Pilgrim's Progress* is possible without recognition on the part of the reader that in the figure of Mr. Greatheart

> Bunyan had in view some stout old Greatheart of Naseby and Worcester, who prayed with his men before he drilled them, who knew the spiritual state of every dragoon in his troop; and who, with the praise of God in his mouth, and a two-edged sword in his hand, had turned to flight on many fields of battle, the swearing drunken bravoes of Rupert and Lunsford.[45]

Macaulay in the early nineteenth century believed in the absolute centrality of the events of the 1640s and 1650s to English liberty, at this stage even more so than the Glorious Revolution of 1688.[46] In his essay on Milton (1825) Macaulay writes with the fervour one associates with nonconformity in his eulogy for 'that great battle':

> Then were first proclaimed those mighty principles which have since worked their way into the depths of the American forests, which have roused Greece from the slavery and degradation of two thousand years, and which, from one end of Europe to the other, have kindled an unquenchable fire in the hearts of the oppressed, and loosed the knees of the oppressors with an unwonted fear.[47]

This reading of the mid-seventeenth century is of a piece with Macaulay's critique of Southey's edition of *The Pilgrim's Progress*. Slightly later in the *Essay on Milton* Macaulay berates public understanding of the English Civil Wars, fed, as he sees it, by the flaws in particular of its historians pre-1825. Most people, he argues, have

---

45   Ibid., p. 459.
46   Worden, *Roundhead Reputations*, p. 228.
47   *Macaulay's Essay on Milton*, ed. John Downie (London: Blackie and Son, 1950), §50, p. 32.

received their knowledge from Hume's *History of England*, a work that demonstrates its author's hatred of religion in terms so voluble that 'he hated liberty for having been allied' with it.[48] In Macaulay's essay on John Hampden he argues that the Civil War was a defence of liberty in the face of 'a direct attack [that] was made by an arbitrary government on a sacred right of Englishmen, on a right which was their chief security for all their other rights'.[49] In 1796, and on the same subject, Southey's views on Hampden were very similar.[50]

Macaulay's lack of doubt about Bunyan's identification of Greatheart with a politicized fire and brimstone army chaplain in the earlier passage quoted, is in marked contrast to Scott, who as stated earlier finds it difficult to adjudge Bunyan's politics from his enrolment in the New Model Army. Far from wishing to separate Bunyan's religious beliefs from his political ideas, Macaulay instead espouses an emphatic, unequivocal certainty regarding the connection between the two. Given the indivisible association of religion with politics in the seventeenth century Macaulay brings to his analysis that keen historical knowledge for which he would be lauded in 1848 when his history of England from the reign of James II appeared.

In his review Macaulay is in full rhetorical flow as he grasps the nettle of Bunyan's political allegory. He is no longer interested in being disinterested and instead plunges the reader into the complexities of seventeenth-century politics and religion. Of Faithful's martyrdom Macaulay writes: 'It is impossible to doubt that Bunyan intended to satirize the mode in which state trials were conducted under Charles II'.[51] The persecutory nature of prosecuting religious and political dissent in the seventeenth century has its corollary in the state trials of the 1790s and beyond, particularly in the manner in which radicals with

---

48   Ibid., §51, p. 33.
49   Macaulay, 'John Hampden', in *Critical and Historical Essays Contributed to the Edinburgh Review*, 3 vols (London: Longman, 1843), II, 426.
50   'The rebel Hambden [*sic*], at whose glorious name / The heart of every honest Englishman / Beats high with conscious pride'; Robert Southey, 'Inscription: For a Column at Newbury'. Southey subsequently modified this sonnet considerably in later editions of the poem. See Nicholes, 'Revolutions Compared', pp. 264–5.
51   Macaulay, in the *Edinburgh Review*, p. 459.

Dissenting or nonconformist affiliations were at the forefront of agitation for reform regarding the franchise, and were persecuted accordingly by both the state and by Church and King mobs. Macaulay, of course, is justly famous as a reforming Whig and is an intellectual product of the legacy of seventeenth- and eighteenth-century aristocratic republicanism that had been transformed by the early nineteenth century from a position that advocated the abolition of monarchy to one that instead emphasized republican idioms to advance a language and policy of opposition framed within the doctrine of a constitutional monarchy.

According to Whig political rhetoric, rebellion against tyranny is not merely justifiable; it is a responsibility of those who believe in liberty and fear oppression. In this respect Macaulay's early work is utterly consistent. The contextual argument forwarded in relation to the politics of *The Pilgrim's Progress*, and Southey's treatment thereof, the essay 'Milton', and the essay 'John Hampden', are all products of their author's Whig political beliefs: his analysis of the period's literature and literary figures is similarly embedded. In this respect, if in little else, Macaulay is at one with other more radical voices of opposition in the period.

The anarchist, political philosopher, and novelist William Godwin's republican *History of the Commonwealth* (1824–8) makes similar claims for the revolutionary events of the mid-seventeenth century. Godwin idolized the Rump Parliament of 1649–53 and wrote positively of the New Model Army, with its politicized theology, in which Bunyan served.[52] Like Blake, Godwin was a product of eighteenth-century Dissent and had been nurtured on *The Pilgrim's Progress*. Although in adulthood he would reject his nonconformist heritage Godwin, a precocious child, had read Bunyan's text half a dozen times by the time he was five years old.[53] Not only does this colour his view of the period's history with its sympathetic understanding of the important role that religious independency played in

---

52 William Godwin, *History of the Commonwealth of England*, 4 vols (London: Henry Colburn, 1824–8), II, 151–2.
53 Peter Marshall, *William Godwin* (New Haven and London: Yale University Press, 1984), p. 14.

the events of 1640–60, it also has its impact upon his fiction. In his most celebrated novel, *Caleb Williams*, Godwin paints a portrait of its eponymous hero and his antagonist Falkland that shares thematic concerns with *The Pilgrim's Progress*: in its analysis of the psychology of anxiety, guilt and despair, is figured the search for election and salvation, and the pursuit of knowledge. More conventionally analysed as a popularization of Godwin's *magnum opus*, *Enquiry Concerning Political Justice* (1793), *Caleb Williams* takes as its governing metaphor a tortuous physical and psychological journey and search for truth. In this respect Bunyan's shadow looms large in Godwin's work, as does more generally the tradition of Puritan spiritual autobiography.

Macaulay's literary criticism has itself come under scrutiny and has been found wanting.[54] Clearly, he is no Hazlitt or Coleridge. Nevertheless, Macaulay is an advocate of literature *in* history, and in his concern not to separate politics from religion is strikingly modern in his methodology. The divisions between Scott and Southey on the one hand, and Macaulay on the other are clear-cut. *The Pilgrim's Progress*, by the common consent of all writers and critics cited in this study is a work of inspirational genius. But there the concord ends, with opinion divided according to political beliefs. Nevertheless, and as Bunyan's most recent biographer has noted, 'together Southey, Scott and Macaulay elevated *The Pilgrim's Progress* to an English classic'.[55]

---

54 See Downie's Introduction to *Macaulay's Essay on Milton*, *passim*.
55 Greaves, *Glimpses of Glory*, p. 626.

Norman Vance

3 Pilgrims Abounding: Bunyan and the Victorian Novel

There are plenty of more or less secular pilgrims and pilgrimages in the more serious Victorian fictions. But do they have much to do with *The Pilgrim's Progress*? It hardly needs to be said that the pilgrimage theme does not begin or end with Bunyan. It can be traced back to the Bible, to Abraham and his descendants, a pilgrim people seeking permanent settlement in Canaan, and to other questing souls identified as strangers and pilgrims on earth. The biblical idea of the pilgrim, someone without assured rights of settlement or citizenship, is clearer in Wycliffe's fourteenth-century translation than in the 1611 Authorized Version of the English Bible in which the actual words 'pilgrim' and 'pilgrimage' occur only twice and three times, respectively. The corresponding Latin terms *peregrinus* and *peregrinatio*, used in the Vulgate, and the words in the original Greek and Hebrew texts which they translate, are more common.[1] Though Wycliffe, working from the

---

[1] See *A Theological Dictionary of the New Testament*, ed. Gerhard Kittel, trans. G. W. Bromiley, 10 vols (Grand Rapids, Michigan: W. B. Eerdmans, 1964–76) under παρεπίδημος and πάροικος. The language of the 1611 Authorized Version (AV), quoted in the examples which follow, is in these instances close to or identical with that of Tyndale's version (1530–7). Some of the principal biblical references to 'pilgrims' and 'pilgrimage' (together with 'strangers', 'sojourners' and 'foreigners', also used to translate the same biblical terms) are Genesis 17:8 (Wycliffe 'the lond of thi pilgrymage, al the lond of Chanaan'; Tyndale and AV 'the land wherein thou art a stranger, all the land of Canaan'; Vulgate 'terram peregrinationis tuae'), Genesis 23:4 (Wycliffe 'a comelyng and a pilgrym'; Tyndale 'a stranger and a foreigner'; AV 'stranger and sojourner'; Vulgate 'advena sum et peregrinus'), Genesis 47:9 ('the days of the years of my pilgrimage'), Exodus 6:4 ('land of their pilgrimage' [ie Canaan]), Exodus 23:9 (Wycliffe 'Thou schalt not be diseseful to a pilgrym [...] ye weren pilgryms in the lond of Egipt'; Tyndale and AV 'thou shalt not oppress a stranger [...]

Vulgate, consistently rendered *peregrinus* as 'pilgrim', Protestant translators used the word 'pilgrim' very sparingly, often substituting 'stranger' or 'sojourner', perhaps because they distrusted the Catholic practice of pilgrimage to particular shrines as an attempt to procure salvation by works alone. In the twentieth article of Philip Melanchthon's Lutheran *Augsburg Confession* (1530) pilgrimages were identified as 'childish and needless works' or 'unprofitable works', grouped with holy-days, particular fasts, services in honour of saints, the use of rosaries and so on as unacceptable substitutes for saving faith.[2]

But the idea, if not the medieval practice, of pilgrimage as lonely and difficult journey is strongly scriptural. It is then developed and reflected in St Augustine's *City of God*,[3] in the Old English poem *The Seafarer*, in the early fourteenth-century *Pèlerinage de la vie humaine*, translated by John Lydgate and known to Chaucer, in Chaucer's *Canterbury Tales*, in Sir Walter Raleigh's poem 'The Passionate Man's Pilgrimage', and – more immediately relevant to Bunyan since we know he owned the book – in Arthur Dent's immensely popular *The Plaine Man's Path-way to Heauen* (1601).

Bunyan's influence, or perhaps more accurately the influence of themes which Bunyan addresses, is of course mediated visually as well as textually. The theme of pilgrimage and the figure of the pilgrim and other images invoked by Bunyan are widely known. They are familiar not just in illustrations of Bunyan such as those by John

---

seeing ye were strangers in the land of Egypt'; Vulgate 'Peregrino molestus non eris. [...] ipsi peregrini fuistis in terra Aegypti'), Psalm 39:12 (Wycliffe 'a comelynge at thee; and a pilgrime, as alle my fadris'; AV 'I am a stranger with thee, and a sojourner, as all my fathers were'; Vulgate 'advena ego sum apud te, et peregrinus sicut omnes patres mei'), Psalm 119:54 'house of my pilgrimage', Hebrews 11:13 'strangers and pilgrims on the earth', 1 Peter 2:11 'I beseech you as strangers and pilgrims'.

2   Philip Melanchthon, *The Confession of Faith which Was Submitted to His Imperial Majesty Charles V at the Diet of Augsburg in the Year 1530*, trans. G. F. Bente and W. H. T. Dau in *Triglot Concordia: The Symbolical Books of the Evangelical-Lutheran Church* (St Louis, Missouri: Concordia Publishing House, 1921), available at http://users.frii.com/gosplow/augsburg.html, accessed 29/11/2004.

3   St Augustine, *The City of God*, XV, 6.

Martin, landscape gardener of the Valley of the Shadow of Death and town-planner and architect in chief of the Celestial City in Southey's 1830 edition of *The Pilgrim's Progress*, but also in seventeenth-century emblem-books such as those by Francis Quarles and George Wither. Bunyan himself made self-conscious use of already familiar didactic images or emblems in the House of the Interpreter in *The Pilgrim's Progress*. John Manning, the most recent analyst of the emblem tradition, has noted that the emblematic illustrations now associated with Bunyan's *Book for Boys and Girls* (1686) were in fact added to the ninth edition of 1724, when the book was re-titled *Divine Emblems: or, Temporal Things Spiritualized, Fitted for the Use of Boys and Girls* and are not so much specifically inspired by Bunyan's text as part of the general visual vocabulary of the age and the culture, available to Bunyan and to everyone else. Manning also points out the longevity of this visual vocabulary, tracing it down to Victorian times in works such as William Holmes's *Religious Emblems and Allegories* (1854).[4]

But if Bunyan brings together and draws on themes and images which were already widely current that enhances rather than limits his usefulness to posterity, including the Victorians. A best-selling popular writer two centuries after his death, he was the most accessible and best-known source for material of wide and enduring interest, a convenient reminder of what was often thought and felt. The pilgrimage, the momentous and difficult journey, may be almost as old as time, but Bunyan's versions of familiar, at times almost archetypal material, whether encountered as text or as illustration, are often the most vivid we have, literally part of what every schoolboy knew at least until the early twentieth century. We know about the vanity of vanities from Ecclesiastes, but it was Bunyan's imaginative realization of a familiar theme in the idea of 'Vanity Fair' in *The Pilgrim's Progess* that gave Thackeray his best-remembered title and a controlling metaphor for his novel to go with it. The influence of Bunyan on Thackeray is clear. Scholars such as Barry Qualls have traced the long shadow of Bunyan in Carlyle's *Sartor Resartus*, in Charlotte Brontë

---

4 John Manning, *The Emblem* (London: Reaktion, 2002), pp. 89, 150.

and in Dickens, particularly in *The Old Curiosity Shop*.[5] Vincent Newey and others have discussed Bunyan's significance in the work of George Eliot, Thomas Hardy and the late-Victorian novelist Mark Rutherford or William Hale White whose family had a connection with Bunyan Meeting.[6] But more can still be said about how Bunyan and Bunyan's Pilgrim contributed to Victorian fiction and Victorian debate and the looming of post-Christian alienation and secular modernity, particularly in the work of Charles Kingsley, Thomas Hardy and Mrs Humphry Ward. And there are of course other essays to be written about Bunyan and those late-Victorian romantics Ralph Vaughan Williams (b. 1872) and John Buchan (b. 1875), author of *Mr Standfast* (1919).

Being imaginatively influenced by Bunyan is of course not the same thing as fully endorsing him or sharing his world-view. Vaughan Williams regarded himself as an agnostic, and Kingsley and Hardy were quite critical in different ways, appropriating Bunyan for their own rather different purposes. Difficult and contentious journeys undertaken out of high principle could be religiously significant, but they could also be significant in other ways. Though at least one modern religious commentator has airily claimed that *The Pilgrim's Progress* 'has no politics'[7] there is at least an implicit politics of injustice and class-division in the trial of Faithful before Lord Hategood and a bigoted jury, derived in part from Bunyan's trial and imprisonment at the hands of Justice Keelin, and in the landowner's aggressive bullying represented in Giant Despair of Doubting Castle. Even before Marx and Marxist commentators, as Jonathan Rose has

---

5 Barry Qualls, *The Secular Pilgrims of Victorian Fiction* (Cambridge: Cambridge University Press, 1982).

6 Vincent Newey, 'Dorothea's Awakening: the Recall of Bunyan in *Middlemarch*', *Notes and Queries*, 31 (1984), 497–9; Vincent Newey, 'The Disinherited Pilgrim: *Jude the Obscure* and *The Pilgrim's Progress*', *Durham University Journal*, 75 (1987), 59–61; Vincent Newey, 'Mark Rutherford's Salvation and the Case of Catherine Furze', in *Mortal Pages, Literary Lives: Studies in Nineteenth-Century Autobiography*, eds Vincent Newey and Philip Shaw (Aldershot: Scolar Press, 1996), pp. 172–203.

7 Rev. Kenneth D. Harvey, 'The best seller that began with a jail sentence', *Belfast Telegraph*, 4 March 1978, p. 7.

shown, nineteenth-century political radicals could read Bunyan as one of them, as a rebel. As early as 1839 we have a secular, socialist *Political Pilgrim's Progress* serialized in the Chartist journal *The Northern Liberator*, tracing a journey from the City of Plunder to the City of Reform.[8] The anonymous author could be sure his readers would be familiar with his literary model.

Bunyan was remembered because he imparted to the idea of the journey or quest, identified by Northrop Frye as the essential form of the romance,[9] a moral seriousness and concentrated brevity which were lacking in Homer's *Odyssey* or Le Sage's *Gil Blas*. For Victorians and Edwardians, as for many of us, Bunyan was often first encountered in childhood, characteristically as a Sunday School prize or a gift from a pious relative. I first read *The Pilgrim's Progress* in a copy which had been given to my father about 1920, when he was seven, and my *Grace Abounding* was originally presented to Mercy Smith of the Senior Bible Class, Cavendish Place Calvinist Independent Chapel, Eastbourne, Christmas 1907. Since childhood is a time of extreme imaginative responsiveness, the imaginative legacy which persists into later life can often be negotiated and renegotiated with varying degrees of nostalgia, detachment, dissent or ironic distance. Jean-Paul Sartre said that he loathed his childhood and all that remained of it,[10] and one would expect Bunyan to have a hard time in the minds of religious renegades who sought to repudiate childhood attitudes. But the imaginative impact of his work was such that he was often loved and remembered even by those who came to loathe or at least to question his theology. A good example is the agnostic Vaughan Williams, whose musical engagement began before 1906 with identifying and arranging a suitably robust folk tune to go with the words of 'Who would true valiant be' in *The English Hymnal*. It ended nearly half a century later with an opera or 'operatic morality'

---

8 Jonathan Rose, *The Intellectual Life of the British Working Classes* (New Haven: Yale University Press, 2001), p. 105.
9 Northrop Frye, *Anatomy of Criticism* (1957; Princeton: Princeton University Press, 1971), p. 187.
10 Jean-Paul Sartre, *Les Mots* (1963), trans. Irene Clephane as *Words* (London: Penguin, 1967), p. 104.

of *The Pilgrim's Progress* performed at the Festival of Britain.[11] The slough of despond and the celestial city are perhaps more durable imaginatively and emotionally than the doctrines of the New Birth or Final Perseverance. Charles Kingsley's friend and brother-in-law, the historian James Anthony Froude, was the son of an archdeacon, younger brother of John Henry Newman's close friend Richard Hurrell Froude, but he drifted away from the assured religious convictions of Bunyan and of the Thirty-nine Articles and caused a scandal which cost him his Oxford fellowship with his agnostic novel *The Nemesis of Faith* (1848). Even so, he lived to write an appreciative study of Bunyan for the English Men of Letters series in 1880, praising the 'substantial flesh and blood' with which Bunyan clothes abstract qualities of character and concluding that even if men might 'never again adopt the letter of Bunyan's creed' they would still revere *The Pilgrim's Progress* as long as they accepted the imperative of moral responsibility.[12]

Kingsley himself revered *The Pilgrim's Progress* on aesthetic as well as moral and religious grounds. Though modern scholars are much less confident than Kingsley and his contemporaries that Guillaume de Deguileville's fourteenth-century *Pèlerinage de la vie humaine* was a direct source, he shrewdly commended the beautiful illustrations in the British Museum manuscript which were published in 1859 as an introduction to Bunyan's visual world. As he wrote to Charles H. Bennett, for whose 1860 illustrated edition he wrote an Introduction, he associated Bunyan with Spenser as one who in his representation of women, shepherds, Mr Greatheart and Faithful had achieved 'the ideal beauty which lifts them into a supernatural and eternal world'.[13]

But the comparison with Spenser was not entirely in Bunyan's favour. Kingsley the novelist welcomed Bunyan's sober 'English-

---

11 See Wilfrid Mellors, *Vaughan Williams and the Vision of Albion* (London: Barrie & Jenkins, 1989), chapter 7 'A Passionate Pilgrim', esp. p. 124.
12 J. A. Froude, *Bunyan* (London: Macmillan, 1880), pp. 166, 181.
13 Kingsley to Charles H. Bennett, 23 January 1859, in *Charles Kingsley: His Letters and Memories of his Life*, ed. F. E. Kingsley, 2 vols (London: Henry S. King, 1877), II, 77.

ness', his character delineation and his use of real people as models. Kingsley the naturalist criticized his apparent insensibility to the natural world. Kingsley the Christian Socialist activist and Anglican clergyman who rather disliked the Baptists in his parish felt, a little unfairly, perhaps, that Bunyan the Puritan had a single-minded concentration on the world to come which led to an over-emphasis on personal qualities such as prudence and determination at the expense of the social virtues and an adventurous openness to the challenges of the world as it is. Spenser, on the other hand, was able to combine the courage of the pilgrim or the questing knight with that of the Baconian scientist alert to the things of the present world. In *The Faerie Queene*, unlike *The Pilgrim's Progress*, Kingsley felt that 'man is considered as striving to do noble work in this world'.[14]

Even so, Bunyan and Spenser combined to provide Kingsley with a model for the manly Christian quest. The hero of his strange incoherent first novel *Yeast* (serial version 1848, first published in book form 1851), a response to Chartism and the crisis of the hungry forties, has the demotically Arthurian name of Lancelot Smith, but his urgent knightly quest against contemporary social evils and injustice is concluded with reference not to Spenser but to Bunyan. Kingsley confirms that Bunyan truly saw

> that there was indeed a land of Beulah, and Arcadian Shepherd Paradise, on whose mountain tops the everlasting sunshine lay; but that the way to it, as these last three years are preaching to us, went past the mouth of Hell, and through the valley of the Shadow of Death.[15]

This emphasis combined the passionate social concerns which Chartists had been able to read into *The Pilgrim's Progress* with something of Kingsley's own moral and religious passion. A similar passion and a similar reformist sense of momentous Bunyanesque journeying to Beulah, the joyful and abundant land on the borders of heaven, animates Kingsley's other novels of contemporary life. In *Alton Locke* (1850), partly based on the experiences of the Chartist

---

14 Preface to John Bunyan, *The Pilgrim's Progress* (London: Longman, 1860), pp. vii–xvi.
15 Charles Kingsley, *Yeast* (London: Parker and Son, 1851), Epilogue.

poet Thomas Cooper, the hero is a working tailor who eventually escapes from London, the insanitary and unjust city of destruction that has almost destroyed him. But the goal of his pilgrimage, the new life in America which stands for Beulah or the land of abundance, flowing with milk and honey, is denied him: 'the great young free New World! – and every tree, and flower, and insect on it new! – a wonder and a joy – which I shall never see'.[16]

Kingsley's later novel *Two Years Ago* (1857) looks back to the Crimean War and a cholera epidemic. By the end of the novel the crusading doctor and sanitary reformer Tom Thurnall has encountered the limitations of his own self-sufficiency and the military humiliation and frustration of a Russian prison, but this largely secular version of the Valley of Humiliation and the battle with Apollyon has a happy ending: he wins through and finds God and the love of a good woman in an England now delivered from war and pestilence, once more a land of joy and abundance. This is another, rather more domestic, version of Bunyan's Beulah, a Hebrew name from Isaiah which means 'married'.

Even in the sprawling fantasy of Kingsley's *Water-Babies* (1863) the theme of quest and pilgrimage derived from Spenser and Bunyan still persists and the text includes an incidental tribute to Bunyan as no poet but 'as wise a man as you will meet in a month of Sundays'. Linley Sambourne's illustration of 'Tom's journey' for the 1886 edition brings out the parallel with Bunyan by furnishing Tom with a substantial wooden staff which corresponds to the pilgrim staff given to Christian in the earliest engraved illustrations of Bunyan's text. But that staff is already traditional. It is in a sense the 'staff of faith to walk upon' specified in Raleigh's poem 'The Passionate Man's Pilgrimage'. Tom's journey, to the Other-end-of-Nowhere, combines the quest idea with moral ordeal, voyage of exploration and scientific expedition, and ends at St Brandan's Isle, yet another version of Bunyan's Beulah, a land of beauty and of song.[17]

But not all pilgrims made such good progress. Thomas Hardy had been fascinated with Bunyan since as a boy of ten he had been

---

16   Charles Kingsley, *Alton Locke* (London: Chapman and Hall, 1850), chapter 41.
17   Charles Kingsley, *The Water-Babies* (London: Macmillan, 1863), chapter 8.

terrified by an illustration of Apollyon fighting Christian.[18] In a notebook dated 1867 he transcribed a favourite passage: 'There, said they, is the Mount Zion, the heavenly Jerusalem, the innumerable company of angels, and the spirits of just men, made perfect'.[19] But in the end the pilgrim's vision faded and the spirit was daunted by the hobgoblins and foul fiends of a sardonic agnosticism. Where Kingsley the Christian Socialist believed that individuals and nations which had lost their way could find it again and find God, and socialist secularizers could hold on to some kind of politico-economic version of the heavenly Jerusalem or the celestial city, Hardy looked for a better future but did not find it, or at least not here and not yet. In Bunyan's Beulah the contract between Bride and Bridegroom is symbolically renewed, and there are traces of this in Victorian pilgrimage novels such as Kingsley's where journey's end for the male protagonist may include the fulfilment of marriage. But in Hardy marriage contracts tend to end badly, if they are ever achieved in the first place. The late poem 'Faintheart in a Railway Train' (1920), in *Late Lyrics and Earlier* (1922), transmutes the pilgrim quest into a lover's quest which never actually happens because Hardy's Faintheart is too timid to get out of the train to speak to the enchanting lady he has observed. This has the effect of returning Bunyan's Faintheart to the more secular business of never winning fair lady, as in the proverb.

Hardy's last novel *Jude the Obscure* (1895) gives the young Jude a distant, delusive glimpse of Christminster or Oxford as Bunyan's heavenly Jerusalem, and that becomes the goal of his life's pilgrimage. But Christminster turns out to be not the bright vision of his dreams but a place of darkness and misery, at least for him. In contrast to Bunyan's Mr Valiant for Truth, whose passing inspired some of Vaughan Williams's most rhetorically effective music, when Jude passes over it is in solitude and despair and the trumpets which sound

---

18   Hardy, letter to J. W. Mackail, 24 December 1924, in *Collected Letters of Thomas Hardy*, eds R. L. Purdy and M. Millgate, 7 vols (Oxford: Clarendon Press, 1978–88), VI, 299.
19   *The Literary Notebooks of Thomas Hardy*, ed. L. A. Björk, 2 vols (London: Macmillan, 1985), II, 463–4.

from the brass band by the river are not sounding for him: they belong to the social world of the university from which he has always been excluded.[20]

Agnostic and incipiently secular negotiations of Bunyan do not have to be quite so dismal. But the biblical sense of the pilgrim as stranger or sojourner without full rights of citizenship or settlement adds an extra dimension of poignancy and tension in agnostic contexts as there is less certainty than in conventionally Christian narrative that there is an ultimate home to go to, a place where the lonely pilgrim can eventually gain full acceptance. Difficult but momentous pilgrimage is a recurring theme in the late-Victorian fiction of Mary Ward, but it does not always end badly. Robert Elsmere, hero of her most famous novel, was once a socially committed clergyman loosely modelled on Charles Kingsley, eventually becoming not so much post-Christian as post-Anglican and vaguely Unitarian. He has worked for social regeneration and a New Brotherhood of Christ which will outlive him, though this has strained his marriage with the religiously orthodox Catherine. At the end of the novel he dreams he is on the brink of the river of Death, described as 'that old familiar image', familiar from Bunyan. He sees old friends on the other side. But he feels no pang of separation for he knows he is about to join them.[21] Soon after, he dies in his wife's arms in an ecstasy of joy, reliving the intensely human moment of delight and relief after suffering when their first child was born.[22] He has found his own version of Bunyan's Beulah, his own renewal of married fulfilment, his own good place.

In a later novel, *Sir George Tressady* (1896), Mary Ward's ultimately heroic Tressady is a wealthy politician and mine-owner, something of a lost soul, unable to find his true place or destiny for most of the narrative, but who gradually learns lessons of compassion and social responsibility through personal pain and difficulty. In his dying moments he has intuitions that his rather desultory life's journey might after all have been a kind of pilgrimage, that he might have been

---

20   For a fuller discussion see my article 'Secular apocalypse and Thomas Hardy', *History of European Ideas*, 26 (2000), 201–10.
21   Mary Ward, *Robert Elsmere* (London: Smith Elder, 1888), chapter 50.
22   Ibid., chapter 51.

guided along his road as the children of Israel were guided in the desert by alternating flame and cloud: 'There was a momentary sense of ecstasy, of something ineffable'.[23] The chastened yet highly charged sense of the numinous, of intuition passing beyond language and image, is characteristic of Mary Ward's almost secular religion: there is emotional certainty, but there are no trumpets, no Shining Ones, no elaborate vision of the Celestial City.

In Mary Ward's *Marcella* (1894), which anticipates some of the themes of *Sir George Tressady* there is a similar effect. The dying social reformer Hallin, based on Arnold Toynbee, knows he is approaching a mystery of the spirit to which the elaborate traditional detail of Dante or Bunyan is irrelevant. It is something dark and unknown to the mind, 'but to the heart it seems unveiled – with the heart, I see'.[24]

That emotional sense of the possibility of ultimate homecoming is something Bunyan shares with Kingsley and Mary Ward, and indeed with Ralph Vaughan Williams, though not perhaps with Hardy. Because the pilgrim is a sojourner and a stranger without rights of citizenship the pilgrim journey involves metaphorical or literal homelessness. But after more than two hundred years Bunyan's vividly timeless narrative offered Victorian sinners and socialists and secular social reformers the prospect of a new home, a new citizenship in the Celestial City, vividly confirming the biblical promise to the faithful of Ephesians (2:19) that they shall be 'no more strangers and foreigners, but fellowcitizens with the saints'.

---

23 Mary Ward, *Sir George Tressady* (London: Smith Elder, 1896), chapter 24.
24 Mary Ward, *Marcella* (London: Smith Elder, 1894), Book 4, chapter 1.

NATHALIE COLLÉ-BAK

4 The Role of Illustrations in the Reception of *The Pilgrim's Progress*

The history of the copious illustrations of *The Pilgrim's Progress* is as convoluted as that of its multitudinous editions. Both reflect the evolution of the reception of Bunyan's most famous prose allegory, but while the publishing history of *The Pilgrim's Progress* has been the object of several studies and accounts,[1] interpretation of its iconography has only lately made its mark on Bunyan scholarship.[2] The recent publication of an Oxford World's Classics edition of the text with the original woodcuts can be taken as a sign of that relatively new and welcome interest.[3] The aim of this essay is to show how the illustrations of *The Pilgrim's Progress* not only reflect the changing reception of the text but also contributed significantly to this reception.

When studying these illustrations throughout the centuries, however, a significant problem surfaces. Most of the critics referring to the early illustrations have argued that they are derivative at best,

---

1 For one of the earliest accounts, see John Brown, *John Bunyan: His Life, Times, and Work* (1885), rev. ed. Frank M. Harrison (London: Hulbert Publishing Company, 1928), and in particular the chapter entitled 'Editions, Versions, Illustrations, and Imitations of *The Pilgrim's Progress*', pp. 439–67. The first part of my doctoral thesis (entitled – translated from the French – 'Illustrating a Classic: A Study of the Editorial and Iconographic Traditions of John Bunyan's *The Pilgrim's Progress* from 1678 to 1850', Université Nancy 2, 2002) also deals with the various editions of *The Pilgrim's Progress*.

2 See in particular Hendrick van 't Veld, *Beminde broeder die ik vand Op's werelts pelgrims wegen. Jan Luyken (1649–1712) als illustrator en medereiziger van John Bunyan (1628–1688)* (Utrecht: Uitgeverij De Banier, 2000).

3 *The Pilgrim's Progress*, ed. W. R. Owens (Oxford: Oxford University Press, 2003).

dull and insignificant at worst. In the nineteenth century they were generally disparaged. In 1859, for example, in a letter addressed to C. H. Bennett and in which he meant to advise the illustrator on how to deal with Bunyan's narrative, Charles Kingsley wrote: 'I feel as deeply as you our want for a fitting illustration of the great Puritan Epic, and agree in every word which you say about past attempts'.[4] In 1885, Bunyan's biographer John Brown stated that 'with the exception of White's "sleeping" portrait the earliest engravings to the work were of the rudest possible kind'. Commenting specifically on Alexander Hogg's 1780 collected edition of Bunyan's *Works*, he noted Hogg's comment that because 'the copper-plates to the old editions had been more a disgrace than an embellishment' this edition had employed 'the most able and renowned artists in the kingdom, so that the illustrations might justly correspond with the dignity and elegance of the works they were intended to embellish'. In Brown's view, however, the new illustrations 'are of no special merit'.[5]

Decades later, in his article devoted to the main illustrators of the first part of *The Pilgrim's Progress*, Frank Mott Harrison continued to deprecate all pre-1860 productions:

> Bunyan's dream was born at a time when woodcut book illustration in England was at a low ebb, and when wood-engravings were rudely designed and coarsely cut. Perhaps no book shows this decadence more than does *The Pilgrim's Progress*, whose first blocks were inferior to the crudest examples of medieval days. [...] Even the climactic revival of wood-engraving (so ably demonstrated by Bewick) had no immediate positive influence on the illustrations of *The Pilgrim's Progress*. It was not indeed until design and engraving became disunited during the 'Sixties' – when that galaxy of wood-engravers including the Dalziels, rose to fame – that Bunyan came to his own.[6]

Later still, in his 1964 article on the American illustrated editions of *The Pilgrim's Progress*, David E. Smith summed up the seventeenth- and eighteenth-century illustrations in two words:

---

4   See *Charles Kingsley, His Letters and Memoirs of His Life*, ed. F. E. Kingsley (1859; Leipzig: Bernhard Tauchnitz, 1881), p. 65.
5   Brown, *John Bunyan*, pp. 441, 445–6.
6   Frank Mott Harrison, 'Some Illustrators of *The Pilgrim's Progress* (Part One)', *The Library*, 3 (1936), 241–63 (244–5).

Crudity and awkwardness – especially in the many pirated editions of the work – were so common as to be the rule. The professional craftsmanship so evident in the work of Luikens [sic] and Sturt rapidly degenerated in subsequent editions of the eighteenth century, when the work of these masters was copied by unskilled amateurs.[7]

Finally, in 1976, in an essay on John Flaxman's drawings (1792), G. E. Bentley Jr. noted that 'before Flaxman's time, the history of the illustrations to *Pilgrim's Progress* had been complex but unenterprizing', and mentioned in particular those 'woodcuts, which were customarily of execrable quality in cheap and vulgar editions'.[8]

While it is true that the series of pictures illustrating the successive editions of *The Pilgrim's Progress* may appear repetitious until the nineteenth century, the negative judgements passed on them by the critics who have found it worth mentioning them at all are not only reductive but also damaging to the study of the reception and interpretation of *The Pilgrim's Progress* by its reading communities through time and across the world. If one can rightly note that *The Pilgrim's Progress* did not need illustrations to become popular in the first place (five non-illustrated editions were issued before Nathaniel Ponder decided to provide the text with images), one can also argue that the story of Christian and his family became *even more* popular once it started being illustrated, and also wonder if it would have endured the passing of time and the erosion of faith had it not been so massively and diversely illustrated.

Considering that until the twentieth century, the illustrated editions of *The Pilgrim's Progress* greatly outnumbered the non-illustrated ones, any study of the evolution of the reception of the work that does not take into account the role played by its rich iconographic tradition[9] is flawed, for the illustrators, like stage

---

7   David E. Smith, 'Illustrations of American Editions of *The Pilgrim's Progress* to 1870', *Princeton University Library Chronicle*, 26 (1964), 16.
8   G. E. Bentley, Jr., 'Flaxman's Drawings for *Pilgrim's Progress*', in *Woman in the Eighteenth Century and Other Essays*, eds Paul Fritz and Richard Morton (Toronto: Samuel Stevens Hakkert, 1976), pp. 246, 248.
9   This is the term used by Gerda S. Norvig in her *Dark Figures in the Desired Country: Blake's Illustrations to 'The Pilgrim's Progress'* (Berkeley: University of California Press, 1993).

directors of plays, have from 1680 onward helped give *The Pilgrim's Progress* its third dimension, bringing it further to life in the eyes and minds of its countless readers. Using evidence from Bunyan's publishers, readers and critics throughout the seventeenth, eighteenth and nineteenth centuries, I will demonstrate how the iconographic tradition of *The Pilgrim's Progress* contributed to its evolving popularity; in other words, how the text was adapted, through its illustrations, to the changing contexts in which, and publics by which, it has been read.

The role of publishers in the illustration of *The Pilgrim's Progress*

First sold separately from the text at an additional cost, then published *with* the text, and later even issued *without* it, the illustrations of *The Pilgrim's Progress* have a history as long and complex as that of its editions.[10] Whether legal or pirated, cheap or costly, printed in Britain or abroad, the majority of the hundreds of editions of *The Pilgrim's Progress* which were published before the early twentieth century were accompanied by illustrations, a tradition which informs us as much about the evolution of the book market as it does about Bunyan's readership. According to the advertisement included at the front of the fifth London edition, Bunyan's first publisher Nathaniel Ponder provided the early readers of *The Pilgrim's Progress* with illustrations in order to satisfy their demand for images.

> The *Pilgrims Progress* having good Acceptation among the People, to the carrying off the Fourth Impression, which had many Additions, more than any preceding: And the Publisher observing that many persons desired to have it illustrated with Pictures, hath endeavoured to gratifie them therein: And besides

---

10 The second chapter of my doctoral thesis deals extensively with the history of the publication of *The Pilgrim's Progress*.

The Role of Illustrations in the Reception of The Pilgrim's Progress

those that are ordinarily printed to this Fifth Impression, hath provided Thirteen Copper Cutts curiously Engraven for such as desire them.[11]

In deciding to include illustrations, Ponder initiated a trend that would be followed by nearly every subsequent publisher of this famous work. Right up to the end of the Victorian era, the majority of publishers reproduced – legally or illegally – series of illustrations that either existed before they acquired copyright on Bunyan's text, or that they ordered especially to supplement it. No doubt what motivated most of these publishers was their awareness of a widespread reading public whose need or passion for pictures in books was likely to boost their sales and profits. A study of the publishing history of *The Pilgrim's Progress* from Bunyan's time onward reveals that behind the lineage of editions (illustrated or not) lay either devout men anxious to pass on the spiritual message recorded by Bunyan (including, for instance, Johannes Boekholt in Holland, or, to a lesser extent perhaps, Nathaniel Ponder in Britain), or opportunist publishers eager to exploit the lucrative potential of the work (the several legal disputes in which Ponder was engaged with unscrupulous printers as early as 1678 testify to this state of affairs), or, from the Romantic period onward, men of letters and art lovers anxious to promote and enhance the aesthetic value of Bunyan's text.

One way to visualize the shifting importance of the illustrations to Bunyan's text is to consider the evolution of *The Pilgrim's Progress*'s title pages through the centuries, and then to estimate the consequences this evolution had on how the book was being read. First, the original title of the allegory was considerably reduced over time by the publishers, passing, on the book covers and title pages of the work's editions, from the original 'The Pilgrim's Progress, from this World, to that which is to come: Delivered under the Similitude of

11 As this 'Advertisement' suggests, the decision to illustrate *The Pilgrim's Progress* in the first place may have owed more to the publisher, Nathaniel Ponder, than to Bunyan himself. However, Bunyan's role may also have been significant. He certainly did not reject the use of illustrations in his work, probably because they served his didactic purpose well, and indeed the fact that *The Life and Death of Mr. Badman* was also illustrated during Bunyan's lifetime is significant evidence of this.

a Dream wherein is discovered, the Manner of his Setting Out; his Dangerous Journey; and Safe Arrival at the Desired Countrey' to the later 'The Pilgrim's Progress, From This World to that which is to come: Delivered under the Similitude of a Dream', until finally (in the 1820s) it was reduced to its simplest form – the one that is known world-wide today – 'The Pilgrim's Progress'.

This reduction seems to have been motivated, at least partly, by the publishers' drive to give more and more details as to the number, nature and origin of the images offered alongside the text, so much so that in late eighteenth- and nineteenth-century editions, the title pages of the work came to play the role of advertising posters promoting not so much the text as its illustrations. One example of the many titles of this kind competing for the attention of readers was:

> The Pilgrim's Progress by John Bunyan. An entire new and complete edition, Embellished with a more superb and elegant Set of Copper-plates than was ever given with any former edition; being elegantly engraved by Burder, Conder, Hall, and other eminent artists ([c. 1790]).

Indeed in most late eighteenth- and early nineteenth-century illustrated editions of *The Pilgrim's Progress*, judging from the book covers and title pages, the illustrations and their creators were given prominence over Bunyan and his dream. In the last quarter of the eighteenth century, the names of the illustrators also started to appear in the book and alongside the text, for most of them now tended to sign their creations. Starting around 1800, 'Lists of Illustrations' were inserted in the volumes, thus legitimizing the image and giving it a formal place and identity distinct from those of the text. Whether in the form of cuts, engravings or lithographs, illustrations progressively invaded the space of the volumes and their pages, and sometimes even of the text itself. Thus, throughout the eighteenth and nineteenth centuries, illustrations to *The Pilgrim's Progress* as well as their creators were gradually given prominence over Bunyan and his dream.

With the illustrations being granted either more space within the published version of the text or more independence from it, so that by the Romantic period editions of *The Pilgrim's Progress* were appearing with *hundreds* of illustrations, the story of Christian and

Christiana was for a time being read *mostly* through its images and no longer through Bunyan's words alone. By the end of the eighteenth century a reader of *The Pilgrim's Progress* could look at the illustrations apart from the text and find in them Bunyan's original narrative (re)told and (re)interpreted in graphic terms. A reader at the beginning of the nineteenth century could even 'read' *The Pilgrim's Progress* mainly or solely through its illustrations, as artists began publishing *Pictorial Pilgrim's Progresses* that either summed up Bunyan's text or totally dispensed with it.

The first half of the nineteenth century, in particular, saw a singular reversal in the iconographic tradition of *The Pilgrim's Progress*. In 1788 Thomas Stothard had issued – separately from the text – a portfolio of engravings of scenes from the allegory which were subsequently included in various editions of *The Pilgrim's Progress* appearing from 1792 onwards.[12] Over the following decades several works 'founded upon' Bunyan's text were published, such as *Bunyan Explained to a Child; being pictures and poems founded upon the Pilgrim's Progress* (1824–5), alongside iconographic versions in which the text became secondary, as in 'Illustrations of *The Pilgrim's Progress*, with excerpts from the text by Frederick J. Shields' (1864). More portfolios of illustrations were produced, some of which were meant to be published with Bunyan's text – for example, *A Portfolio of Outline Drawings, Illustrations of The Pilgrim's Progress, prepared for the Edition issued to the subscribers of the Art Union of London* (1844) – while others were to be issued independently from it, such as Mrs Douglas-Mackenzie's *Twenty-four Designs Illustrating The Pilgrim's Progress* [1836], or Claude Reignier Conder's *Pictorial Scenes from Pilgrim's Progress* (1869).

The *Portfolio of Outline Drawings* by Henry C. Selous published by subscription in 1844 is a particularly interesting example of the status illustrations to *The Pilgrim's Progress* could be accorded in this period. It was introduced by the following advertisement:

---

12 A copy of the Stothard portfolio is among the Bunyan collection at the Bedford Central Library (reference 80222). For further details of the history of these engravings, see Brown, *John Bunyan*, p. 447; Harrison, 'Some Illustrators', p. 248.

> Nearly Ready, *Price One Guinea*, a New Illustrated Edition of Bunyan's *Pilgrim's Progress* [...]. This Work will be Embellished with Twenty-One Additional Designs in Outline, Engraved by Mr. Charles Rolls from a Series of Drawings made expressly for this Edition by Mr. H. C. Selous, after the manner of those Engraved by Mr. Henry Moses, and issued by the Art-Union of London. The Text will be also further Illustrated by numerous Wood-Cuts, Engraved by Mr. John Bastin, likewise from original Drawings by Mr. Selous. The Bibliographical Notice will contain Facsimiles of several curious Illustrations from the earliest Illustrated Editions of *The Pilgrim's Progress*. To the Subscribers of the Art-Union of London. This Edition is especially adapted to be bound with the Engravings issued by the Society, when it will present an *Uniform Series* of Forty-Three Plates, *illustrating nearly every page of the work, independently of the Wood-Cuts*. A certain number of copies will be issued in a wrapper, for the *Subscribers* only, at *Seventeen Shillings*, on production of their official receipt for the current year: application, however, must be made within a reasonable time after the distribution of the Prints by the Art-Union of London.[13]

The imminent publication of this new lavishly illustrated edition is presented as a significant cultural event. What is interesting is obviously not so much the fact that a new illustrated edition should be launched onto the market, but rather that this edition should have been especially arranged to 'welcome' illustrations solicited and rewarded by the Art-Union of London. The drawings by Selous had in fact won a competition launched in 1842 by the Committee of the Art-Union of London,

> for a consecutive series of designs in outline, illustrative of some epoch in British History, or the work of some English author. Expression, beauty of form, and correct drawing, apart from colour and all effects of light and shade, were pointed out as the qualities the Committee were anxious to realise in the series.

The series by Selous

> was selected as the most worthy of reward, and being deemed of a high order of merit, the drawings, increased in number by the liberality of the artist from ten

---

[13] Henry C. Selous, *A Portfolio of Outline Drawings, Illustrations of The Pilgrim's Progress, prepared for the Edition issued to the Subscribers of the Art Union of London* (London: H. M. Holloway, 1844).

to twenty-two, were at once placed in the hands of Mr. Henry Moses, to be engraved for the Society.[14]

Here we have an example of how the text of *The Pilgrim's Progress* was occasionally used as a pre-text for artistic expressions and treated as secondary to the image.

We can also see this prioritization of the image over the text in a comment by Bernard Barton, written to accompany an illustration drawn by H. Melville, engraved by W. Floyd and issued in an 1836 pictorial version of the story.

> The text of Bunyan gives little aid, in this subject, to the fancy of the artist. 'So, in the process of time, Christian got up to the Gate. Now over the Gate there was written, "Knock, and it shall be opened unto you". He knocked, therefore, more than once or twice.' The arrival of Goodwill the porter, and the colloquy between him and the Pilgrim, may be omitted, as not directly bearing on aught given in the plate; its conclusion, however, must be quoted, as it refers to the most striking and effective part of the engraving. 'A little distance from this Gate there is erected a strong Castle, of which Beelzebub is the Captain, from thence both he and them that are with him shoot arrows at those that come up to this Gate, if haply they may die before they can enter it.'[15]

Here the image is given utmost importance, both materially and interpretatively speaking, while the text is reduced to extracts dispersed throughout the commentaries devoted to the plates. Bunyan's original narrative has given place to an iconographic narrative, and the image has become the text.

It is clear from this discussion that the illustrations considerably affected the way *The Pilgrim's Progress* was marketed, both in Britain and abroad. From an examination of the illustrations' relationship with Bunyan's *book* and of the effect that relationship had on its publishing history *as book*, we turn now to an examination of the relationship of

---

14   Ibid.
15   *Illustrations of the Pilgrim's Progress: Accompanied with Extracts from the Work, and Descriptions of the Plates, by Bernard Barton. And a Biographical Sketch of the Life & Writings of Bunyan by Josiah Conder* (London: Fisher, Son & Co.; Paris: Quai des Grands Augustins, n.d.), p. 38.

the illustrations to Bunyan's *text* and the effect that relationship had on its reception *as text*.

The interplay between the illustrations of *The Pilgrim's Progress* and its reception

As is well-known by Bunyan scholars, although *The Pilgrim's Progress* became instantly popular it was not the subject of any sustained *literary* criticism before the Romantic period.[16] Partly as a result of this, evidence of Bunyan's early readers and of how they interpreted the allegory of the pilgrims is scarce. Such evidence could potentially be found in personal statements, such as those recorded in diaries, letters or memoirs, but unfortunately, locating these random statements is no easy task.[17] Another source of information does exist though, one that has not been considered as such yet, and that is the illustrations which have accompanied the text ever since 1679 and 1680.[18] For if the publishers of the work were quick to satisfy the request of the public for images, they no doubt did so with representations that pleased this public somehow, or that at least aroused its interest. As a result, one can perceive in the early illustrations of *The Pilgrim's Progress* a reflection of the way early readers apprehended it.

This view seems to be corroborated by the fact that in the personal accounts written by later readers of the allegory (such as

16   See Introduction in *The Pilgrim's Progress: A Selection of Critical Essays*, ed. Roger Sharrock (London and Basingstoke: Macmillan, 1976), pp. 19–22.
17   See W. R. Owens, 'The Reception of *The Pilgrim's Progress* in England', in *Bunyan in England and Abroad*, eds M. van Os and G. J. Schutte (Amsterdam: VU University Press, 1990), pp. 91–104.
18   Robert White's famous 'sleeping portrait' of Bunyan appeared as early as 1679 in the third London edition, but the first illustration of a specific episode of the pilgrimage – a depiction of the martyrdom of Faithful at Vanity Fair – is to be found in one of the fifth London editions of 1680. For reproductions, see *PP*, facing p. 1 and p. 96.

those one can find reported in scholarly works dealing with readers and readership), it is usually not only Bunyan's text that is vividly remembered but also – and sometimes particularly – its accompanying illustrations.[19] One example of the impact the illustrations had or might have had on nineteenth-century readers is provided by Samuel Bamford's recollection of *The Pilgrim's Progress* as expressed in his memoirs *Early Days* (1848–9):

> The first book which attracted my particular notice was 'The *Pilgrim's Progress*' with rude woodcuts; it excited my curiosity in an extraordinary degree. There was 'Christian knocking at the strait gate', his 'fight with Apollyon', his 'passing near the lions', his 'escape from Giant Despair', his 'perils at Vanity Fair', his arrival in the 'land of Beulah', and his final passage to 'Eternal Rest'; all these were matters for the exercise of my feeling and imagination.[20]

It is certainly not coincidental that all of the narrative events that Bamford recalls are those that have been repeatedly illustrated. The fact that he should remember *The Pilgrim's Progress* as a book combining text *and* image is also telling. A Lancashire weaver and a self-taught man, Bamford no doubt found in the illustration an apt companion to the text, one that potentially escorted him through the principal episodes of Bunyan's dream.

That a nineteenth-century man assessing his intellectual growth and his progress as a reader should recall the impression made on him by an illustrated edition of *The Pilgrim's Progress* is remarkable enough; that a twentieth-century writer should have the central figure and narrator in one of his books do so is all the more astounding. In *Hearing Secret Harmonies*, the last of Anthony Powell's famous

---

19   See in particular, Richard D. Altick, *The English Common Reader 1800–1900: A Social History of the Mass Reading Public 1800–1900* (Chicago: University of Chicago Press, 1957); Q. D. Leavis, *Fiction and the Reading Public* (London: Chatto & Windus, 1965); Margaret Spufford, *Small Books and Pleasant Histories: Popular Fiction and its Readership in Seventeenth-Century England* (London: Methuen, 1981); David Vincent, *Literacy and Popular Culture, England 1750–1914* (Cambridge: Cambridge University Press, 1989).

20   Quoted in Patricia Anderson, *The Printed Image and the Transformation of Popular Culture 1790–1860* (Oxford: Clarendon Press, 1991), p. 40.

sequence of twelve novels, *A Dance to the Music of Time* (1951–75), Nicholas Jenkins resorts to childhood memories of *The Pilgrim's Progress* in order to convey the powerful feelings generated in him by a dramatic situation:

> Some of the cult [...] were straying about in the neighbourhood of the Castle, because a blue robe was visible at some distance from where I stood. Its wearer was crossing one of the playing-fields. [...] Watching the approaching figure, I was reminded of a remark made by Moreland ages before. It related to one of those childhood memories we sometimes found in common. This particular recollection had referred to an incident in *The Pilgrim's Progress* that had stuck in both our minds. Moreland said that, after his aunt read the book aloud to him as a child, he could never, even after he was grown-up, watch a lone figure draw nearer across a field, without thinking this was Apollyon come to contend with him. From the moment of first hearing that passage read aloud – assisted by a lively portrayal of the fiend in an illustration, realistically depicting his goat's horns, bat's wings, lion's claws, lizard's legs – the terror of that image, bursting out from an otherwise at moments prosy narrative, had embedded itself for all time in the imagination. I, too, as a child, had been riveted by the vividness of Apollyon's advance across the quiet meadow. Now, surveying the personage in the blue robe picking his way slowly, almost delicately, over the grass of the hockey-field, I felt for some reason that, if ever the arrival of Apollyon was imminent, the moment was this one.[21]

Once again, it is not only the power of Bunyan's prose that is here confessed to have made a lasting impression on young minds, but also that of the illustrations which 'assisted' the text. In this particular case, the forceful 'image' created by hearing of the text being read aloud was reinforced by the 'realistic' and vivid image offered by the illustrator of that particular edition.

If the illustrations played a significant role in shaping the two reading experiences reported above, one real and the other fictional, they probably did so for countless other Bunyan readers, learned or not. Such testimonies as these, though scarce, are extremely precious since they give us an idea of how readers from different eras and backgrounds have accessed and appreciated the allegory, and show us that the illustrations were definitely part and parcel of their

---

21 Anthony Powell, *Hearing Secret Harmonies* (1975; London: Flamingo, 1983), ch. 6, p. 216.

acquaintance with the text. Whether taken as reading guides, interpretative tools or pleasing ornaments (or all of those at the same time), the illustrations of *The Pilgrim's Progress* must necessarily have altered its perception by readers, and consequently contributed to shaping its reception through the years.

These testimonies aside, then, the best indicators of Bunyan's readers and reception could be the illustrations themselves. A survey of the corpus of illustrations from 1680 to the end of the nineteenth century informs us of the varying ways in which illustrators interpreted the allegory at that time, and accordingly, of the varying ways in which its readers enjoyed it then. What is to be noticed first is that the varied treatment that Christian's and Christiana's pilgrimages received via the illustrations generally depended on the type of edition they were meant to adorn, and on the type of public these were aimed at. Looking at the two ends of the wide range of *The Pilgrim's Progress* editions and illustrations, one can perceive how the original woodcuts and their numerous copies helped a more or less literate portion of society to read and enjoy Bunyan's narrative, while the more elegant and artistic series engraved first on copper and then again on wood or later on steel contributed to popularizing the text among the literary- and art-minded. Looking at the whole range of editions and illustrations, one can also get an idea of the motley nature of Bunyan's wide-ranging reading public, and realize how much of their own times and minds the illustrators put into their creations.

The critics who have negated the value of what could be described as the artistically or aesthetically *inferior* series of illustrations (in other words, most of the production before Stothard's time) have in fact underestimated their impact on the public, and so doing, have neglected key factors in the reception of the work. To some extent, they have overlooked the very special bond that the early series of illustrations created between *The Pilgrim's Progress* and a good portion of its seventeenth- and eighteenth-century public. In short, they have bowed to the judgement of the literati who had decided for a time that *The Pilgrim's Progress* was not worthy of attention, more so than to that of the majority of the book's readers, who were avidly consuming the dozens of illustrated editions being launched successively or simultaneously on the book market.

It is significant, if also perhaps ironic, that recognition of *The Pilgrim's Progress* as a work of literary art should have coincided with the publication of an illustrated edition. In 1830, John Murray published an edition of *The Pilgrim's Progress* which came to be known as the 'Southey edition'.[22] Not only was this richly illustrated edition accompanied by a lengthy Introduction written by poet Robert Southey, it was also the origin of commentaries written by Thomas Babington Macaulay and Sir Walter Scott and published respectively in the *Edinburgh Review* and the *Quarterly Review*.

Scott's commentary is of special interest for us since after reassessing the popularity of Bunyan's allegory, and dealing with the characters and poetic qualities of the text, it addresses the question of illustration.

> We must not omit to mention, that this edition of *The Pilgrim's Progress* is adorned with a great variety of woodcuts, designed and executed with singular felicity, and with some highly finished engravings after the rich and imaginative pencil of John Martin. Thus decorated, and recommended by the taste and criticism of Mr. Southey, it might seem certain that the established favourite of the common people should be well received among the upper classes; as, however, it contains many passages eminently faulty in point of taste, (as, indeed, from the origin and situation of the author, was naturally to be expected,) we should not be surprised if it were more coldly accepted than its merits deserve. A dead fly can corrupt a precious elixir – an obvious fault against taste, especially if it be of a kind which lies open to lively ridicule, may be enough, in a critical age like the present, to cancel the merit of wit, beauty, and sublimity.[23]

The illustrations that 'adorn' or 'decorate' this new edition, which is itself recommended by a man of 'taste', are here presented as sort of amends for the faults of the text, and judged likely to arouse the interest of the British aristocracy. According to Scott, it is clearly the 'rich and imaginative' engravings that ornament the edition, much more so than the text they accompany, that *could* prompt Bunyan's

22 *The Pilgrim's Progress. With A Life of John Bunyan by Robert Southey Esq.* [...] *Illustrated with Engravings* (London: John Murray and John Major, 1830).
23 Scott's review of the Southey edition, *Quarterly Review*, 43 (1830), reprinted in *The Pilgrim's Progress: A Selection of Critical Essays*, ed. Roger Sharrock, pp. 64–5.

reputation among the upper classes. 'Thus' illustrated (that is, by a famous artist), recommended by a distinguished poet, and promoted by men of letters, *The Pilgrim's Progress* was finally bound to be accepted by the intellectual elite.

It was precisely when *The Pilgrim's Progress* finally achieved recognition among the literary ranks that it attracted a new type of publisher who was ready to invest more in its illustration, and with him a class of illustrators who were also distinguished artists. Once it had been approved by these arbiters of literary taste, Bunyan's work was issued in much more elegant forms, by which I mean editions as well as illustrations. With the cheap or middle-range editions continuing to appear with their cheap or middle-range illustrations alongside more refined ones, *The Pilgrim's Progress* embarked on an editorial and iconographic career that was as diversified as its newly expanded reading public.

The Pilgrim's Progress found continued – or rather renewed – success as it came to be read with different eyes and from different backgrounds. Having opened itself up to an extremely wide range of readers, it was treated by an extremely wide range of illustrators as a doctrinal exposition, a religious allegory, an adventure story, or a literary artefact – or a combination of these – and was consequently interpreted, both literally and graphically speaking, in multiple ways and fashions. A chronological study of its corpus of illustrations thus shows that the successive representations of Christian's and Christiana's pilgrimages reflect more the evolution of its readership than they do any literary truth about the text. Bunyan's work had the potential to reach across time and cultures, but the illustrations undoubtedly facilitated that reach.

Conclusion

The at times gradual, at times brutal mutations evidenced in both successive and simultaneous series of illustrations of *The Pilgrim's Progress* show us essentially two things. The first is that although the images may have started out as physical auxiliaries to the allegory, they gradually grew in material and interpretative importance until, by the beginning of the nineteenth century they either invaded the space of the text or pervaded a space of their own, so that they not only carried a separate identity from the narrative but could also tell the story of the pilgrims without Bunyan's text even being present. The second is that the presence of illustrations in the book and alongside the text inevitably altered the way readers accessed and interpreted the journey to the Celestial City.

Whether used to serve didactic purposes in relating the allegory's Christian message to a pre-literate readership at home or to illiterate peoples abroad, or further to dramatize the already powerfully-imagined action for the lettered, the illustrations were always more than simply visual baggage to the text of *The Pilgrim's Progress*. Not so much adornments of the book, they were rather significant extensions of the narrative and therefore became instruments in its evolving reception, especially at a time when the reading public in England was shaping – as well as being shaped by – what has been termed 'print culture'. As they portrayed Christian's and Christiana's pilgrimages over and over again, the illustrations provided a wide range of interpretations of Bunyan's text for a wide range of readers in a wide range of contexts – historical as well as geographical and cultural. They sustained the work's popularity through an extended period of time that witnessed the decline of Puritanism as well as changes in tastes, sensibility and mentality; and through an expanded geographical space that reaches as far as the numerous translations of the work have travelled.

As they were continuously adapted to their target publics and their historical and cultural environments, the illustrations that have supplemented the text of *The Pilgrim's Progress* from 1680 onward in

Britain and abroad can thus be read as meaningful attempts at capturing Bunyan's original narrative and at rendering it in a language – albeit a graphic one – intelligible to a diverse readership. In that sense they can be said to have influenced a reading public's interpretation of an important text. Because they could speak to a larger, even illiterate public, the illustrations of *The Pilgrim's Progress* throughout the seventeenth, eighteenth, and nineteenth centuries helped countless readers to concretize the text, thus reinforcing its impression on their minds and their memories of the crucial moments in the narrative – or rather, of those moments deemed crucial by generations of illustrators. It may also be argued that they helped to secularize the narrative for an expanding lay readership, all the while emphasizing its religious dimension for those readers who still found strength in its Christian message. By 1830, when *The Pilgrim's Progress* was finally admitted into the English literary canon, its success was owed not only to the brilliance of Bunyan's imagination and the power of his vernacular prose, but also to the illustrations' prominent role in sustaining the text's popularity and helping advance its interpretation.

Mary Hammond

5 *The Pilgrim's Progress* and its Nineteenth-Century Publishers

There are a number of key analyses of the reception of *The Pilgrim's Progress* in the nineteenth century with which I wish to engage in this essay. Important as they are, I want to argue that these analyses do not sufficiently explain the central but crucially changeable place which Bunyan's best-known work occupied in Britain's imagination during this period, mainly because they do not take account of its varied and colourful publishing history – a history which is demonstrably responsive to social change, the declining fortunes of empire, and the inexorable secularization of culture.

Most of the best-known critical approaches to Bunyan's text over the past 150 years or so centre on its questionable status as 'classic' literature and/or the idea of its authentic theological message. In 1831, reviewing a new edition by Robert Southey, Macaulay famously described *The Pilgrim's Progress* as one of the few literary works which the critical minority had learned from the lower classes to appreciate, and argued that it owed its status to popular consensus: 'That wonderful book, while it obtains admiration from the most fastidious critics, is loved by those who are too simple to admire it'.[1] This view held sway for several decades, passing into truth it seemed by virtue of pure repetition. In 1876, for example, in one of the literature-based 'St. James's Lectures: Companions for the Devout Life' delivered in St James's Church in Piccadilly, the Very Reverend J. S. Howson, Dean of Chester, devoted several long passages to Macaulay's assessment as a way of backing up his claim that *The Pilgrim's Progress*

1   Macaulay, review of Southey's edition of *The Pilgrim's Progress*, *The Edinburgh Review*, 54 (December 1831), in *Critical and Historical Essays contributed to the Edinburgh Review by Lord Macaulay* (London: Longmans, Green, Reader, and Dyer, 1874), p. 186.

provided 'common ground for persons of the highest education, and for those whom we commonly term the working classes'.[2] And this is by no means an isolated case. Much more recently, though, Barbara Johnson has suggested that while Southey's edition and Macaulay's review together represented the first serious attempt 'to turn *The Pilgrim's Progress* into literature',[3] in the end this attempt was to prove unsuccessful. 'What was a foundational text for the working class,' she claims, 'became a children's book for the upper class family'.[4] More recently still, Michael Davies has argued that while the canonization of *The Pilgrim's Progress* as a literary classic was in fact achieved during the nineteenth century, this was at the cost of its original nonconformist message.[5] For Davies, canonization meant secularization, and a corresponding loss of textual power.

These somewhat contradictory readings all centre, nevertheless, on a rather essentialist notion of the book's status in the nineteenth century, arguing primarily about whether it was or was not recognized by the discerning as a 'classic', and if so when. This, I think, is something of a missed opportunity. What I want to do here is to revisit the complex nineteenth-century publication history of *The Pilgrim's Progress* in order to add to, and perhaps in some cases to challenge, some of the views that have held sway among literary critics. As I hope to show, Bunyan's best-known work was by no means relegated to the status of a children's book during the Victorian era. On the contrary, it appeared in a vast number of editions for a wide range of readers, including but by no means predominantly children. As a staple of many a classics list, it also – for some readers at least – had an assured status as literature. And while its theological meaning was certainly recast in new ways for new audiences, it would be a mistake to see

---

2   'Lecture VI, *The Pilgrim's Progress*, by the Very Reverend J. S. Howson, DD, Dean of Chester', in *The St. James's Lectures: Companions for the Devout Life* (London: John Murray, 1876), pp. 114–15.

3   Barbara A. Johnson, *Reading 'Piers Plowman' and 'The Pilgrim's Progress': Reception and the Protestant Reader* (Carbondale and Edwardsville, Ill.: Southern Illinois University Press, 1991), p. 165.

4   Ibid., p. 8.

5   Michael Davies, *Graceful Reading: Theology and Narrative in the Works of John Bunyan* (Oxford: Oxford University Press, 2002), p. 351.

this as an impoverished a-historicism. The most valuable history of this text, as of any text, I want to suggest, is the history of its relationship with its publishers, its editors and its readers, those who were, in the end, responsible for meanings which were as plural and multifarious as the nineteenth-century 'reading public' itself.

In the number and diversity of its appearances, *The Pilgrim's Progress* reflects of course the fate of many an out of copyright work in the nineteenth century as literacy increased, new markets for cheap literature opened up, and widespread middle-class anxieties about the newly literate masses being provided for with seditious or immoral rubbish were answered by the creation of a canon of harmless, serious, must-read classics. But *The Pilgrim's Progress* is a particularly useful example to track through these enormous social and cultural changes, precisely because of its doctrinal content. Its shift from the theological and historical specificity of seventeenth-century nonconformity, through its didactic moral usefulness in Victorian Britain, to its final status as an English 'classic' might, as Davies has argued, mean that over time we have erased its more radical elements, privileging individual literary genius over the powerful forces of marginalized religious belief. But this shift mirrors in important ways the larger shift from a religious to a secular culture which occurred in Britain during this same period and achieved its greatest rate of acceleration in the nineteenth century. In terms of publishing history as well as literary criticism, *The Pilgrim's Progress* is an important milestone on the road from the Bible to the novel.

Surviving early nineteenth-century editions tend to demonstrate through their quality and price a thriving adult middle-class readership for the book even before Southey's edition, and despite what Barbara Johnson suggests, this adult readership continued. Johnson does note that in the preface to Joshua Gilpin's 1811 edition, which was one of the first to 'correct' the vernacular spelling and remove the 'coarseness' as though envisaging a youthful readership, Gilpin nonetheless speaks of the book in terms of his lifelong relationship to it as child, father, adult and critic.[6] But this is not an isolated incident as Johnson implies, or even confined to the early 1800s. Throughout the century,

---

6   Johnson, p. 8.

edition after edition as well as many published lectures on the text refer to its wide appeal, to its power to speak, as the Reverend James Black put it in his 1873 edition, 'to the churchgoer, the poet and the philosopher as well as to the child'.[7] The Dean of Chester, whose claims for the ability of *The Pilgrim's Progress* to unite all classes we have already noted, claims further that the book 'is a link [...] between the old and the young. While children are entertained with it, and read it with eager pleasure and curiosity, the aged never lose their sense of its solemn beauty.'[8] As late as 1904, the Reverend Cecil E. Bolam was claiming during his lecture to the Lincoln Diocesan Higher Reading Society that, not only do 'its vivid pictures delight children' we should not forget how 'its knowledge of character enchained Swift and Dr Johnson'.[9] There were certainly hundreds of editions produced for children at this time, but this needs to be seen as part of the enormous diversification of the publishing industry into targeted niche markets, rather than as a dominant trend. Adult editions continued to multiply right alongside those produced for children – and in a few instances the boundary between implied audience groups is not easily demarcated. A Sunday school prize presented to a child, for example, was often designed to last a lifetime, its durability proudly advertised alongside its morality and its design as an inducement to the teacher or the Board of Governors to purchase this edition over a competitor's.

Nor should we read the popularity of *The Pilgrim's Progress* with children as evidence of its failure to be assimilated into the canon amongst the discerning. As early as 1826 an edition published by Rivington announced itself as a literary classic. This edition is well bound in leather, accompanied by a scholarly preface, and followed by a two-page list of other books in this 'British Classics' series, which include Burney's *Evelina*, Sterne's *Tristram Shandy*, Fielding's *Tom Jones* and Defoe's *Robinson Crusoe*. Rather an odd mixture to surround a book about clean living for spiritual rewards, perhaps, but an

---

[7] The Rev. James Black, *The Christian Life: An Exposition of Bunyan's Pilgrim's Progress*, 2 vols (London: James Nisbet, 1873), I, 2.
[8] *The St. James's Lectures*, p. 114.
[9] The Reverend Cecil E. Bolam, lecture given to the members of the Lincoln Diocesan Higher Reading Society (published privately, 1904), p. 8.

indication, I think, that for the middle classes able to afford it, at least, this pre-Southey edition was regarded as a work of literature, part of a series for adults rather than for children. The preface to this edition states of Bunyan himself that 'since more attention has been paid by men of critical taste to his *Pilgrim's Progress*, he has been admitted into a higher rank among English writers'.[10] This is an early example of *The Pilgrim's Progress* being accorded a high status as literature – and it is perhaps significant that the edition contains none of Bunyan's marginalia. Like Gilpin's, this is a cleaned up, aestheticized version, ostensibly rescued through diligent editorship from its author's ignorance and indicative of the fact that *The Pilgrim's Progress* was apparently heading for a safe career as a solid English classic.

But cultural concerns about the necessary control of different types of reading matter for different audiences – in their infancy in the Georgian period when Jane Austen was lampooning them in *Northanger Abbey* – deepened as the century wore on and industrialization exacerbated and accelerated the permeability of boundaries – both social and intellectual – which might once have been considered secure. During the eighteenth century Bunyan's text had apparently been safely left to perform its spiritual work on the working classes unaided, while the middle classes enjoyed it equally as literature. But in the nineteenth century it began to be appropriated by publishers and editors in a new and different way. What we find in editions from the 1840s to around the early 1880s is an abundance of footnotes, and sometimes even whole chapters, devoted to didactic exposition of Bunyan's text, apparently in an attempt both to illuminate and possibly even to control its interpretation.

We should not take this phenomenon to mean, as Johnson suggests it does, that during this period publishers were producing editions only for the lower classes, the learned classes having continued to toss de-theologized editions of *The Pilgrim's Progress* to their children while disdaining to read it themselves.[11] On the contrary, we

10 *John Bunyan's 'The Pilgrim's Progress', to which is affixed a critical Preface and the Author's Life, written by himself with a copious index* (London: Rivington, 1826), pp. v–vi.
11 Johnson, p. 237.

still see the regular appearance of new editions which, judging by their production values, were aimed at well-to-do adults, as well as their children, and there occupied an apparently unproblematic place as 'serious literature'. George Virtue's expensively produced and beautifully illustrated 1850 edition, for example, provides a full 'life' of the author, and a text 'collated for the first time with the early editions, and the phraseology of all his works'. It seems unlikely that this is language – or an edition – aimed at children. Rather, it takes the form of a representation of authentic authorial intention – a long-standing scholarly approach to classic literature which was only to reach the lower classes at the end of the century: 'It was neither the design nor the wish of the Editor to introduce a single word of his own into this version of *The Pilgrim's Progress*,' the editor explains. 'He undertook the labour of collating and annotating the Edition with the oldest copies of all Bunyan's works, just that Bunyan alone might speak, and only in his own words; a right which has been too long withheld from him.'[12] James Nisbet and Co.'s even more expensive, leather-bound, gilt-edged edition of 1860 contains no editorial extras whatsoever, apparently unworried by the possibility that its readers might not understand it. Cambridge University Press's small but nicely produced edition of 1862 is likewise devoid of editorial commentary.

But alongside these editions – what we might call the elite of Bunyan publishing during mid-century – there sprang up a flourishing market for the didactic edition. The target audience for some of these editions is clearly middle-class patriarchs: several of them advise the heads of households to read from them daily to families and servants, and as such they seem to be performing the function of a domestic sermon. Even in editions apparently designed equally for private reading (in that they lack any exhortation to read from them to others) the expository footnotes provide a range of explanations, adjustments and even additions to Bunyan's text which point to a widespread concern that it might somehow be misunderstood – to the ultimate detriment of the soul of the reader.

---

12 *The Pilgrim's Progress collated, for the first time, with the early editions, and the phraseology of all his works* (London: George Virtue, 1850), p. xvii.

In 1857, for example, Nelsons reissued, on cloth over boards with thin paper, a cheap version of William Mason's didactic 1813 edition. This was evidently considered suitable for presenting as a Sunday school prize, since the British Library's copy contains a plate inscribed to one Sarah Dee in recognition of her good conduct in Sunday School.[13] It contains Bunyan's marginalia (often excised from previous versions due, as one later editor ironically remarks, to some perceived 'raciness' in the author's language[14]) but it also contains numerous biblical references plus copious footnotes designed, it seems, to control the reader's interpretation as well as to provide guidance through the text. By and large this control works in less-than-subtle ways, often taking the form of exhortations to read Bunyan alongside the Bible, and to apply Bunyan's allegory to the individual spiritual life, but it was also, as Barbara Johnson has suggested of the 1813 edition, clearly meant in addition to prevent any sinful consumption of the text as entertainment.[15] Mason's long footnote to the awakening of Bunyan's Dreamer with a 'lamentable cry' reads:

> The cry of an awakened sinner, who sees his own righteousness to be as filthy rags: [...] Reader, was this ever your case? Did you ever see your sins, and feel the burden of them, so as to cry out [...]? If not, you will look on this precious book as a romance or history which in no way concerns you; you can no more understand the meaning of it, than if it were written in an unknown tongue: for you are yet carnal, dead in your sins, lying in the arms of the wicked one, in false security. But this book is spiritual; it can only be understood by spiritually quickened souls.[16]

---

13 We should be careful, though, about assuming that this made it a book for children; Sarah Dee's good conduct by 25 October 1857, when she received the book, had apparently lasted 'over a period of twenty years', which might mean that she was either a Sunday School teacher, rather than a pupil, or that she had progressed form one role to the other.
14 *The Pilgrim's Progress As John Bunyan Wrote It* (Elliot Stock: London, 1895), p. viii.
15 Johnson, p. 229.
16 *The Pilgrim's Progress*, with explanatory notes by William Mason (London: T. Nelson and Sons, 1857), pp. 11–12.

This sentiment might have come from earlier in the century, but its reissue in the 1850s indicates a continuing belief in its relevance, however partial, and it is in fact part of a larger trend in this period.

Explicitly engaging with the implied reader's spiritual peril, this edition makes frequent reference to the contemporary world, a world which is lamentably neglectful of Bunyan-esque devotion, and more full of Worldly-Wises and By-Ends than Christians. In fact, many of these annotated editions seem to be particularly exercised by Bunyan's depiction of Christian's meeting with Mr By-Ends and his three friends, in which the relationship between earthly and heavenly rewards is discussed. William Mason devotes several long footnotes to this episode, in which Mr By-ends and his friends are castigated for displaying 'worldly wisdom, infernal logic, and the sophistry of Satan',[17] though he seems content just to warn his readers against glorifying wealth. In response to Hopeful and Christian's conversation with Mr Hold-the-World about the relationship between faith and worldly goods, Mason's footnote marks disgustedly:

> We hear this language daily from the money-loving professors, who are destitute of the power of faith, the reasoning of godliness. [...] But in opposition to all this, the Holy Spirit testifies, 'the love of money is the root of all evil' (1 Tim. vi. 10) and a covetous man is an idolater (Col. iii. 5). Hear this and tremble, ye avaricious professors. Remember, ye followers of the Lamb, ye are called to let your conversation be without covetousness (Heb. xiii. 5). Your Lord testifies 'Ye cannot serve God and mammon' (Luke xvi. 13).[18]

In the end, Mason exhorts his reader to behave like Christian in all dealings with such 'money-loving professors' and, having ascertained the sinfulness of their characters, simply to walk away:

> Mind how warily these pilgrims acted to this deceitful professor. They did not too rashly take up an ill opinion against him; but when they had full proof of what he was, they did not hesitate one moment but dealt faithfully with him, and conscientiously withdrew from him. Love should always move slowly in

---

17 Ibid., p. 120.
18 Ibid., pp. 120–1.

receiving a report, but ever deal faithfully when it is made plain that men are not what they profess to be.[19]

But the idea that a true Christian should spurn all worldly goods and offers of advancement for the hard road to Heaven, even if it really was palatable in 1813, was far more problematic at the time of this book's reissue in 1857 when the nation's infrastructure depended heavily and far more publicly on progress of a material rather than a spiritual kind. Chartist rebellions had already indicated increasing class restlessness and a refusal to tolerate hardship. The railways were spreading modernity – and inevitably also consumer culture – across the nation. The Nelson reissue of Mason is certainly the last edition I have been able to find which condemns earthly riches outright: subsequent editions find the problem much more difficult to dispel with chapter and verse alone.

By 1873, in the Reverend James Black's edition entitled *The Christian Life: an Exposition of Bunyan's Pilgrim's Progress*, for example, this warning against the worship of money has become somewhat more ambivalent. This book is one among many produced in the last half of the century by clergymen who appropriated Bunyan's text in the service of their religious offices, a service which appears to have had two main functions, a public and a private. On the one hand, studying and annotating *The Pilgrim's Progress* seems to have become in this period one of the last examples of 'intensive' as opposed to 'extensive' reading practices, and like many earlier examples of this type of reading it had a personal, devotional nature. But on the other hand, exhorting the lower classes to study Bunyan's text seems to have become a way of sermonizing in the new church of contemporary publishing, turning ordinary people back to the increasingly neglected Bible via the much more palatable medium of fiction. Like Mason, Black is concerned to prevent the work from being misunderstood, though unlike Mason he seems inclined to allow his readers to appreciate it as a good story as long as they also get the religious message. Justifying this edition of *The Pilgrim's Progress* in his preface, he explains:

19   Ibid., p. 117.

> While from a cursory perusal, its general scope and meaning may be gathered, it has been very generally felt to require explanation in order to its deeper, hidden meanings being apprehended, as well as the singularity of its conceptions, the accuracy, fertility, and beauty of its imagery being fully perceived and appreciated.[20]

But the book's main purpose is unmistakably didactic, Black taking the position of a mediator between God and the reader by downplaying the role of the editor, referring to himself throughout in the third person: 'It is hoped,' Black finishes,

> that his [i.e. his own] Exposition may be somewhat helpful to the better understanding of Bunyan's immortal allegory, and thus, through the Divine blessing, in promoting the faith, hope, and comfort of devout readers.[21]

The Pilgrim's Progress must have seemed like a Godsend to a beleaguered clergy worrying about declining congregations. It was still popular, and it was a good read. As Black remarks, it was a useful sort of bridge between God and Everyman:

> 'The Pilgrim's Progress' is the word of God translated into Christian experience. By the pious, it has therefore ever been reckoned a valuable companion to the Bible and, next to it, has been placed above every other religious book.[22]

In this period this was probably particularly true of the working classes. A decade later, when Edward G. Salmon conducted a survey of what the working classes read, he found that most working class homes apart from the very poorest owned at least a Bible and a copy of *The Pilgrim's Progress*.[23] For the middle classes this was probably quite reassuring. At least since the Chartists and the 1848 revolutions in Europe, the idea of mass literacy had been inextricably tied up with fears about the spread of sedition. By the 1870s these fears had proved unfounded, and the over-riding concern – particularly following the

---

20 Black, I, iii.
21 Ibid., p. iv.
22 Ibid., p. iii.
23 Edward G. Salmon, 'What the Working Classes Read', *Nineteenth Century*, 20 (July 1886), 115.

introduction of compulsory elementary education – was that the working classes would read trashy fiction instead. This, it was supposed, would turn them into bad workers and mothers, juvenile delinquents, prostitutes and thieves. But fiction was what most readers wanted and increasingly bought. Types of literature, and the notion of policing those types, therefore became increasingly important. This is a crucial backdrop to the ways in which a text like *The Pilgrim's Progress* is integrated into and adapted by middle-class culture at this specific historical moment. *The Pilgrim's Progress* is clearly an important text to impress upon readers if one is concerned about their sliding morals. But its somewhat archaic Puritanism has to be adapted and reinterpreted to suit a modern, wealthy, industrialized world power. These concerns, as Black's edition demonstrates, are very evident in the late 1870s, when the expository footnote or chapter is at its height.

Black's edition, issued in two volumes in 1873 and 1875, is cloth over boards, and less expensively produced than Nisbet's of 1860. It would have been available to a largely middle class audience either by private subscription from a circulating library or by outright purchase, and also – although probably less easily – to the lower classes via the second-hand bookstall, the public library, the parlour and the pulpit. Its didactic purpose is everywhere evident, and no pains have been spared to make its message plain and relevant to a contemporary audience. Its layout is particularly significant in this regard. Chapters are arranged and divided into roughly equal parts, purely in accordance with their editor's need to provide more or less explanation on a given passage of Bunyan's text. Bunyan's own marginal comments provide chapter headings, and at its most intensely expository points, for every two pages of Bunyan there are at least ten of Black. Compared with Bunyan's original – and with the many editions from this period which are free of editorial intervention – this edition is wordy in the extreme. The first volume consists of 493 octavo pages, the second of 515 – and between them they deal only with Bunyan's first part.

What made so much exposition necessary? In Black's view, *The Pilgrim's Progress* aimed 'to represent in general outline the experience of all Christians in all possible external circumstances' (another claim for the work's universality).[24] But what if some of these Christians were not poor Pilgrims, and had no intention of eschewing all worldly goods, but were instead the wealthy and powerful? And what if the poor listeners and readers worked for a wealthy industrialist whose labour was devoted to the accumulation of capital? Were they to see him as a hypocrite? As we have seen, the Mr By-ends episode seems explicitly to disavow the possible co-existence of material and spiritual wealth, and Mason agreed wholeheartedly. Black's answer to this problem is different, though, managing to combine spiritual and earthly duties in a manner that justifies an apparently unequal and (in Bunyan's terms) even ungodly situation, both at home and in the Empire. 'It is beyond dispute the will of his Creator that man should have secular employment of one kind or another', Black assures his reader. 'Agriculture, trade and commerce, which supply food and raiment, and the materials for progress and civilization, make labour a necessity.'[25] Devotion is all very well and good in its place, but as Black goes on to explain, those who shut themselves up in pious seclusion are simply selfish:

> [these people] have no-one's welfare at heart except their own. If their example were followed to a large extent, how could benevolent institutions for the poor, the diseased, and the blind be supported, church ordinances be maintained, and the knowledge of salvation be diffused over the earth?

Clearly, for Black, and no doubt for the middle class patriarch reading aloud to his household, to a large extent the end justifies the means, and public displays of good works (which rely, of course, upon wealth) are synonymous with true piety. And how does a person witnessing these good works know whether they have been done out of true faith and charity, or merely represent lip service? Well, that's apparently for God alone to know. This is all very convenient, of course, for the middle-class patriarch himself, and for his family. Devotion and wealth are not antithetical. There is no need to spend one's life in a private devotional journey, forsaking all but Christ. And as for the servant and the factory worker listening to this, he or she

24 Black, I, 5–6.
25 Black, II, 176.

apparently had simply to trust that between them God, the Reverend Black and the boss knew what they were doing.

The role of the clergyman is equally thoroughly discussed in this edition. In his exposition of the scene in which Mr Two-Tongues assures Christian that a parson can be more effective and more godly if he suits his sermon to its audience, Black explains that Two-Tongues is a man who,

> rather than preach the Gospel, without adding to it or diminishing from it, corrupting or diluting it, with all fidelity and boldness, whether they should hear or forbear, would study their prejudices and sins, by presenting it in a certain form to one, and in a different light to another, so as not to displease any.[26]

However, Black finds it far less easy to swallow Bunyan's ideas about the worldly power of the clergy. If offered a more lucrative living, he explains, the clergyman should not turn it down for fear of displeasing a God who demands self-sacrifice, but simply make sure that his motives for accepting advancement are the right ones:

> There are many enquiries which his sense of duty and accountability will compel him to make before he seek or accept that preferment – such as whether the benefice would come to him directly in the natural course of events, or as the result of illegal methods resorted to by interested parties; whether his ministrations would be acceptable and profitable to the parishioners there; and whether his labours were likely to be productive of more abundant fruit to a larger number of souls in hat new sphere than in the one he presently occupied.[27]

And how are modern parishioners to know that their comfortable, well-connected parson is acting unselfishly? According to Black they are, once again, simply to trust in God and their betters, since 'It is by the motive from which an action is done that the Searcher of Hearts determines its moral rightness and worth'.[28]

Black's is one of the most thorough of the expository editions, but it simply represents a more fully fleshed version of a very common

---

26   Ibid., p. 183.
27   Ibid., p. 193.
28   Ibid., p. 194.

editorial procedure in this period. There were many such editions of Bunyan appearing across the middle decades of the century, available to a wide range of readers in a range of formats. To give just one more example, an edition in thirty-six monthly parts was issued by Cassell from 1878 to 1881. It too contains extensive annotations by a Reverend gentleman bent on instructing his readers in correct Christian living in a specifically Victorian context, in this case the Rev. R. Maguire, DD, Rector of St Olave, Southwark. This is a book to study, not just to read, a supporting text for the Bible rather than the other way around. At seven pence per part it would have been available to all but the very poor, a supplement to Cassell's range of 'Popular Educators' advertised in the back of this edition at four pence per part, a price which put them 'within the means and capacity of all'.

Around the early 1880s, though, there was another sea change in published interpretations of *The Pilgrim's Progress* which can be illuminated by a look at the sales of other religious texts in the same period. In May 1881, a joint venture by the Presses of the Universities of Oxford and Cambridge made publishing history when a Revised Version of the New Testament was released. It sold a million copies in twenty-four hours and was widely pirated across the Atlantic at enormous cost. But a mere five years later, when their revised version of the Old Testament was released, it had nowhere near such sales, and in fact both Bibles were finally over-printed and became something of an embarrassment to the Presses.[29] The cult of the Bible was over. In 1887, one of the year's best-selling novels was Mrs Humphry Ward's *Robert Elsmere*, the story of a clergyman who loses his faith in institutionalized religion and ends up converting the working classes by reading to them from literature and improvising his own versions of the scriptures, rather than reading directly from the Bible. The secularization of British culture was proceeding apace, and it was reflected in reading habits. In his seminal analysis of the period's literary trends, Peter Keating confirms that the production of publications of a decidedly religious character dropped from 37% in 1875 to 21% by 1903 while during this same period the production of

---

29 Peter Sutcliffe, *The Oxford University Press: An Informal History* (Oxford: Oxford University Press, 1978), pp. 51–2.

newspapers, novels and magazines doubled or even trebled, easily absorbing the new reading public and their rising disposable incomes.[30] For the first time, new readers bought secular literature more often than they bought religious texts. For *The Pilgrim's Progress*, this change in reading habits meant a new phase. It continued to be issued as widely as ever, but it was increasingly marketed as literature, as a must-have classic for the self-educated, rather than as theology or as a conduct book.

In 1887, the same year that *Robert Elsmere* appeared, Hodder and Stoughton published the first part of the Reverend J. A. Kerr Bain's book *The People of the Pilgrimage: An Expository Study of 'The Pilgrim's Progress' as a Book of Character*. Here there is a recognizable shift towards literary analysis, albeit through the use of character as a determinant of moral fibre and Christian values. The Victorian cult of character, at its height in the 1850s and 60s when Samuel Smiles published his first self-help volumes was still in vogue thirty years later. It marked a particular moment in the successful integration of Protestantism and capitalism, a shift from heaven to earth via bourgeois man's public performance of goodness (as seen in Black's edition, discussed above). For the Reverend Kerr Bain, Bunyan's characters are easily divided into categories. Christian, Faithful, Hopeful, Christiana and the boys are categories by themselves in the first volume, and then in the second volume (1888) come the minor characters divided into Helpers, Hosts, Deceivers and Enemies. On the one hand, these categories are used to exemplify the virtues of 'moral earnestness', 'truth' and 'sensibility', and their opposites. But on the other hand they are unmistakably also pieces of literary criticism, used to explore plot and narrative drive. 'In *The Pilgrim's Progress*', the introduction tells us, 'character is not an ornament merely, nor an adventitious excellence, but a constituent

---

30 Peter Keating, *The Haunted Study: A Social History of the English Novel 1875–1914* (London: Secker and Warburg, 1989), pp. 32–4.

substance. [...] The creation and management of character [...] is a foremost aim of the book as work of art.'[31]

The divide described by Johnson between three types of Bunyan reader in the nineteenth century – the Protestant, the 'lettered' and the 'secular' – as they emerge through her examination of the publication history of *The Pilgrim's Progress*,[32] seems to have thoroughly broken down by this time. We might at this stage want to question whether it had ever existed as comprehensively as she suggests, and wonder into which of these categories Johnson would slot the Operative Institution's 1858 edition, a translation of *The Pilgrim's Progress* into Hebrew. But in the Kerr Bain book, at least, we are certainly seeing clear evidence of the text's diversification for a rapidly widening market.

One of the first critical studies of *The Pilgrim's Progress*, this book entirely omits Bunyan's text to concentrate on his characterizations. It is far less interested in theology than in literature, explaining the relative absence of 'Deceivers and Enemies' in Bunyan's second part, for example, as a structural decision on a par with – if not actually greater than – any theological motive: 'In the later Part the circumstances are less inviting to this class of traveller; and Bunyan seems to have felt [...] that he had done fair justice to that class in what he had already written'.[33] As for Mr By-ends and his friends who so troubled mid-century commentators, Kerr Bain admits that the present age is a far more worldly one than Bunyan's, but he seems rather less troubled by it than his predecessors and has apparently accepted that the essence of Bunyan's message in this regard has lost its power:

> What, then of the spirit which pervades our own age and country? It would be pleasing to be able to say that it is not a worldly spirit; yet, predominantly, it is no other than this. [...] Worldliness has long been refining itself among us, but it is worldliness still. [...] Material prosperity, secular civilisation, worldly cul-

---

31 Rev. J. A. Kerr Bain, *The People of the Pilgrimage: An Expository Study of 'The Pilgrim's Progress' as a Book of Character*, 2 vols (Edinburgh and London: Macniven and Wallace and Hodder and Stoughton, 1887), I, 22.
32 Johnson, p. 217.
33 Kerr Bain, II, 294.

ture, the embellishment of and enjoyment of life – the magnifying of these excellent things is not very ready to alarm us, even if it be done in the porch of the Church itself, or perhaps in its pulpit.[34]

We should not, though, he warns, allow ourselves to be fooled even now into accepting these things as the real thing, 'even if they slide into the place of Christianity while they are courting its fellowship'. True faith is still apparent to God, and while in a modern world 'there are few of the sophistries of our four pupils of Gripeman which might not thrive', according to Kerr Bain we really should not worry about them over-much since for such sinners these sophistries will simply 'adorn the way to a like fate with theirs'.[35] The removal of piety to a private, personal sphere recognizable only by God, the acceptance of worldly progress as inevitable and not entirely blameworthy, and the enthusiastic response to Bunyan's text as a work of art seem complete here in this work, and they signal a new era for *The Pilgrim's Progress*.

The classics series, which consecrated *The Pilgrim's Progress* as a canonical text once and for all and effectively marked the end of editorial theology, was very much a product of this period. Produced and marketed to assist the self-advancement of the new Board School educated generation, these series sprang up in their dozens until by the 1890s there were literally hundreds of them. They had been around in one form or another since at least the early part of the century (as my example of the Rivington edition of *The Pilgrim's Progress* in their 'British Classics' series of 1826 demonstrates), but by its end every publishing house seemed to have its series of classics. For ideological as well as economic reasons the texts thus canonized were almost exclusively conservative, male-authored, edifying, instructive and clean (as well as out of copyright), a persuasive counter-measure, in other words, to the seductive qualities of the new best-selling novel.

But each series also had to have an edge over its competitors, and this is where *The Pilgrim's Progress* burgeons into a whole host of new formats to appeal to its widest-ever range of markets. Nelson's

---

34   Ibid., p. 292
35   Ibid., p. 293.

sixpenny 1902 version, for example, is presented without the footnotes that were such a feature of the same publisher's 1857 reissue. The marginalia and Biblical references have been removed, and the punctuation and spelling have been modernized for easy reading. The same is true of the first World's Classics edition of 1902, though after Oxford University Press took over the series in 1905 the marginalia were put back and a preface was added in line with the Press's reputation for authentic scholarship (by this time part of an all-important brand name appeal).

Special editions of *The Pilgrim's Progress* reached a range of other markets too. In 1891, for example, Pitman's produced an edition written entirely in shorthand for the use of lower middle class trainees practising to become secretaries and clerks. In 1898 Pearson produced a large ornate version with lavish illustrations and no pretensions to literary merit or moral didacticism or anything other than a kind of prototype coffee table appeal. In 1895, Elliot Stock produced an edition which has to be the pinnacle of biblio-worship and the cult of the author in this period. Significantly entitled *The Pilgrim's Progress As John Bunyan Wrote It*, it is a careful facsimile of the first edition. The preface draws attention to the wrong spellings, both Bunyan's and the printer's, and declares that

> no pains have been spared to make this facsimile an exact reproduction of the original first edition. Even as regards typography, it is strictly a lineal descendant of that of 1678, for the type now used has been cast from moulds made in 1720, which were taken from the Dutch type used for that first issue. The paper, too, is a close imitation of that manufactured two centuries ago.[36]

This edition is claiming a new high ground – consecration at the level of the text, in which literature has become one of the 'higher' art forms, and the author practically a god.

Not everyone went to these lengths to get close to the deified original, of course. Edmund Venables referred somewhat disparagingly to Elliot Stock's 'literal reprint' in the Introduction to his own Clarendon Press edition of 1900:

---

36 *The Pilgrim's Progress As John Bunyan Wrote It* (London: Elliot Stock, 1895), p. vii.

> Literal accuracy has not been sought for in the present edition. The object of the series of which it forms a part is not to reproduce archaeological curiosities, but to present some of the chief works of our leading authors in a form which will throw no needless obstacles in the way of the less advanced students of English literature. Pedantic fidelity to the original text would have impeded the progress of the student without any advantage to the philologist.[37]

But in the end, this aim is no less lofty than Elliot Stock's – or, indeed, William Mason's, or the Reverend James Black's. In the turn of the century literary marketplace the scholarly edition was a strong contender in the good works stakes: replacing missionary with literary editorial zeal and self-denial with self-help, but apparently still bent on saving the people from themselves.

It has been my aim here to add some nuances to previous accounts of *The Pilgrim's Progress* in the nineteenth century, where it has sometimes been regarded as in some way either relegated to the nursery or so divorced from its historical seventeenth-century context that it suffers as a text. On the contrary, I have tried to suggest, the astonishing number and diversity of appearances by *The Pilgrim's Progress* during the nineteenth century demonstrate that its appeal – and its value for historians – lies as much in its adaptability as in its historical specificity. As the Reverend R. H. Haweis, editor of the Pearson 'coffee table' edition of 1898 puts it: 'It is not necessary here to discuss Bunyan's theology. It was neither better nor worse than that of his age. [...] But in providing what the people really wanted, Bunyan was a master.'[38] This was patently true whether what 'the people' wanted – or perhaps more specifically in this case, what editors and publishers thought they ought to have wanted – was a spiritual tour guide, a book to read to their children, a way of understanding a rapidly changing world, or a classic for the suburban bookshelf. In surveying the publication of this important text across

---

37   *The Pilgrim's Progress*, ed. Edmund Venables (Oxford: Clarendon Press, 1900), p. xxxviii.

38   *The Pilgrim's Progress*, illustrated by George Wooliscroft Rhead, Federick Rhead and Louis Rhead (London: Pearson, 1898), pp. vi–viii.

several decades of a century during which it was at the forefront of cultural debate, we are able to learn a great deal about the changing relationships between readers, writers, literature and faith.

Isabel Hofmeyr

6 Evangelical Realism: The Transnational Making of Genre in *The Pilgrim's Progress*

As writing on the topic has long recognized, genre is best conceptualized as a process and an institution.[1] Genre happens both inside and outside texts and its operations must necessarily be spread across a number of different but interacting sites. How might these processes of genre operate if these sites are spread across different parts of the world?

This question has become increasingly central to literary studies as it takes a transnational and globalizing turn. In his recent work *What is World Literature?*, David Damrosch suggests how such transnational genre-making might occur. He examines a particular category of texts, namely those that circulate widely beyond their original culture. These texts constitute what he defines as world literature: 'My claim is that world literature is not an infinite, ungraspable canon of texts but rather a mode of circulation and of reading'. As such texts circulate, they mutate: 'The shifts a work may undergo [...] do not reflect the unfolding of some internal logic of work in itself but come about through often complex dynamics of cultural change and contestation'.[2] The model suggested here is that the genre being of a text cannot be determined solely by its internal textual logic. Indeed, its textuality may turn out to be a relatively weak force that can be overridden by other factors as it circulates into and between different societies.

This article investigates these issues in relation to *The Pilgrim's Progress*, a text translated into some 200 languages and hence almost

---

1 See Tony Bennett, *Outside Literature* (London: Routledge, 1990); Rick Altman, *Film/Genre* (London: British Film Institute, 1999).
2 David Damrosch, *What is World Literature?* (Princeton: Princeton University Press, 2003), pp. 5–6.

an ideal type for understanding how genre works transnationally. The transnational presence of Bunyan has for a long time attracted little attention, but this situation is fortunately beginning to change and a number of scholars have begun to investigate the topic.[3] An international conference on Bunyan held in Bedford in 2004 included a number of papers discussing Bunyan in translation and Bunyan in the Third World.[4]

By drawing on and extending this scholarship, this essay offers a case study of how *The Pilgrim's Progress* undergoes generic redefinition through its international circulation. The particular instance I consider is the case of topographical realism in *The Pilgrim's Progress* and how this aspect of the text, despite being only marginally 'realistic', came to be defined generically as intensely 'real'. I argue that such a reading has to be understood as a function of the text's circulation, and examine interpretations of *The Pilgrim's Progress* that emerged in and between three overlapping domains. The first of these is the realm of evangelical readers whose methods of applied reading (i.e. applying the text to one's life circumstances) could be adapted to construe Bunyan's landscape as realistic. I examine the application of such evangelical realism in two settings. The first is Bedford, Bunyan's home town from whence emanated some of the most realistic readings of the topography of *The Pilgrim's Progress*. The second comprises a selection of evangelical translations of Bunyan's famous text and the ways in which these construct the 'real'. In conclusion, I return again to Bedford and focus on the Bunyan Meeting House and two of its pastors whose uses of Bunyan illuminate the ways in which versions of *The Pilgrim's Progress* from various parts of the world were configured to produce differing versions of realism.

---

3 See Isabel Hofmeyr, *The Portable Bunyan: A Transnational History of The Pilgrim's Progress* (Princeton: Princeton University Press, 2004); Tamsin Spargo, *The Writing of John Bunyan* (Aldershot: Ashgate, 1997).

4 Among these papers were Sylvia Brown, 'Bunyan among the Eskimos: Missionary Translations of *Pilgrim's Progress* into Inuktitut'; Arlette Zinck, 'Two Cree Translations of *The Pilgrim's Progress*'; and Henk Van 't Veld, 'Desired or Imposed? *The Pilgrim's Progress* in the Third World'.

Bunyan's Topographical Realism

The question of realism in *The Pilgrim's Progress* constitutes a major strand in Bunyan scholarship.[5] This scholarship has demonstrated that Bunyan's realism is distributed across a number of features, including his characterization, his focus on ordinary people, his deployment of homely detail, and his use of language, dialogue, setting and landscape. There is ample evidence in the text to support most of these categories. The evidence in relation to landscape is, however, less certain. As several commentators have indicated, the topographical setting of the text is not geographically convincing. The landscapes lack particularity and the book relies on a series of 'standard-issue' backdrops: mountains, hills, rivers, vineyards, orchards, gardens. At times, of course, features of this topography are minutely described, but in Ian Watt's words, such passages are 'incidental and fragmentary'.[6] Overall the weight of opinion suggests that Bunyan's topography is pre-realistic and romance-like.[7] Indeed James Turner concludes that Bunyan's sense of place is pre-Cartesian: 'ways of seeing which assume a three-dimensional continuum of space cannot be applied to Bunyan's vision'.[8]

Yet, these analyses notwithstanding, there is an implicit assumption in much Bunyan criticism that the text unfolds in seventeenth-century Bedford. This tendency is particularly marked in analyses of

---

5   See in particular Dorothy Van Ghent, *The English Novel: Form and Function* (New York, Harper, 1961); Arnold Kettle, *An Introduction to the English Novel*, 2 vols (London: Hutchinson, 1965); Michael McKeon, *The Origins of the English Novel 1600–1740* (Baltimore: Johns Hopkins University Press, 1987); Richard Kroll, 'Defoe and Early Narrative' in *The Columbia History of the British Novel*, ed. John Richetti (New York: Columbia University Press, 1994).
6   Ian Watt, *The Rise of the Novel* (1957; Harmondsworth, Penguin, 1983), p. 28.
7   See Paul Salzman, *English Prose Fiction 1558–1700* (Oxford: Clarendon Press, 1985).
8   James Turner, 'Bunyan's Sense of Place' in *The Pilgrim's Progress: Critical and Historical Views*, ed. Vincent Newey (Liverpool: Liverpool University Press, 1980), p. 95.

Bunyan by nineteenth-century scholars of English literature. C. H. Firth comments:

> Bunyan's feeling for natural beauty is very keen, but it is the landscape of his native Midlands which pleased him most. [...] Woods and green fields, rich meadows and softly-sliding waters attract Bunyan's imagination most.[9]

Charles Kingsley sees the book as deeply rooted in the people and scenery of the Midlands. Bunyan's characters are 'not merely life-portraits, but English portraits: men of the solid, practical unimpassioned midland race'; they are 'quiet folk going about Bedford town in slop-breeches, bands and steeple-hats'. His landscape is similarly indigenous:

> Born and bred in the monotonous midland, [Bunyan] has no natural images beyond the pastures and brooks, the towns and country houses, which he saw about him. He is as thoroughly 'naturalist' in them as in his characters.[10]

This impression lingers in contemporary discussion. Christopher Hill remarks: 'the countryside through which [Christian] passes is clearly England'.[11] Paul Salzman comments on the 'Bedford sloughs' in *The Pilgrim's Progress*.[12] Douglas Chambers points to the 'recognizable topography of England, its street fairs and its country houses'.[13]

If instances of topographical realism are in fact few and far between, how did this view of the text as firmly rooted in the countryside of Bedford come into being? One answer can be extracted from existing explanations of how *The Pilgrim's Progress* as a whole came to be read realistically.[14] This historiography indicates that

9   *The Pilgrim's Progress*, ed. C. H. Firth (London: Methuen, 1908), p. xxxv.
10 *The Pilgrim's Progress*, ed. Charles Kingsley (London: Longman, Green, Longman & Roberts, 1860), pp. ix–xiv.
11 Christopher Hill, 'Bunyan's Contemporary Reputation', in *John Bunyan and his England 1628–88*, eds Anne Laurence, W. R. Owens and Stuart Sim (London: Hambledon Press, 1990), p. 9.
12 Salzman, *English Prose Fiction*, p. 244.
13 Douglas Chambers, *The Reinvention of the World: English Writing 1650–1750* (London: Arnold, 1996), p. 22.
14 See Richard L. Greaves, 'Bunyan through the Centuries: Some Reflections', *English Studies*, 64 (1983), 113–21; N. H. Keeble, '"Of Him Thousands Daily

Bunyan's 'realism' is a nineteenth-century phenomenon. Before this, the major method for reading the book was evangelical and didactic and the text was treated as a spiritual manual. This style of reading was shifted by a number of factors. The popularization of a Romantic aesthetic foregrounded Bunyan's depictions of ordinary life and made this a focus of interpretative attention. Robert Southey's edition of 1830 shifted Bunyan's reputation decisively, and the growth of English literature as a discipline conferred further value on him and institutionalized his texts as 'realistic'. Implicit in such analyses is the assumption that evangelical and realistic readings are necessarily somewhat at odds. This was a view encouraged by evangelical readers themselves. In the preface to his edition of *The Pilgrim's Progress* in 1790, George Burder famously warned evangelical readers against falling into the trap of reading the book 'merely as a Novel'.[15]

This tendency to separate evangelicalism and realism is strengthened by the rise of secular approaches to Bunyan. While these latter views recognize Bunyan as a religious figure, they hold that his texts are most profitably read through a secular rather than an evangelical lens. Similarly, in Marxist approaches, nineteenth-century evangelical reading strategies are seen as weakening or in some cases erasing Bunyan's 'real' message of political radicalism.[16]

Evangelical Realism

Yet, are evangelical and realistic ways of reading necessarily at odds? A consideration of testimonies from nineteenth-century Nonconformist readers can throw some light on this issue. The first point to emerge from these accounts is that most readers relied on multiple reading

Sing and Talk": Bunyan and his Reputation', in *John Bunyan: Conventicle and Parnassus*, ed. N. H. Keeble (Oxford: Clarendon Press, 1988), pp. 241–63.
15 *The Pilgrim's Progress*, ed. George Burder (London, 1786), Preface.
16 Christopher Hill, *A Tinker and a Poor Man: John Bunyan and his Church, 1628–1688* (New York: W. W. Norton, 1988), pp. 375–6, 380.

strategies. In childhood, the text was generally consumed as romance, a 'reading' technique which at times relied heavily on the illustrations:

> As a picture book 'The Pilgrim's Progress' is the rival of any volume of fairy-tales. No ogre in fairy-land was ever more terrifying than Apollyon. [...] All these things excited the imagination like the adventures of Jack the Giant-killer or Ulysses.

In this account, the pictures were the source of pleasure and delight, the text itself 'a slough of sermonizing'.[17]

As Nonconformist readers grew older, they would have been introduced to evangelical reading strategies, first at Sabbath day readings at home, and then at Sunday school, in church, and church-related groups which arranged events, lectures and reading programmes around *The Pilgrim's Progress*.[18] Such readings could be deepened by undertaking one's own intensive reading of the text with the aid of manuals like *Half-hours with Bunyan's Pilgrim's Progress* (1856) and *Some Daily Thoughts on The Pilgrim's Progress* (1917).

But what did these evangelical reading strategies entail? Evangelicalism as a social phenomenon is well understood.[19] Theologically, it is a doctrine of salvation by faith rather than by good works or the sacraments. Phenomenologically, it entails a particular style of conversion: a burdensome awareness of sin followed by an overwhelmingly emotional experience of conversion. Its reading protocols are less well understood, beyond the fact that didacticism was important.[20] One way to gain some insight into evangelical reading strategies is via

---

17 Augustine Birrell, 'John Bunyan Today', *The Bookman*, 73:435 (1927), 151.
18 Hofmeyr, *The Portable Bunyan*, pp. 58–62.
19 See D. W. Bebbington, *Evangelicalism in Modern Britain: A History from the 1730s to the 1980s* (London: Unwin Hyman, 1989); idem, *The Nonconformist Conscience: Chapel and Politics 1870–1912* (Boston: Allen & Unwin, 1982); Stuart Piggin, *Making Evangelical Missionaries 1789–1858: The Social Background, Motives and Training of British Protestant Missionaries to India* (Abingdon: Sutton Courtenay Press, 1984); Susan Thorne, *Congregational Missions and the Making of an Imperial Culture in Nineteenth-Century England* (Stanford: Stanford University Press, 1999).
20 See Margaret Nancy Cutt, *Ministering Angels: A Study of Nineteenth-century Evangelical Writing for Children* (Wormley: Five Owls Press, 1979).

the most popular nineteenth-century evangelical form, the religious tract. Tracts were believed to have extraordinary powers of possession and enchantment, and were thought to possess an authority through which they could compel dramatic conversions.[21]

In part, of course, these ideas are driven by the heady combination of the novelty and power of mass print being used to produce texts considered to have religious and spiritual authority. The potency of this combination can be detected in the early nineteenth-century belief – common amongst evangelical Protestants – that through the Bible alone the world could be converted. In this scenario, the Bible, distributed far and wide, would convert any person who encountered it.[22] The Bible and associated texts such as tracts could become mini-missionaries: they could precipitate conversion; guide and instruct readers; and carry important messages and advice. Famously, of course, this style of reading was practiced by Bunyan himself. In *Grace Abounding*, texts both written and printed exercise a compulsive force over him.[23] The religious document for him was a site of intense power.

In keeping with these notions, *The Pilgrim's Progress*, which was deeply woven into Nonconformist life, became an emotionally powerful conduct book or spiritual manual which was applied to everyday religious problems and dilemmas. One favoured reading strategy was to imagine oneself as one of the characters and apply their words to one's own situation. Take for instance the following example from a Scottish cleric who wrote an introduction to an edition of *The Pilgrim's Progress*:

---

21 See Isabel Hofmeyr, 'Mini-missionaries: The Travelling Text as Evangelical Trope', *Yearly Review* (University of Delhi), 12 (2004), 77–93; idem, 'Transnational Textualities', in *Mixed Messages: Materiality, Textuality, Missions*, eds Jamie Scott and Gareth Griffiths (London: Palgrave Macmillan, in press).

22 Leslie Howsam, *Cheap Bibles: Nineteenth-Century Publishing and the British and Foreign Bible Society* (Cambridge: Cambridge University Press, 1991).

23 John Bunyan, *Grace Abounding to the Chief of Sinners*, ed. W. R. Owens (London: Penguin, 1987), pp. xx–xxiii; Maxine Hancock, 'Bunyan as Reader: The Record of *Grace Abounding*', *Bunyan Studies*, 5 (1999), 68–96.

> An experienced Christian woman, who had undergone a critical surgical operation which all but deprived her of the power of speech, when asked how it was with her, with difficulty whispered out, *'The jewels are all safe!'* We had had as the subject of our reading shortly before, the passage in the 'Pilgrim's Progress' in which the assault upon Little Faith is described. He was robbed of his 'spending money' – i.e., his present comfort, but he could not be deprived of his interest in Christ – the 'jewels' were 'all safe'. [...] These incidents are referred to, not as at all singular, but as specimens of what is constantly taking place in town and country in connection with their reading and exposition of the 'Pilgrim's Progress'. They also serve to show, what might be much more largely illustrated, that the language of this book has become to a striking extent, the language of the people when they would give expression to their personal Christian experience.[24]

The type of reading suggested here is close to that outlined by Michael Davies. He suggests that to read Bunyan as an analytically removed aesthetic object is to undertake a modern form of interpretation. If read evangelically, *The Pilgrim's Progress* cannot be treated as 'writing that we operate on from a distance'. Instead we need to entertain a different mode of reading: one that entails 'faithful action',[25] or put in slightly different terms, an activist reading in which the text is applied to circumstances and behaviour.

Characters in *The Pilgrim's Progress* then became important sites of imaginative identification: the readers' subjectivity is projected onto the character. Characters become 'real' and can be read as 'real' people. Underlining this tendency to make character 'real' was the link that all evangelical editions made between *The Pilgrim's Progress* and Bunyan's autobiography *Grace Abounding to the Chief of Sinners*. One commonplace of such commentaries was that the characters in *The Pilgrim's Progress* dramatized Bunyan's own spiritual experiences and dilemmas. This link further strengthened the 'realism' of character in Bunyan by indirectly conferring the

---

24 J. H. W., 'Introductory Notice', in *The Pilgrim's Progress* (Edinburgh: Andrew Stevenson, n.d.).
25 Michael Davies, *Graceful Reading: Theology and Narrative in the Works of John Bunyan* (Oxford: Oxford University Press, 2002), p. 221.

Evangelical Realism 127

authenticity of spiritual autobiography, and the aura of psychological realism which it carried, onto *The Pilgrim's Progress*.[26]

This method of applied reading could easily be extended to other features of the text. As any number of readers' testimonies may demonstrate, the practice of applying bits of *The Pilgrim's Progress* to one's surroundings was commonplace. Like many Victorian children, Robert Blatchford acted out episodes from the story, turning parts of his house into topographical features of the book: the stairway, Hill Difficulty; the dark lobby, the Valley of Death.[27] In some cases, the application of the text was even more literal, as in the case of the Methodist James Mellor who landscaped his Cheshire garden as a Bunyan trail.[28] This constant investment in the text meant that readers inhabited it with tremendous intensity. As Blatchford explains, fans of the text could turn vaguely rendered descriptions of landscape into experiences of intense realism, if not hyperrealism:

> We remember many of Bunyan's scenes because he tells us so little about them. Of the Hill Difficulty he tells us nothing but that it was a hill and steep; of the footpath across the Giant Despair's demesne he tells us little but that it ran hard by the hedge; and we remember these things because we have all seen steep hills and hedgerow paths, and because we at once adopt a hill or path from the pictures in our memories. It is small wonder, then, that these places are real to us. They *are* the places we know, but they are *our* places, not Bunyan's, and real as they are to me, and real as they are to others, they are not the *same* to any two of us. Macaulay's Valley of Humiliation, Doubting Castle, and Hell Gate are not mine, nor yours. Each of us paints his own picture, puts it into Bunyan's frame, and cries out 'wonderful'.[29]

Through a life-long investment in *The Pilgrim's Progress* in which the text was made applicable to everyday life, readers could overwrite passages of vague topographical description by filling in the gaps with profuse and intense detail. It is a reading strategy on to which the procedures of the English novel could map themselves with relative ease. Since for thousands of readers, character and setting already

---

26   *Grace Abounding*, ed. Owens, p. xxiii.
27   Robert Blatchford, *My Favourite Books* (London: Walter Scott, 1900), p. 192.
28   Anon, 'Devotion to Progress', *Period Garden* (December 1993), pp. 86–91.
29   Blatchford, *My Favourite Books*, pp. 213–14.

existed as an intensely inhabited site, this could be filled with new details. These could be items of dress like Kingsley's 'slop-breeches, bands and steeple-hats' or Firth's assertion that the pilgrim's road is 'very like a common English seventeenth century high-road'.[30]

For such interpretations to take hold, readers had to accept some degree of overlap between English literature and evangelicalism. This co-habitation had been some time in the making: Dissenting Academies, for example, had been one of the sites for the emergence of English as a discipline and several scholars of English literature were to emerge from evangelical backgrounds.[31] Unsurprisingly then, turn-of-the-century accounts of Bunyan, such as John Kelman's *The Road: A Study of John Bunyan's Pilgrim's Progress* (1912), situate Bunyan both in older evangelical traditions of commentary and in the emerging canon of English Literature.

Some ardent Nonconformist readers resisted such attempts to mingle evangelical and secular readings. Looking back on his schooling, one Baptist commented on the experience of studying Bunyan for matriculation (probably in the 1920s):

> And so it was that I came to know Bunyan in the first place as the master of vivid, forceful and colloquial English; as an allegorist who made his characters live; as a storyteller who was preparing the way for the novel that was to emerge with Fielding, Richardson and Smollett.

For this writer, however, such literary interpretations represented a distraction from the text's true meaning: 'it is the religious significance of the book that has given it its worldwide appeal'.[32] While such views no doubt lingered on amongst 'hardliners', the mixed-mode of evangelical reading strategies overlaid with English literature protocols gained ground. However, with increasing secularization, particularly post-First World War, the evangelical tide began to

---

30   Kingsley, p. x; Firth, p. xxviii.
31   See D. J. Palmer, *The Rise of English Studies* (London: Oxford University Press, 1965), pp. 15–28.
32   *The Baptist Times* (30 October 1947), Newspaper Cuttings, Bunyan Collection, Bedford Library.

recede, leaving secular literary interpretations as the dominant and authoritative mode of reading.[33]

Today, we inevitably view matters somewhat teleologically, and consequently Evangelical approaches tend to appear as prior to, and hence less important than, modern secular criticism. However, a brief look at Bunyan's home town, Bedford, the site which produced many of the key ideas of topographical realism in *The Pilgrim's Progress*, will demonstrate how often the most intense forms of realism went hand in hand with evangelical modes of reading.

Evangelical Realism in Bedford

The Bunyan tercentenary witnessed a flood of books on the 'immortal tinker'. One sub-set of this comprised books on Bunyan in Bedfordshire: Albert J. Foster's *Bunyan's Country: Studies in the Bedfordshire Topography of The Pilgrim's Progress* (1901); Charles G. Harper's *The Bunyan Country* (1928); A Colonial Pilgrim's *Footsteps of The Pilgrim's Progress: A Key to the Allegory* (n. d.); and C. Bernard Cockett's *Bunyan's England: A Tour with the Camera in the Footsteps of the Immortal Dreamer* (1948). As their titles indicate, these books featured the sites associated with Bunyan's life in and around Bedford, linking features of the local topography to scenes in *The Pilgrim's Progress*. The intention was to embed *The Pilgrim's Progress* firmly in the Bedfordshire countryside. Foster explains his method thus:

> It is simply an attempt to show that [Bunyan] reproduced in the first part of *The Pilgrim's Progress*, scenes and localities which were familiar to him. [...] We propose to take the scenes described on the wayfarer's journey, and to give to each its local habitation and its name, so far as it is possible, and to show that Bunyan's imagination was stimulated by what he saw around him.[34]

---

33 Hofmeyr, *The Portable Bunyan*, pp. 217–27.
34 Albert J. Foster, *Bunyan's Country* (London: H. Virtue, 1901), p. 18.

These books included maps in which landmarks in and around Bedford were identified with topographical features of the story. These landmarks were in turn further popularized through guide books for walking, cycling and motoring around Bedfordshire.

One context for understanding this Bunyan-in-Bedford movement is the 'invention' of late nineteenth-century versions of Englishness.[35] A central plank of this intellectual movement was an attachment to the southern shires of England as the ideal setting and landscape for the newly imagined forms of nationhood.[36] The interest in Bedfordshire needs to be seen as part of this intellectual development. Also central to late nineteenth-century Englishness was the idea of English literature itself and Bunyan of course registered increasingly strongly on this radar. The combination of Bunyan and Bedford was hence a powerful one, drawing together English literature and the magical southern shires. In this potent cathexis, the topographical material on Bunyan in Bedford increasingly seeped into the English literary scholarship and vice versa.

Read through the lens of these English literature scholars, the Bedfordshire topography material may appear to have little to do with evangelical modes of reading. However, if we turn to examine some of the architects of this topographical project, it soon becomes evident that one impulse behind this application of the text to the Bedfordshire countryside arose from long-standing evangelical habits of reading. One early 'designer' of excursions to, and lectures on the topographical sites in and around Bedford was Richard Poynter (also known as the 'second John Bunyan'). As a press notice of 1888 indicated, Poynter's lectures and guided walks showed

> beyond doubt that most or many of the pictures or illustrations in 'The Pilgrim's Progress' have their origin in the neighbourhood of Elstow, and Mr Poynter is able with pride and satisfaction to point out on the spot such scenes as By-Path

---

35 See Brian Doyle, *England and Englishness* (London: Routledge, 1989); *Englishness: Politics and Culture 1880–1920*, eds Robert Colls and Philip Dodds (London: Croom Helm, 1986).
36 Alan Howkins, 'The Discovery of Rural England', in *Englishness*, eds Colls and Dodds, p. 62.

Meadow; Vanity Fair; The Palace Beautiful; The Wicket Gate in Elstow Church; The Slough of Despond.[37]

The popularity of Poynter's lectures attracted imitators and the market was soon crowded. In the 1920s in the lead-up to the tercentenary, Poynter felt it necessary to explain that he was

> not prepared to plan out step by step the pilgrim journey on a map of Bedfordshire. It was a spiritual journey, and [...] it is not incumbent to make a pilgrim go straight from place to place as we now have it in Bedfordshire, but to state the spots and sites we have that agree with Bunyan's own description of the most notable places to which he takes Christian, and which are full of soul-inspiring lessons.[38]

Poynter's irritation no doubt arose from the growing secularization of such tours. For someone who had helped pioneer the genre, the point of such excursions was to inculcate 'soul-inspiring lessons' in which the application of the text to the landscape was an extension, not a replacement of evangelical methods of reading. Yet, by the 1920s, Poynter's evangelical views were rapidly losing ground. Bunyan as a figure in the public domain was increasingly subject to secular forms of viewing and consumption. As these secular modes became more prominent, they inevitably overshadowed evangelical views and pushed these into the background.

Translation and Evangelical Realism

Virtually all translations of *The Pilgrim's Progress* are evangelically driven and most of them arose out of the Protestant missionary movement. This evangelical imperative marks these translations in

---

37 R. H. Poynter, *Syllabus of Bunyan Lectures* (Bedford: Robinson, 1912), back cover.
38 'Local Scenery of "The Pilgrim's Progress": Account of a Lecture by R. H. Poynter', *Bedfordshire Standard* (24 December 1924), Newspaper Cuttings, Bunyan Collection, Bedford Library.

various ways: they are often hasty; they are done in bits and pieces as missionaries try and work out what will appeal to their new constituencies of readers; they are done by teams of first-language converts and second-language missionaries in a process that often produces a hybrid form of translation. Importantly, they are translations designed to speak unequivocally and directly to the target audiences of missionaries.[39]

These circumstances tend to promote a target- rather than source-inclined translation. For Protestant missionaries the text was a key evangelizing 'device' and they hence sought a style of translation that could make the text take hold as soon as possible. The audiences that missionaries encountered generally had no prior knowledge of the text and so could not fill in the 'gaps' in the way that established evangelical readers were able to do. As far as possible, the text had to be made realistic. For converts involved in translation there was also a desire to produce realistic translations. Converts were generally the major brokers of Christianity. Missionaries were often culturally and spiritually remote from those they sought to convert. Converts needed texts they could use and they had a vested interest in making sure that these texts could speak to their new audiences.

Drawing evidence from two specific translations of *The Pilgrim's Progress* (Sesotho and Afrikaans) as well as observations on others, one can discern some of the ways in which translations naturalize the text. One obvious strategy, as I have indicated elsewhere,[40] is that geographical references are generally indigenized. In the Sesotho version, the arbor in which Christian takes his nap and loses his scroll is *Mokhoro a pholileng*, an outhouse or hut where fire is made. In the same translation, proverbs are Sothoized. 'A bird in the hand is worth two in the bush'[41] appears as 'U se ke ua toepa letlalo la phokojoe e sa tsamaea': 'Don't hope for the jackal's skin when [the jackal] is no longer there'.[42] In the Afrikaans translation, the wilderness becomes

---

39 Hofmeyr, *The Portable Bunyan*, pp. 76–97.
40 Ibid., p. 235.
41 *PP*, p. 74.
42 John Bunyan, *Leeto la mokreste*, trans. Adolphe Mabille and Filemone Rapetloane (1986; Morija: Morija Sesuto Book Depot, 1988), p. 20.

'woestyn' (desert); the Slough of Despond, *'moeras van Kleinmoedigheid'* (Marsh of Faintheartedness); and in the scene of the Delectable Mountains the sheep are translated not as *skape* but *vee* (cattle or stock), since shepherds are most often seen with cattle, not sheep which are normally left to their own devices.[43]

These attempts to localize translations also emerge from Moses Mubitana's translation of Bunyan's text into Ila (a language spoken in present-day Zambia). His account of the trial of Faithful and Christian at Vanity Fair has been back-translated into English (The Voice). It is clear from key terms in this passage that the translation has been indigenized: 'king/prince' becomes 'chief'; 'town' becomes 'village'; 'jury' becomes 'members of the court'. However, the indigenization of the text extends beyond terminology. Compare for example the indictment of Christian and Faithful in the two versions. In the original we read

> That they were enemies to, and disturbers of their trade; that they had made commotions and divisions in the town, and had won a party to their own most dangerous opinions, in contempt of the law of their prince.[44]

In the Ila translation this passage reads thus:

> That they were their enemies, and again that they spoilt their trade; just as they brought commotion and division into the village so again they turned some of the people to their notorious thinkings because they wished to dishonour the law of their Chief.[45]

There are several important differences between the two passages. In the first extract Christian and Faithful are described as 'enemies to [...] their trade [i.e. the trade of Vanity Fair]'. Their crime in other words inheres in creating public disorder which in turn disrupts commerce. In the Ila passage, their crime is slightly different and comes in

---

43   John Bunyan, *Die Christen se Reis na die Ewigheid* (Cape Town: Nederduits Gereformeerde Kerk-uitgewers van Suid-Afrika, n. d.), pp. 11, 18, 142.
44   *PP*, p. 141.
45   Anon., 'The Voice of Africa: A Bit of Bunyan by Moses Mubitana', *Africa*, 16 (1946), p. 179.

two discrete parts: Christian and Faithful are enemies of the village *and* they disrupt trade.

A second difference between the two passages lies in the type of disturbance created. In the first passage, the two had 'made' division and disturbance whereas in the Ila the offence seems stronger, since the two introduce an entirely new state of affairs by bringing in 'commotion and division' where none apparently existed. The third difference pertains to the 'law of the prince'. In the first passage, the crime is that Christian and Faithful through their seditious ideas have weaned subjects away from their legitimate superiors: the two processes (of harbouring seditious ideas and disturbing the hierarchies of authority) appear seamlessly related. In the second passage, the two processes are more discrete. Christian and Faithful appear to wish to attract people to their ideas with the express purpose of dishonouring the person of the Chief. Offending the chief appears to be the primary objective, attracting followers a subsidiary motive. A further dimension of their crime is that these offences are ongoing (they commit the offences 'again'), something not evident in the original where the offences appear to be one-off affairs.

The Ila passage needs to be read in the context of the politics of African Christianity and chiefly authority. In a situation where converts were often drawn from those who were not beneficiaries of the existing social order, Christians were targeted by chiefs whose authority was threatened by radical and egalitarian versions of Christianity. As Christianity gained a foothold in African societies, communities were at times fiercely divided between 'traditionalists' and converts. Christians were labeled as enemies and as being responsible for introducing division where none was deemed to have existed. In this context, Christians were often seen to be inflammatory and to be seeking out conflict by disrespecting the authority of chiefs. These conflicts were endemic in many communities and rumbled on for decades. Judged against this context Mubitana's translation introduces linguistic choices and ideological emphases that would encourage Christian readers to naturalize the text and to experience it as closely related to, and hence applicable to, their particular circumstances.

It is possibly these types of translation strategies that contributed to the perception of *The Pilgrim's Progress* as 'realistic'. In one account of Tiyo Soga's legendary 1868 translation into Xhosa (a language spoken in present-day South Africa), a reviewer reported the following:

> A missionary, traveling in Kaffraria [a Xhosa-speaking area in the Eastern Cape], a short time ago, happened to have in his possession a proofsheet [of the Xhosa version of *The Pilgrim's Progress*], containing a description of the conflict [between Christian and Apollyon]. Having read this to a native he was asked if the writer had himself witnessed the scene, and being informed that this was the translation of an allegory, the native in great astonishment replied – that it appeared to him impossible for any one but an eye-witness to have given such a description.[46]

Allowing for the trope of the 'awe-struck native' which lurks in this passage, the excerpt does none the less point to a perception that the translation was inviting the reader to imagine the text as unfolding in a familiar world. Indeed, the Introduction to Soga's translation encourages readers to place themselves in the text and to undertake the kind of evangelical realistic reading we have been discussing.

> Folks! Here is a book for you to examine. The book tells the story of a traveller who walks the road which many of you would like to travel. Accompany the traveller whilst slowly trying to make acquaintance with each other – stopping to take rest whilst listening to things the traveller tells and reports to you; move along with the traveller to his destination, the end of his journey.[47]

Another very famous instance of 'realistic' translation of *The Pilgrim's Progress* was the 1835 Malagasy version undertaken in Madagascar, the large island off Africa's eastern seaboard. Briefly, the context in which this translation was produced was an episode of intense persecution of Christian converts sparked by a change of monarch in the Merina royal court. The London Missionary Society (LMS) had been invited into Madagascar in 1820 by the king Radama. Eight years later he died and his successor, Ranavalona, outlawed

---

46 Quoted in John A. Chalmers, *Tiyo Soga: A Page of South African Mission Work* (Edinburgh: Andrew Elliot, 1877), p. 342.
47 'Intshayelelo' (Introduction), *Uhambo lo Mhambi* (*The Pilgrim's Progress*), trans. Tiyo Soga (1868; Lovedale: Lovedale Press, 1965), p. 7. My thanks to Monde Simelela for the translation.

Christianity. Missionaries had to flee and converts were ruthlessly punished.[48] Before the missionaries left, one of their number, David Johns, completed a translation of *The Pilgrim's Progress*. Several copies were written out by the converts and passed from hand to hand. In letters from converts which were smuggled out to the LMS, the Malagasy Christians invoked Bunyan regularly and quoted passages in the book which matched their circumstances. Accounts of their persecution were frequently cited in LMS publicity.[49] A tour through England in 1839 of six converts who had managed to escape raised the profile of the Malagasy Christians and their use of *The Pilgrim's Progress*. Indeed, the episode came to occupy a pivotal role in LMS historiography and was featured extensively for at least a century afterwards in their publications.

Reports of how the converts used the text stressed its links to features of the society and landscape of Christians in Madagascar: 'The many graphic delineations of Christian life, as then existing in Madagascar, which the incomparable work contains, cause it to be prized, next to the Scriptures, as their most valued treasure'.[50] Another account stressed questions of topography:

> The friends [Malagasy converts] often, as they travelled talked of their favourite 'Pilgrim's Progress', and compared themselves to Christian. Once their way lay along a hill so steep and slippery from the heavy rains that they could hardly keep their footing; this they called 'the Hill Difficulty'.
>
> Another time they had to cross a wide and deep stream by a single plank some height above the water. The narrow bridge shook at every step, and the women asked if there was no way but this. They were told there was no other, and they then called to mind how Christian had found that there was no way to

---

48 See Bonar A. Gow, *Madagascar and the Protestant Impact: The Work of British Missionaries, 1818–95* (London: Longman, 1979), pp. 1–39.

49 See William Ellis, *History of Madagascar*, 2 vols (London: Fisher, n. d.), II, 516; idem, *Faithful unto Death: The Story of the Founding and Preservation of the Martyr Church of Madagascar* (London: John Snow, 1876); *The Report of the Directors to the Fiftieth General Meeting of the Missionary Society usually called the London Missionary Society* (London: London Missionary Society, 1844).

50 Ellis, *Faithful unto Death*, p. 93.

Evangelical Realism

the Celestial City but through the deep river. This encouraged them, and they passed over safely.[51]

This passage is accompanied by an engraving showing a Malagasy setting. In the background are tall trees in a tropical forest. In front, three tiny figures make their way over a huge abyss by means of a fallen tree trunk. The caption says 'A Bridge in Madagascar – P. 323'. The page reference indicates that we are meant to link this image to the extract on the fugitives escaping by means of the narrow plank over the stream. The circumstances depicted in the image and the text, are slightly different. The text describes a group of people crossing a wide and deep stream by means of a plank, whereas in the image we see three people crossing an abyss by means of a horizontal tree trunk.

However, in both instances, we are being asked to witness, and to apply a particular reading strategy. In the case of the converts' narrative, we see them applying the text to their circumstances both evangelically and topographically. In looking at the picture and reading the caption, our task is to apply the picture to the text. In doing this, we can imagine the type of terrain through which the converts pass more vividly and in that process obtain confirmation for ourselves of how *The Pilgrim's Progress* can be applied topographically to a range of environments. The book from which this account comes is a popular Protestant mission publication and its readers were in all probability accustomed to the idea of applying *The Pilgrim's Progress* to their own surroundings. The passage on the Malagasy Christians reinforces this reading strategy from afar.

Another feature of translated texts which underlined this method of reading was the indigenized illustrations that began to appear in foreign language versions from at least the mid-1800s.[52] These attracted considerable comment and interest and were frequently displayed or shown in magic lantern events. The illustrations were invoked to demonstrate the 'universality' of the text and to illustrate

---

51 Frances Arnold-Foster, *Heralds of the Cross or the Fulfilling of the Command: Chapters on Missionary Work* (London: Hatchards, 1885), p. 323.
52 Hofmeyr, *The Portable Bunyan*, pp. 173–90.

its capacity to be applied to any ecology or environment. Discussing a set of Japanese illustrations, one commentator said:

> These are very characteristic, especially the portraiture of Mr. Worldly Wiseman, who appears before us in the very ideal of a smug, self-satisfied Pharisee; the picture of the three Shining ones coming to Christian with wonderful Japanese head dresses; and the scenes of Vanity Fair Crowded with incident, and depicting the revels and delights dear to the Japanese Heart. [...] Christian appears as a native Chinaman, and the Palace Beautiful as a Chinese pagoda.[53]

In some editions, there was a miscellany of illustrations, so that on one page the reader might be asked to imagine Christian as a seventeenth-century Puritan in Bedford, and then a few pages later to visualize the story unfolding in a tropical forest, and then to witness Christian and Hopeful welcomed to heaven by a host of Victorian angels.[54] Such editions are almost the ideal version of an evangelical realist text: as one reads one has to imagine the text as applicable to an ever-changing set of environments.

These translations and illustrations were all used as publicity material back home. As Susan Thorne has demonstrated, Nonconformists used the foreign mission project to add value to their political cause at home.[55] Translations of *The Pilgrim's Progress* formed an important plank in these campaigns and were featured in mission exhibitions, book displays, magic lantern evenings, press reports, sermons and lectures.[56] All of these underlined the book as one that could take root in many different societies and appear as real to them as it did to audiences at home.

Thus far we have examined a series of evangelical reading strategies that promoted realism in different parts of the world. How did such dispersed readings come to be brought into dialogue? How did they interact with and shape each other? To answer this question we turn again to Bedford and the Bunyan Meeting House to examine

---

53   John Brown, *Bunyan's Home* (London: Ernest Nister, n. d.).
54   See John Bunyan, *Zamlendo wamkrisitu kwa ana* (n. p.: Church of Scotland Mission, 1902).
55   Thorne, *Congregational Missons*, pp. 1–22.
56   Hofmeyr, *The Portable Bunyan*, pp. 63–7.

the way in which two of its pastors – John Brown and C. Bernard Cockett – assembled different versions of Bunyan.

Bunyan Meeting House: John Brown and C. Bernard Cockett

As the spiritual home of one of the world's most important evangelical writers, the Bunyan Meeting House has always been something of an international crossroads. Visitors from different parts of the world have made it a site of pilgrimage both to see the building but also the relics of Bunyan that it housed. Between 1849 and 1866, the Bedford Theological Seminary under John Jukes (another pastor of the Meeting House) served as an institution to train agents for the LMS.[57] Once out in the field, some of these Bedford-trained missionaries sent back copies of translations of *The Pilgrim's Progress*. These formed the core of a collection that was to be built up and displayed in the church (and subsequently the Museum). Indeed, for missionaries from a Congregationalist or Baptist background, the Meeting House was a powerful symbolic point: one missionary imagined the proselytizing of the world stretching from 'Mandalay to Mill Street' (the location of the church).[58]

For any pastor called to this congregation, an important dimension of the job description was to curate the memory of Bunyan. The pastors who took this task on most enthusiastically were John Brown, who held the position from 1864 to 1903 and C. Bernard Cockett, the incumbent from 1925 to 1931. The different emphases that they brought to the position provide a useful insight into the changing configuration of Bunyan in a transnational domain.

---

57   H. G. Tibbutt, 'The Dissenting Academies of Bedfordshire II – Bedford', *Bedfordshire Magazine*, 6:41 (1957), 8–10.
58   *Bedfordshire Times* (25 May 1928), Newspaper Cuttings, Bunyan Collection, Bedford Library.

In his history of the Meeting House, H. G. Tibbutt remarks that 'Brown's ministry coincided with an awakening of interest, both locally and nationally, in John Bunyan'.[59] Brown himself played a key role in this revival. From the 1860s onwards he immersed himself in Bunyan, and went on to produce one of the first authoritative biographies based on intensive archival and oral historical research.[60] In addition, Brown interested himself in how Bunyan might be projected in Bedford and beyond.[61] His hand is evident in the erection of a statue of Bunyan in Bedford in 1874 and in the campaign to place a memorial in Westminster Abbey, and it was Brown who systematized the collection and display of Bunyan artefacts that formed the nucleus of what is today the Bunyan Museum.[62] By some accounts, he arranged the first national exhibition of these relics. Another task he took on was to collect and display editions and translations of Bunyan's work.[63]

At the same time as he promoted Bunyan as a national figure, Brown was fully apprised of his transnational status. Through the Congregational Union he was active in mission circles and was well-informed on mission translations of Bunyan. He would have known missionaries who translated the text, some of whom sent him copies for display. For Brown, Bunyan's local and global presences were inseparable. As his daughter's biography indicates and as Brown himself notes, his interest in Bunyan was in part sparked by the number of visitors who arrived at the Meeting House from all parts of the world in search of Bunyan sites.[64]

---

59   H. G. Tibbutt, *Bunyan Meeting Bedford 1650–1950* (Bedford: Trustees of Bunyan Meeting House, n. d.), pp. 71–2.
60   See John Brown, *John Bunyan: His Life, Times and Work* (London: Isbister, 1900).
61   See Flora Ada Keynes, *Gathering up the Threads: A Study in Family Biography* (Cambridge: W. Heffer, 1950), pp. 22–4.
62   Ibid.
63   Cyril Hargreaves and M. Greenshields, *Catalogue of the Bunyan Meeting Library and Museum, Bedford* (Bedford: Bunyan Meeting House, 1955), Preface.
64   Keynes, *Gathering up the Threads*, p. 22; Brown, *John Bunyan*, p. v.

As a noted scholar of Bunyan, Brown had links to scholars working in the emerging field of English literature. In the preface to his biography of Bunyan, he thanks Edward Arber, Professor of English Language and Literature at Sir Josiah Mason's College, Birmingham for assistance. He would also certainly have had links to other English literature scholars, particularly those in the 'new' universities with their strong Nonconformist roots. His discussions of Bunyan in the biography and elsewhere demonstrate that he was well-read in the literary debates of the day.[65]

Brown then had a firm grasp on Bunyan as a figure of Bedford, as an evangelical writer with a transnational presence, as a writer who had been widely translated, and as a figure in the emerging canon of English literature. His discussion of *The Pilgrim's Progress* draws all of these strands together. He portrays the book both as an evangelical classic (a book of 'heart-experience') and as a story firmly rooted amongst the common folk of Bedford. As a book concerned with ordinary people, the text can take its place in the emerging canon of the English novel. In Brown's view, the strength of *The Pilgrim's Progress* lies in the way it combines an evangelical concern with a sympathetic depiction of the 'lowliest life' in a 'commonplace region'. It is this combination which allows the book to travel so widely:

> it is one of the few books that can easily make themselves at home among nations the most diverse. It lends itself so readily to idiomatic thought and dialectic variety, and so livingly touches the universal heart beating under all nationalities.

His view of the text as 'universal' also emerges in his discussion of 'Editions, Version, Illustrations, and Imitations of the "Pilgrim's Progress"'. Here Brown discusses the local and international versions of the text not as two disparate spheres of activity but as one continuous set of developments. For him, then, Bunyan as an important figure in English literature is inseparable from his evangelical standing and his international circulation.[66]

---

65   Brown, *John Bunyan*, p. 300.
66   Ibid., pp. 298, 299, 453–82.

Read today Brown's claims of the text's 'universality' may sound partial and ideologically driven. However, in the context in which Brown operated his thinking was about as 'universal' as one could hope for. The point emerges more clearly if we turn to Cockett, a supporter of more vehement versions of Imperialism which produced a rather different kind of Bunyan.

Cockett, an Australian Baptist, was called to the Meeting House in 1925, three years before the 1928 tercentenary celebrations. Unsurprisingly, he was drawn into the management of the event and became a key player in the proceedings both in Bedford and nationally.[67] He appeared at numerous events; delivered speeches and sermons; and produced a raft of newspaper articles. He also published several popular works on Bunyan. These included *Bunyan's England: A Tour with the Camera in the Footsteps of the Immortal Dreamer* and *John Bunyan's England*, done for the Homeland Association. These books drew strongly on traditions of Bunyan-in-Bedford topographical writing.

Like Brown, Cockett was interested in Bunyan both as an evangelical figure, as a figure rooted in Bedford, and as an international presence. However his version of Bunyan's internationalism was narrower than Brown's and was rooted in the British settler communities of Empire. He evinced almost no interest in non-English versions of *The Pilgrim's Progress* and instead focused on Bunyan as a figure of importance to 'white' communities outside England: 'Bunyan charms especially the visitor from Scotland, the Dominions and the United States'.[68] In one of his numerous tercentenary writings, Cockett describes some Australians visiting Bedford:

> Last Sunday three Australian attended the Bunyan Meeting House, after traveling ten thousand miles by land and sea, in order that they might pay a pilgrimage to Elstow, where, 60 years ago, a father had attended the services in the upper room of the Moot Hall on the Village Green. They walked on hallowed ground, for it was the first time they had come 'Home'. Ancestral memories surged through them as they visited the place, sanctified by family

---

67 Tibbutt, *Bunyan Meeting*, pp. 90–6.
68 C. Bernard Cockett, *Bedfordshire Standard* (16 February 1927), Newspaper Cuttings, Bunyan Collection, Bedford Library.

tradition. In such a spirit people from all part of the earth will visit the haunts of the Immortal Dreamer of Bedford Town, and myriads, unable to leave their native shores in the body will wing their way in spirit to this sacred corner of the British Commonwealth.[69]

Superficially the extract appears committed to ideas of Bunyan's internationalism: 'people from all part of the earth' will imaginatively visit Bedford and share in Bunyan's memory. However, as phrases like 'ancestral memory' and 'family tradition' indicate, the 'people' who will think of Bunyan are in fact 'white'. Elsewhere in Cockett's writing, this racialization of Bunyan is more explicit:

England is a garden, and the wild flower in Bunyan's genius is blossoming into strange beauty in 1928, his Tercentenary, for the whole world honours his memory. Visitors from the Dominions coming 'Home', Americans of British ancestry and pilgrims of all nationalities long to drink at the ancient springs of life and literature in these sea girt isles. John Bunyan […] is one of the great names of our race.[70]

Here the claim of universality – 'pilgrims of all nationalities' – is explicitly circumscribed by race. For Cockett, then, Bunyan's importance resides in his evangelicalism, his realism and his international standing but only amongst settler communities. For Brown, by contrast, Bunyan's status was linked to his circulation across barriers of both language and race.

The shift from Brown to Cockett meant a narrowing in the meaning of Bunyan's internationalism. Bunyan was no longer a figure for all Protestants, only those who were 'white'. This shift in turn formed part of a larger process of sloughing off Bunyan's transnational presence. In some quarters, Bunyan's over-association with colonized bodies and societies appeared as a 'problem', and in response there was a new focus on Bunyan as a national writer and a shifting of his transnational presence into the background.[71]

---

69 Cockett, *Bedfordshire Standard* (25 May 1928), Newspaper Cuttings, Bunyan Collection, Bedford Library.
70 Cockett, *John Bunyan's England* (London: Homeland Association, 1928), Foreword.
71 Hofmeyr, *The Portable Bunyan*, pp. 217–27.

One side effect of this nationalization process was to claim his realism as indigenously inspired, as emerging from the very soil of Bedfordshire itself. For this claim to hold, Bunyan had to be loosened from the societies in which he had been indigenized and made 'real'. This process is aptly illustrated in an 1896 Macmillan school version of *The Pilgrim's Progress* published for use in Indian schools. In the Introduction, the book is shaken free of its naturalization in India and turned it into a 'universal' story: 'the pilgrim called "Christian" is not a fakir or ascetic, as the Indian youth is apt to suppose; he is every ordinary Christian man'. The Introduction continues to explain that the story is 'not restricted to any individual, any age, or any country, for it is the universal human theme of man's struggle with the moral evil that is in him or influencing him'. Inevitably, however, this universality is strongly associated with English and Englishness, not least by the seventeen pages of explanatory notes which root the text in England.[72]

The impulse to read Christian as a fakir is one that earlier evangelical versions would have encouraged in their translations and illustrations. Now, however, this interpretation is declared wrong and is supplanted with a reading in which the story is apparently universal but also 'really' English.[73] This 'realism' had initially been predicated on, and validated by the circulation and indigenization of the text in a wide range of settings. The impulse behind this circulation had been evangelical and international and in this context, inclusion of such modes of reading added value to Bunyan. As secular and national styles of reading became dominant, these transnational modes were sloughed off. It was now exclusion, rather than inclusion which added value to *The Pilgrim's Progress*.

---

72 John Morrison, *Bunyan's Pilgrim's Progress in Modern English* (London: Macmillan, 1896), pp. vii–viii.

73 That this injunction had little effect is apparent from a book written some one hundred years on in which Bunyan is discussed as an Indian mystic saint putting forward Sufi concepts. These 'have established the reputation of John Bunyan as the greatest English mystic saint of the seventeenth century' (M. G. Gupta, *Mystic Symbolism in Ramayan, Mahabharat and The Pilgrim's Progress* (Agra: M. G. Publishers, 1993), p. 178).

In conclusion, let us return to our opening comments on genre as a phenomenon made transnationally. In relation to Bunyan's realism, one uncertain plank of the generic platform was the lack of specificity in topography of his allegory. However, through a series of evangelical reading strategies that applied the texts to a range of circumstances, these 'gaps' could be filled in to produce the illusion of an abundant spatial realism. Through translation and illustration undertaken in various parts of the world and reflected back in England, the capacity of the text to adapt itself to multiple topographical environments was confirmed. The text's claims to realism were hence strengthened. The rise of English literature, in part indebted to older evangelical reading strategies massively strengthened the idea of Bunyan's realism. As the national emphasis in English literary studies gained ground, the idea of Bunyan as a writer rooted in seventeenth-century England took shape while his transnational standing diminished in importance. Bunyan emerged as a writer steeped in highly particular and localized forms of realism and hence as an early practitioner of the English novel.

As this essay has attempted to demonstrate, this process needs to be understood as being shaped in and by the text's circulation pathways. To return to Damrosch, it is not the text alone which can determine its outcomes. In some cases, textual features can be generically reshaped or overwritten. To grasp how these protocols of genre unfold both inside and outside the text, we need to lift our eyes from the page and look out across the globe the better to grasp the text and its worlding.

RICHARD DANSON BROWN

7 Everyman's Progresses: Louis MacNeice's Dialogues with Bunyan

Bunyan was not just a writer Louis MacNeice admired: he was also a protagonist in one of his poems. 'The Streets of Laredo' is an ebullient parody of a cowboy ballad which reconfigures war time London as the nightmarish Laredo.[1] Into this lapsarian world, Bunyan makes an apocalyptic entrance:

> Then twangling their bibles with wrath in their nostrils
> From Bonehill Fields came Bunyan and Blake:
> 'Laredo the golden is fallen, is fallen,
> Your flame shall not quench nor your thirst shall not slake.'[2]

The uncertain, shifting tone of this passage is characteristic of what I will call MacNeice's dialogue with Bunyan. At one level, Bunyan and Blake appear almost as a comic millenarian chorus, 'twangling their bibles' as a country singer would 'twangle' a guitar, freely adapting

[1] For a reading of the poem in relation to the ballad, see John T. Irwin, 'MacNeice, Auden, and the Art Ballad', *Contemporary Literature*, 11 (1970), 58–79, who notes the 'appropriateness' of the use of Bunyan and Blake in terms of MacNeice's critique of London-Laredo (p. 68).

[2] Louis MacNeice, *Collected Poems*, ed. E. R. Dodds (London: Faber and Faber, 1979), p. 217; hereafter cited as *CP*. The original text of the poem reads 'From *Bunhill* fields came Bunyan and Blake' (my emphasis), the actual name of the Dissenters' burial ground in the London Borough of Islington; see MacNeice, *Holes in the Sky* (London: Faber and Faber, 1948), p. 13. For *Eighty-Five Poems* (London: Faber and Faber, 1959), MacNeice changed the text to 'Bonehill'. This almost certainly demonstrates his awareness that 'Bunhill' 'is probably a euphonious corruption of Bonehill, since the site was apparently a repository for bones before 1549'; *The Official Guide to Bunhill Fields* (London: The Corporation of London, 1991), p. 6. I am grateful to W. R. Owens for alerting me to the origins of the name.

Revelation, appearing as an embodiment of zealous indignation with 'wrath in their nostrils' and moral nostrums to chill the heart of the flintiest of sinners. (Appropriately enough, Johnny Cash recorded a powerful version of the original ballad on his final album, *The Man Comes Around*, the title song of which revisits the imagery and agendas of Revelation.)[3] Read in this spirit, the stanza undermines the traditions of Protestant apocalyptic, and the values of the poet's father, Bishop John MacNeice. Bunyan and Blake are ludicrous biblical strummers rather than inspired writers.

Yet in the context of the poem as a whole, Bunyan's profile is less fixed. Bunyan and Blake enter the poem after Sir Christopher Wren – 'His big wig a-smoulder' – has gleefully realized that the destruction of Laredo means fresh business for architectural entrepreneurs: '"Let them make hay of the streets of Laredo; / When your ground-rents expire I will build them again."' The city is corrupt: '"loot is still free on the streets of Laredo"', while the fate of 'Tom Dick and Harry the Wandering Jew' points to its culpable failure to find a place for the victims of war: '"They tell me report at the first police station / But the station is pancaked – so what can I do?"' In such a milieu, Bunyan and Blake articulate the sense that Laredo has become a type of Babylon, or Amalek from the Book of Samuel, whose citizens are 'utterly destroyed' by Saul (1 Samuel 15), and whose King, Agag, is alluded to in the poem's first line. The comic demeanour of Bunyan and Blake does not undermine the indictment which they level; '"Your flame shall not quench nor your thirst shall not slake"' is both a literal description of the ruin of London and a hellish warning of punishments yet to be inflicted.

'The Streets of Laredo' provides an initial context for understanding MacNeice's relationship with Bunyan. Though he was not a constitutive influence in the way that Yeats, Eliot or Auden were, during the later 1940s and 1950s, Bunyan provided MacNeice with raw narrative materials and metaphors which inform his poetry and drama. 'The Streets of Laredo' signals MacNeice's receptivity to Bunyanesque apocalyptic and locates his imaginary Bunyan in the

---

3   Johnny Cash, *American IV: The Man Comes Around* (American Recordings, 2002).

significant context of popular literature and song. As he was to observe in *Varieties of Parable*, 'Bunyan was of the people and wrote for the people'.[4] Despite his own upper middle class origins as the son of a Church of Ireland bishop, as a non-doctrinaire Socialist, and (after 1941) as a BBC radio producer, MacNeice retained the ambition to write 'for the people' throughout his career. Yet the suspicion explicit in 'The Streets of Laredo' alerts us to the fact that MacNeice's response to Bunyan is inflected by his own secular humanism and his ongoing dialogue with his father's religion. In this essay, I read *Varieties of Parable*, the radio play *Prisoner's Progress* and the poem 'The Blasphemies' in the light of their critical dialogue with the Bunyanesque.

* * *

Though he wrote a novel in his early twenties, MacNeice was lukewarm about prose fiction. 'It seems to me that most novels are full of padding, of which we get quite enough in life.'[5] Such indifference is striking in the light of Auden's enthusiasm for the form; in 'Letter to Lord Byron', Auden discerns a moral hierarchy which separates 'unobservant, immature and lazy' poets from high-minded novelists like Jane Austen: 'novel writing is / A higher art than poetry altogether'.[6] Despite collaborating with Auden on *Letters from Iceland* (in which the 'Letter to Lord Byron' first appeared) MacNeice would have dissented from this judgment. Yet his later essay 'Pleasure in Reading' identifies a select group of prose works 'which come very high on my list of enjoyables': *The Pilgrim's Progress*, *The Golden Ass*, the *Alice* books and *The Day of the Triffids* are described as examples of 'poetic

4   Louis MacNeice, *Varieties of Parable* (Cambridge: Cambridge University Press, 1965), p. 43; hereafter cited as *VoP*.
5   Louis MacNeice, *Selected Literary Criticism of Louis MacNeice*, ed. Alan Heuser (Oxford: Clarendon Press, 1987), p. 232.
6   W. H. Auden, *The English Auden*, ed. Edward Mendelson (London: Faber and Faber, 1977), p. 171. See also Auden's 'The Novelist' (an idealized portrait of Christopher Isherwood), which contrasts the more immediately startling gifts of the poet with the longer term work of the novelist: 'he / Must struggle out of his boyish gift and learn / How to be plain and awkward' (p. 238).

fantasy'.[7] MacNeice's preferred fiction is indicative of his interest in popular forms and his anti-realist bias. So 'realism in the photographic sense is almost played out': *The Day of the Triffids* exemplifies a compromise between the competing discourses of realism and parable, resulting in a text which is 'closer to Spenser than the main tradition of the English novel' (*VoP*, p. 26). MacNeice's prejudice against the novel was chiefly a reaction against realism; imaginative prose – including *The Pilgrim's Progress* – which could be exempted from the taint of realism did engage his interest.

In *Varieties of Parable*, 'poetic fantasy' is translated into the umbrella term 'parable'. Despite, or rather because of, its congruence with Christianity, MacNeice had misgivings about the term: 'it suggests something much too narrow for my purpose, namely the parables of the New Testament' (*VoP*, p. 1). Yet parable has become a touchstone for describing the poetry of MacNeice's last three volumes, *Visitations*, *Solstices* and *The Burning Perch*. Peter McDonald's characterization of MacNeice's parable, as 'both an unfinished idiom and one which is of itself unfinishable', aptly describes the terrain of poems like 'The Truisms' and 'Charon'.[8] However, it immediately suggests a distinction between MacNeice and Bunyan: despite the many deviations along the narrow path, Christian and Christiana arrive at the Celestial City – Bunyan had no use for ambiguous closures or unfinished idioms. How then did MacNeice assimilate Bunyan into his own discourse of parable? What was it which MacNeice imported from Bunyan into his later works?

Varieties of Parable articulates the difficulties which Bunyan poses for a modern reader. According to MacNeice, English readers frequently cannot cope with Bunyan's theology, because 'Bunyan is too near to us. Whatever his religion or lack of religion, every Englishman has to some degree inherited the Puritan Revolution [...] if Bunyan's beliefs are not his, Bunyan's *experience* to some degree must be' (*VoP*, p. 20).[9] There is some slippage between the first

---

7   MacNeice, *Selected Literary Criticism*, p. 233.
8   Peter McDonald, *Louis MacNeice: the Poet in his Contexts* (Oxford: Clarendon Press, 1991), p. 176.
9   Original emphasis.

person plural 'Bunyan is too near to *us*' and the earlier remark '*they*' – again referring to the English – 'cannot stomach a writer who held such beliefs'.[10] By implication, MacNeice's Irish identity meant that he did not fully share English reticence about Bunyan's theology. He was critical of the sermonizing tendency in Bunyan's writing, especially as he compared *The Pilgrim's Progress* with *The Faerie Queene*:

> Some of Spenser's figures [...] are not allegorical at all. Bunyan has none of this variety. His material is *all* sermon material. Why then does his story haunt us in an age when sermons are considered unreadable? The answer [...] is sleight-of-hand. [...] Bunyan starts with his overt theme – which is the orthodox Puritan gospel – but, thanks to his own intense experience and also his acute observation, the pulpit abstractions become concrete and speak with the voice of human beings. (*VoP*, p. 45)

This sense of the problematic universality of *The Pilgrim's Progress* is present throughout *Varieties of Parable*. In an earlier passage, MacNeice argues that

> provided he will forget his sectarian or anti-religious prejudices, anyone ought to be able to identify with Christian. For Christian is Everyman again, and his quest can stand for any quest that begins in anguish and ends in self-conquest and death (*VoP*, p. 29).

This sort of claim will be familiar to most teachers of Bunyan: don't worry too much about the theology, we urge; *The Pilgrim's Progress* is a work of existential fiction. To paraphrase Graham Hough's account of Hazlitt's reading of *The Faerie Queene* (in a book MacNeice admired) don't meddle with the theology and it won't meddle with you.[11] As we shall see, MacNeice performs a poetic variation on this approach in 'The Blasphemies', which concludes with a similar assertion of the ontological validity of all quests.

---

10   My emphases.
11   Graham Hough, *A Preface to 'The Faerie Queene'* (London: Duckworth, 1962), p. 9. See MacNeice's review of Hough in *Selected Literary Criticism*, pp. 237–9.

So MacNeice was aware both of the historical specificity of Bunyan's ideology and of universality of his fictions. His Bunyan is a popular writer, who uses fiction to put across the 'orthodox Puritan gospel'. However, Bunyan's work remains compelling because of its use of parable not because of its ideology. Yet as MacNeice's hesitations about English reactions to Bunyan indicate, he was himself a product of what Terence Brown calls the 'puritan tradition'.[12] As *The Strings are False* records, the young MacNeice grew up in the almost exclusively protestant milieu of Carrickfergus ('The cook Annie [...] was the only Catholic I knew and therefore my only proof that Catholics were human'), in which his core beliefs were shaped by his father's tormented piety ('because of his conspiracy with God I was afraid of him') and the scarifying warnings of the 'Mother's help'.[13] This leads to a terror of damnation in its own way every bit as lurid as Bunyan's:

> I had done so much wrong I knew I must end in Hell and, what was worse, I could imagine it. Sometimes when Miss Craig had jerked me and thumped me into bed she would look at me grimly and say: 'Aye, you're here now but you don't know where you'll be when you wake up'.[14]

Though John MacNeice was liberal politically and theologically,[15] such fears had a constitutive impact on MacNeice's thinking. Though

---

[12] Terence Brown, 'MacNeice and the Puritan Tradition' in *Louis MacNeice and his Influence*, eds K. Devine and A. J. Peacock (Gerrards Cross: Colin Smythe, 1998), pp. 20, 33.

[13] Louis MacNeice, *The Strings are False: An Unfinished Autobiography*, ed. E. R. Dodds (London: Faber and Faber, 1965), pp. 41, 38.

[14] Ibid., p. 42.

[15] According to Robert Welch, John MacNeice 'had Puritan leanings'; see 'Yeats and MacNeice: A seminar with Francis Stuart' in *Louis MacNeice and his Influence*, p. 10. John MacNeice's puritanical liberalism is manifest in *Carrickfergus and its Contacts*. In the chapter on 'The Coming of the Presbyterians', MacNeice passes from scepticism about the League and Covenant to a generous tribute to the evangelical achievements of Northern Irish Presbyterianism; see John MacNeice, *Carrickfergus and its Contacts* (London: Simpkin, Marshall, Ltd.; Belfast: W. Erskine Mayne, 1928), pp. 47–8. This must be counterbalanced by an awareness of Bishop MacNeice's commitment to Home Rule and his long hostility to Carson and the Unionists.

The Strings are False makes no direct allusion to Bunyan, it is clear from other sources that he read *The Pilgrim's Progress* at any early age. In his travel book, *I Crossed the Minch*, the sight of fishing nets in the Hebrides reminds a horrified MacNeice of his early reading: 'I had always thought of nets as evil because of an illustration in *The Pilgrim's Progress*'.[16] Bunyan, or rather the Bunyanesque, is a significant presence in MacNeice's poetry throughout his career. *Collected Poems* begins with 'The Creditor', written in 1929, which figures the speaker as God's debtor:

> The peacefulness of the fire blaze
> Will not erase
> My debts to God for His mind strays
> Over and under and all ways
> All days and always. (*CP*, p. 3)

Though the edgy word play owes much to modernist tricksiness, the sense of a radical debt to God which cannot be 'erase[d]' is strikingly Bunyanesque. For all the apparent 'peacefulness of the fire-blaze', the poem's deity is omnipresent: his intrusive 'finger probes [...] All days and always'. The much later *Autumn Sequel* (1954) relates a dream which has a bearing both on MacNeice's relationship with his father and on the power Christian theology retained for him:

> Tom, Dick and Harry, peeping, dirty, red
> In the face with shouting, bunting and paper caps,
> While tiers and tiers below, where all the gangways led
>
> Down to the round arena, newspaper scraps
> Capered around the foot of three tall black
> Crosses and through the noise I foresaw the world collapse
>
> In my father's mind in a moment, who at my back
> Was still coming up, coming up. This was the worst
> Of my dreams and I had the worst of it, in the lack

---

16 Louis MacNeice, *I Crossed the Minch* (London: Longmans, Green and Co, 1938), p. 27.

Of my own faith and the knowledge of his, the accursed
Two-ways vision of youth. (*CP*, p. 422)

What is most striking about this disturbed and disturbing poetry is what we might call the two-ways vision of the adult poet: while on the one hand, the text depends on the reader's knowledge of the writer's faithlessness, on the other, through its empathetic focus on his the fragility of his father's faith, it ennobles and dramatizes Christian belief. MacNeice's scepticism, in other words, was hard-won and flourished in the teeth of his ongoing anguish about his rejection of his father's values.[17] *Autumn Sequel* enacts this anguish poetically and suggests some of the charge which Bunyan held for MacNeice: though the poem ostensibly imitates Dante in its canto structure and elegant *terza rima*,[18] the economical evocation of the crucifixion recalls the similarly terse description of the passion in *The Pilgrim's Progress*: 'He ran thus till he came to a place somewhat ascending; and upon that place stood a *Cross*, and a little below in the bottom, a Sepulcher' (*PP*, p. 37). The chief difference is what for Bunyan is a moment of individual revelation which relieves Christian of his burden is transposed by MacNeice to a nightmarish public show, where the crucifixion is staged in an arena for the entertainment of the undifferentiated audience of 'Tom, Dick and Harry'. Although *Varieties of Parable* claims that 'anyone ought to be able to identify with Christian', my reading of MacNeice's dialogue with Bunyan suggests that in his case such universalism is enriched by his proximity to and critical sympathy with Bunyan's mentality.

* * *

---

17 MacNeice relates the same dream in *The Strings are False*, where it illustrates the limitations of his rebellion against his father's values: 'Anthony [Blunt] too had a father a clergyman and we both resented the fact that our parents assumed us to be Christian, though neither of us would have dared to stand up in their presence and die for our lack of faith' (pp. 100–1).
18 On MacNeice's debt to Dante, see Steve Ellis, 'Dante and Louis MacNeice: A Sequel to the *Commedia*', in *Dante's Modern Afterlife: Reception and Response from Blake to Heaney*, ed. N. Havely (Basingstoke: Macmillan, 1998).

Everyman's Progresses 155

MacNeice's Introductory Note for *Prisoner's Progress*, first printed in the *Radio Times*, defines it as a parable:

> *Prisoner's Progress*, like two earlier programmes of mine, *The Dark Tower* and *One Eye Wild*, is a parable play. The hero of each [...] is [...] a lost soul and [...] an unheroic figure. But in each case the hero finds himself at the end.[19]

MacNeice thus saw the new play in relation to previous successes like *The Dark Tower* (first broadcast in 1946 and published with other radio scripts in 1947).[20] Brown suggests that the 'plain-style quest romance' of *The Pilgrim's Progress* was a key influence on *The Dark Tower*, a play which revitalizes Browning's 'Childe Roland to the Dark Tower Came' as an allegory of the struggle against fascism.[21] *Prisoner's Progress* is still more indebted to Bunyan. Though the Note makes no allusion to him, given the title, this was unnecessary. A parable centered on 'an unheroic figure' who 'finds himself in the end' is as evocative of *The Pilgrim's Progress* as *Prisoner's Progress*; it is certainly proleptic of *Varieties of Parable*'s existential account of Christian as Everyman quoted above. MacNeice's play rewrites Bunyan's fiction in the context of the Second World War; it is a miniature embodiment of universalist readings of *The Pilgrim's Progress*, in which Bunyan's values are reimagined in secular terms.

Prisoner's Progress is set in a prisoner-of-war camp during a war between the Greys and the Browns. Though MacNeice suggests he used colours as a way of emphasizing the play's symbolic dimensions (*SP*, p. 151), identities rapidly decode into British and German: the camp commandant speaks in a sinister version of English by phrase book ('Here man has guards, man has wire, here all the night man has searchlights. Therefore man here must be happy' (*SP*, p. 157)) and the main protagonists' relationship is evoked through quotations from

---

19 Louis MacNeice, *Selected Plays of Louis MacNeice*, eds A. Heuser and P. McDonald (Oxford: Clarendon Press, 1993), p. 151; afterwards cited as *SP*.
20 For the context of *Prisoner's Progress* in MacNeice's career at the BBC, see Barbara Coulton, *Louis MacNeice in the BBC* (London: Faber and Faber, 1980), pp. 141–3, though she has little to say about the play's literary contexts and misprints the hero's name as 'Walters'.
21 Terence Brown, 'MacNeice and the Puritan Tradition', p. 33.

'The Ancient Mariner' and 'The Definition of Love'. The central character, Thomas Waters, whose name recalls both the Waters of Death from *The Pilgrim's Progress* and the protagonist of the ballad 'True Thomas',[22] is an illegitimate, depressive divorcee. He is an archetypal MacNeicean figure, a 'lost soul' with no pretensions to heroism.

The action centres on Grey attempts to escape from the camp, which is inconveniently located beside an enormous mountain. Though labelled by his fellow prisoners as a 'Very strange bird indeed' (*SP*, p. 158), Waters's mountaineering prowess earns him a place on the escape team. The prisoners tunnel into a Neolithic passage-grave, which is compared with 'New Grange in Ireland' (*SP*, p. 166). Archaeological implausibility notwithstanding (such monuments are usually found close to the sea in Western Europe),[23] the passage-grave is a symbolic property, which aligns the play's geography with that of *The Pilgrim's Progress*: it is a narrow way which leads to possible redemption. The grave also brings the prisoners into contact with female prisoners from an adjoining camp. In the final scenes, Waters and Alison (a poetry-loving kindred spirit) get out of the grave before being shot by pursuers as they flee over the mountain.

Prisoner's Progress is littered with details which recall *The Pilgrim's Progress*. Yet the play is not just an assemblage of Bunyanesque touches: rather, it uses the template of Bunyan's fiction for secular purposes. MacNeice notes that he used quotations to endow naturalistic dialogue with symbolic and poetic undertones (*SP*, p. 151). In so doing, he adopts one of the basic structuring devices of *The Pilgrim's Progress*, the use of biblical quotation and allusion. MacNeice's quotations are more catholic in range: the play samples from English poetry, nursery rhyme and popular songs. The black cook, Catsmeat, performs a shifting repertoire of nursery rhymes and songs as a sinister chorus: his signature tune, 'Comin' Round the Mountain'

---

22   This was a favourite of MacNeice's; see *VoP*, p. 8.
23   See Warwick Bray and David Trump, *A Dictionary of Archaeology* (Harmondsworth: Penguin, 1972), pp. 172–3. MacNeice note concedes the implausibility of the incident while observing that 'certain prisoners in North Africa did make their escape through an ancient Roman underground gallery' (*SP*, p. 151).

points relentlessly to the fact of the prisoners' incarceration. The solitary quotation from the Bible, when Waters performs Job's curse of the day of his birth and the night of his conception, emphasizes the differences between MacNeice and Bunyan. MacNeice juxtaposes Waters's intense investment in the despair of the biblical text with the blasé this-worldliness of the am-dram loving Padre, who only hears in Waters's recitation an opportunity to cast him in his production of *The Importance of Being Earnest*:

> WATERS 'And that which I was afraid of is come unto me. I was not in safety, neither had I rest, neither was I quiet; yet trouble came.'
> (*Shutting of heavy book*)
> PADRE Bravo, Waters! Never mind the slips. I can see you've an actor's memory. Chasuble, we'll have you as Chasuble. (*SP*, p. 163)

Though MacNeice follows Bunyan in using the Bible as a symbolic and rhetorical resource, the text invoked bespeaks his own values and agenda. The Book of Job articulates for Waters what he cannot state himself: a sense of existential alienation. In contrast, *The Pilgrim's Progress* makes little use of Job. Mr Hold-the-World quotes from Eliphaz's temporizing advice to Job, while Christian cites the Lord's terrifying description of the horse to Hopeful,[24] but Job's curse does not figure in the narrative. MacNeice uses a biblical text notable for its absence of comfort or reassurance; Waters insists that he prefers the Old Testament as the Padre attempts to cheer him up with something 'soothing' from the Gospel (*SP*, p. 162). MacNeice imitates Bunyan's technique to produce a modern effect of estrangement and isolation. Earlier in the same scene, Waters says, 'That mountain up there, it's always been between me and the sun' (*SP*, p. 161). While the symbols and techniques of the play recall Bunyan, there are invested with different symbolic values: this mountain is horrific, not delectable, while the biblical text encapuslates despair rather than bringing comfort.

* * *

---

24   See *PP*, pp. 100, 126.

According to *Varieties of Parable*, Bunyan's central attraction to MacNeice was his ability to capture existential predicaments in simple, persuasive language. I turn now to one of MacNeice's late masterpieces, 'The Blasphemies', which adapts the terminology and preoccupations of *Grace Abounding*.

'The Blasphemies' is keyed into the central anxieties of Protestant belief and psychology. It imitates *Grace Abounding* both in its thematic concern with blasphemy and as a spiritual autobiography; however, MacNeice's autobiography uses his experience not as an instance of what Bunyan calls '*the Grace of God towards me*' but as symbol of modern neurosis.[25] The ambiguity of the sin against the Holy Ghost frames the poem: it is conundrum which the protagonist never untangles. As a seven-year-old, he relives the psychological torments of Bunyan and Christian:

> The sin against the Holy... though what
> He wondered was it? Cold in his bed
> He thought: If I think those words I know
> Yet must not be thinking – Come to the hurdle
> And I shall be damned through thinking Damn (*CP*, pp. 507–8)

The poem recalls passages in *Grace Abounding* and *The Pilgrim's Progress*:

> In these days, when I have heard others talk of what was the sin against the Holy *Ghost*, then would the Tempter so provoke me to desire to sin that sin [...]

> Just when he was come over against the mouth of the burning Pit, one of the wicked ones got behind him, and stept up softly to him, and whisperingly suggested many grievous blasphemies to him, which he verily thought had proceeded from his own mind.[26]

Though Bunyan records his lived uncertainty about 'what was the sin against the Holy *Ghost*', as he writes the story, he is in no doubt that his perplexity arises directly from the machinations of 'the Tempter'.

---

25   John Bunyan, *Grace Abounding to the Chief of Sinners*, eds John Stachniewski and Anita Pacheco (Oxford: Oxford University Press, 1998), p. 4.
26   Ibid., p. 31; *PP*, p. 65.

Similarly, *The Pilgrim's Progress* locates Christian's temptation to blaspheme at 'the mouth of the burning Pit', insisting that the confusion induced by the temptation is a direct product of the malevolent intervention of 'one of the wicked ones'. Vera Camden suggests that 'Blasphemy is a sin of the flesh, waged against the spirit'.[27] For Bunyan, the combatants in this struggle are both human and supernatural. In *The Strings are False*, however, MacNeice explores his childhood 'obsession with the Sin against the Holy Ghost' without any of the ambiguity of 'The Blasphemies':

> I had discovered what this sin was and I could not help committing it. It consisted in saying 'Damn God' and once you had said that you were lost. I never said these words aloud but I could say them in my mind as distinct from just thinking them. [...] I would use my willpower not to say them but the strain was too great, I could not go to sleep till I had said them, so I said them in my mind and was lost.[28]

'The Blasphemies' lacks such expository contexts. It evokes the spiritual crisis induced by the fear of blaspheming, leaving the reader embroiled in the protagonist's inner conflict: 'He swore to himself he had not thought / Those words he knew but never admitted' (*CP*, p. 508). The pathos of the poem, however, lies in its revitalizing of a seventeenth-century mentality; like the crucifixion passage in *Autumn Sequel*, 'The Blasphemies' relies on the reader's awareness of modern secular values and the residual authority of Christian theology. We can see this in the choice of the word 'hurdle'. The boy seems to be anticipating posthumous judgement, yet 'hurdle' is a confusing word since it does not mean bar or dock. More plausibly, it relates to the sledges on which traitors were dragged through the streets to their execution.[29] 'Come to the hurdle/I shall be damned through thinking Damn' fuses judgement and execution in one terrified word; MacNeice may have remembered Bunyan's fear of execution in *Grace Abounding*: 'I was also at this time so possessed with the thought of

---

27 Vera Camden, 'Blasphemy and the Problem of Self in *Grace Abounding*', *Bunyan Studies*, 1:2 (1989), 8.
28 MacNeice, *The Strings are False*, p. 59.
29 See *OED* 1. c. which cites Ford's *Perkin Warbeck*: 'Let false Audeley / Be drawn upon an hurdle from Newgate / To Tower-hill'.

death, that oft I was as if I was on the Ladder, with the Rope about my neck'.[30]

The dialogue between 'The Blasphemies' and Bunyan works on a number of levels. Though Christian fears uttering 'many grevious blasphemies', as *Grace Abounding* makes clear, Bunyan's understanding of the sin against the Holy Ghost depended on a notion of what is essentially a single act of despairing repudiation of God's mercy. The terrible temptation *'to sell and part with Christ'*[31] draws its horrified energies from Bunyan's reading of the story of the Italian protestant Francesco Spira, whose conviction of his own reprobation arises out of his decision to deny his faith to save his family: 'I knew that justification is to be expected by Christ; and I denied, and abjured it; to the end I might keepe this fraile life from adversitie, and my children from povertie'.[32] It is in this context which the title of MacNeice's poem should be read: his protagonist does not commit a single act of blasphemy; his life is a series of overlapping blasphemies; each decade and each stanza rehearses a new form of derogation, or more precisely, a new form of moral failure.

Despite these sources, the poem is almost wholly undidactic: its blasphemies are not sins so much as habits of mind, attitudes through which the protagonist mirrors and experiences the intellectual life of his times. In asking 'what is a joke about God if you do not/Accept His existence? Where is the blasphemy?' MacNeice enacts the movement from theism to scepticism common among intellectuals of his class (*CP*, p. 508). Inevitably, the text registers a lack of symmetry between modern and early modern vocabularies. This is particularly evident in the third stanza, which loosely reimagines the secular humanism of the 1930s:

---

30 Bunyan, *Grace Abounding*, p. 91.
31 Ibid., p. 40.
32 *A Relation of the Fearefull Estate of Francis Spira, in the yeare, 1548*, trans. Nathaniel Bacon (London: Phil. Stephens and Christoph. Meredith, 1638), pp. 55–6. For Bunyan's reading of Spira, see *Grace Abounding*, pp. 45–6; for early modern conceptualization of despair and the sin against the Holy Ghost, see John Stachniewski, *The Persecutory Imagination: English Puritanism and the Literature of Religious Despair* (Oxford: Clarendon Press, 1991), pp. 38–44.

> Rising thirty, he had decided
> God was a mere expletive, a cheap one,
> No longer worth a laugh, no longer
> A proper occasion to prove one's freedom
> By denying something not worth denying.
> So humanism was all and the only
> Sin was the sin against the Human –
> But you could not call it Ghost for that
> Was merely emotive; the only – you could not
> Call it sin for that was emotive –
> The only failure was not to face
> The facts. But at thirty what are the facts? (*CP*, p. 508)

The language of *Grace Abounding* jostles with that of humanism. At one level, the poem endorses the protagonist's adult sense that God has become 'a mere expletive', yet both in the texture of the verse and the consciousness which it represents, progressive values are held in the poetic balance and found wanting. MacNeice juxtaposes the language of sin with that of humanism to produce a formulation which is at once accurate and deliberately impoverished: 'The only failure was not to face / The facts'. A failure to face the facts is not the same thing psychologically or rhetorically as the sin against the Holy Ghost; what the protagonist gains in self-awareness he loses in poetic resonance.

Hence it is no surprise that the fourth stanza attempts to assimilate the categories of traditional Christianity to the contemporary world: 'I can use my childhood symbols / Divorced from their context, Manger and Cross / Could do very well for Tom Dick and Harry' (*CP*, p. 508). The appearance of the perennially ominous trio 'Tom Dick and Harry' (onlookers at *Autumn Sequel*'s crucifixion and immigrants to Laredo) points to the hollowness of the analogy: as the final stanza firmly underlines, 'Tom Dick and Harry were not Christ' (*CP*, p. 509). Though MacNeice attempted similar symbolic appropriations in plays like *Prisoners' Progress* and *The Dark Tower*, 'The Blasphemies' remains undeceived about this kind of symbolic sleight-of-hand: 'how can a cross / Be never your fault?' (*CP*, p. 508).

How then does the poem correlate its Bunyanesque concerns with its secular agenda? Even though MacNeice displays the diminishing rhetorical returns in the shift from the Holy Ghost to humanism, the poem remains resolutely sceptical: 'whether there was a God or not / The word was inadequate' (*CP*, p. 509). A return to Bunyan's beliefs would be similarly inadequate: 'The Blasphemies' uses Bunyan's vocabulary not to turn against modernity, but to insist that the fictive motifs of *The Pilgrim's Progress* can remain in imaginative play. By the end of the poem, the protagonist defines himself as 'a walking / Question but no more cheap than any / Question or quest is cheap' who reiterates the question with which the child begins the poem: 'The sin / Against the Holy Ghost – What is it?' (*CP*, p. 509). It seems to me that 'The Blasphemies' is structured around existential questions which derive their rhetorical and moral consequence from their dialogic engagement with Bunyan. The poem articulates the protagonist's dilemmas via allusions to Bunyan which in turn demarcate MacNeice's world from Bunyan's. In such a world, the existence of God remains conjectural and ultimately tangential to the broader experiential 'quest' on which all blasphemers – that is, all people – are engaged.

My sense of the dialogue between MacNeice and Bunyan has emphasized the rhetorical differences between seventeenth-century Puritanism and twentieth-century humanism which surface in 'The Blasphemies'. As *Varieties of Parable* demonstrates, MacNeice was a sensitive reader of the styles of early modern parabolists. Citing T. S. Eliot's remark that 'good verse should show the virtues of good prose', MacNeice draws analogies between Spenser and Herbert's verse and Bunyan's prose: 'If Herbert's verse, like much of Spenser's, has the virtues of prose, Bunyan's prose has the virtues of good conversation' (*VoP*, pp. 46–7). As Terence Brown observes, Mac-Neice 'exploited an essentially puritan English tradition of writing';[33] 'The Blasphemies', I suggest, not only dialogues with Bunyan, it incarnates in its poetic form – its plain-style idiom – MacNeice's version of this tradition. Through its combination of existential questions, fluid syntax in which conversational tone, stanzaic structure and metrical impact are seamlessly interwoven, and the precise articulation of different states of mind – 'No Hell at seventeen feels empty' – the poem revitalizes early modern styles (*CP*, p. 508). Indeed, much of what is striking in *Solstices* and *The Burning Perch* derives from

---

33 Terence Brown, 'MacNeice and the Puritan Tradition', p. 33.

MacNeice's re-evocation of this puritan English tradition for his own distinctive purposes.

* * *

This essay suggests that complex psychological, spiritual and literary issues were at stake for MacNeice in his reading of Bunyan. While his work epitomizes universalist appropriations and rereadings of *The Pilgrim's Progress*, MacNeice never altogether loses sight of the historical specificity of Bunyan's beliefs. Inasmuch as Bunyan's theology recalls that of John MacNeice, Bunyan remains a profoundly ambivalent figure in Louis's oeuvre. While MacNeice may have wanted his Everyman figures to appear as secular versions of Christian, it is part of their peculiar power that Protestant ideology is so readily detectable below the surface of his parables. The fire-breathing, prophetic Bunyan of 'The Streets of Laredo' remains in MacNeice's mind throughout his dialogues with Bunyan. Conducive and sympathetic though he found *The Pilgrim's Progress*, MacNeice refused to remake Bunyan in his own image.

JULIE CAMPBELL

8 'A Mighty Maze of Walks': Bunyan's *The Pilgrim's Progress* and Beckett's *Molloy*

Samuel Johnson, as we know from Boswell, praised John Bunyan highly.

> His 'Pilgrim's Progress' has great merit, both for invention, imagination, and the conduct of the story; and it has had the best evidence of its merit, the general and continued approbation of mankind. Few books, I believe, have had a more extensive sale. It is remarkable, that it begins very much like a poem of Dante; yet there was no translation of Dante when Bunyan wrote. There is reason to think that he had read Spenser.[1]

Samuel Taylor Coleridge praised Bunyan no less highly.

> This wonderful work is one of the very few books which may be read over repeatedly at different times, and each time with a new and a different pleasure. [...] The Pilgrim's Progress is composed in the lowest style of English, without slang or false grammar. If you were to polish it, you would at once destroy the reality of the vision. For works of imagination should be written in very plain language; the more purely imaginative they are the more necessary it is to be plain.[2]

It is pleasing to hear such high praise from Johnson, especially as we have learned to consider the Augustan age as a time when invention and imagination were denigrated. The eulogy from Coleridge is far less surprising, as he is writing during an era when 'imagination' and

---

[1] See James Boswell, *The Life of Samuel Johnson, LL.D.*, 2 vols (London: J. M. Dent, 1949), I, 470–1.

[2] Coleridge, in a passage dated 1830, in *Coleridge on the Seventeenth Century*, ed. Roberta Florence Brinkley (Durham N.C.: Duke University Press, 1955), quoted in *The Pilgrim's Progress: A Selection of Critical Essays*, ed. Roger Sharrock (London and Basingstoke: Macmillan, 1976), p. 53.

'plain language' were valorized. However, Johnson, in line with Augustan thinking, also looks to sources as a basis for Bunyan's 'invention': he decides that Bunyan cannot have read Dante, but may well have read Spenser. The text all three writers will have had in common, of course, is the Bible, to which Johnson fails to refer.

But perhaps some of the similarities Johnson points towards have a wider significance: the choice of a journey, or quest, as a narrative form has a very long pedigree. Every culture, it seems, has, and always seems to have had, stories which tell of journeys. The journey creates a strong narrative structure, with a beginning (setting off), middle (the journey itself) and an end (the successful achievement of the goal, or the return home). The narrative interest can centre on the events that occur on the journey, such as the successful passage through difficult terrain, the various obstacles to be overcome, and, most of all, the encounters along the way – with other travellers, and with friends and foes who either help or hinder the traveller.

The reader can identify with the hero very directly, whether it is Odysseus finally reaching home and being reunited with Penelope; the seventh son of a seventh son gaining riches and marrying a princess, or Parsival gaining sight of the Holy Grail. A journey is something we can easily understand and participate in imaginatively, and experience delight and satisfaction in its successful outcome. The pervasiveness of the journey narrative is inescapable, whether secular or spiritual: myths, legends, chivalric romance, folk tales, fairy stories; many novels, poems and plays feature journeys and quests, as do many films, and even detective fiction and spy stories follow the basic formula of the quest narrative. Northrop Frye describes such narratives as being about 'the unending, irrational, absurd persistence of the human impulse to struggle, survive, and where possible escape', and he notes especially 'how intense is the desire of most readers of romances for a happy ending'.[3]

---

3   Northrop Frye, *The Secular Scripture: A Study of the Structure of Romance* (Cambridge Mass. and London: Harvard University Press, 1976), p. 136.

Vladimir Propp has proposed an underlying system to which such stories adhere to a greater and lesser degree.[4] It seems that the quest narrative is an archetypal story, and one that accesses materials from what C. G. Jung terms the 'collective unconscious', which he suggests is hidden beneath both the surface consciousness, and the layers of the 'personal unconscious' in all of us. Jung describes the contents of the collective unconscious as

> of definitely unknown origin, or at all events of an origin that cannot be ascribed to individual acquisition. These contents have one outstanding feature, and that is their mythological character. It is as if they belong to a pattern not peculiar to any particular mind or person, but rather to a pattern peculiar to *mankind in general*. [...] Therefore they are of a *collective nature* [...]. From these layers derive the contents of an impersonal, mythological character, in other words, the archetypes.[5]

If we view the quest narrative as archetypal it encourages us to say, as Roger Sharrock does, that 'the journey as an image of human life from birth to death is of universal appeal'.[6] Coleridge declares that Bunyan's 'piety was baffled by his genius'; that the poet in Bunyan 'had the better' of the preacher.[7] In other words, by choosing such a universally appealing form, which seems to find an echo in us all, Bunyan captures his readers' imaginations, and their undivided attention, and gets in touch with something lying deep down beneath the conscious mind. This is one very good reason why, as Johnson notes, the work sells so well, was and is read so widely, and has such a central place in the cultural consciousness of our society. If *The Pilgrim's Progress* is a wish-fulfilment fantasy on the part of Bunyan, redolent of 'his own yearning' and 'inner struggle',[8] his readers, too, wish for, and find pleasure in, its fulfilment.

---

4   Vladimir Propp, *The Morphology of the Folktale* (Austin, TX: University of Texas Press, 1986).
5   C. J. Jung, *Analytic Psychology: Its Theory and Practice. The Tavistock Lectures* (1935; London: Routledge, 1968), pp. 40–1.
6   *The Pilgrim's Progress: A Selection of Critical Essays*, ed. Sharrock, p. 18.
7   In ibid., p. 53.
8   Sharrock, Introduction, in ibid., p. 13.

Alongside Bunyan's successful choice of the journey format, there is also his decision to narrate it as dream – a very effective strategy. The full title, as on the original title page, is: *The Pilgrim's Progress from This World to That Which is to Come: Delivered under the Similitude of a DREAM Wherein is Discovered The manner of his setting out, His Dangerous Journey, and Safe Arrival at the Desired Country.*[9] It is all there: the journey will be dangerous and the outcome will be successful – what more could a reader desire? But notice the prominence of the word 'dream'. It is central on the page, in large, thick, block capitals. The decision to give the narrative this 'dream' aspect is a master stroke. Dreams are something we can all identify with, for just as we all journey through our lives, we also all dream. In his 'Apology' Bunyan defends his 'method' or what he calls '*my Scribble*' (p. 3). '*May I not write in such a stile as this?*' he asks (p. 4). It is an allegory, and as such 'It is dark' and 'it is feigned' (p. 5), but '*God*', '*the Prophets*', '*Christ, his Apostles too* [...] *used much by Metaphors / To set forth Truth*' (p. 6). It is a good and fitting defence. But writing it 'under the similitude of a dream' also provides a fitting explanation for the darkness of the story. When we dream we all come into contact with allegory, with '*Dark Clouds*', '*Shadows and Metaphors*' and with '*Figure, or Similitude*' (pp. 5–7).

Dreams have been read as prophesies through the ages and as obscure messages in need of interpretation. Freud in *The Interpretation of Dreams* speaks of 'the people of classical antiquity' and how 'they took it as axiomatic that dreams were connected with the world of superhuman beings in whom they believed and that they were revelations from gods and daemons'.[10] He cites many instances of dream exegesis, from classical times right up to the time in which he was writing, and includes Joseph's interpretation of Pharaoh's dream as foretelling the famine to come. And of course the importance of dream analysis in Freud's psychoanalytic theory and practice is a clear example of how dreams continue to be regarded as a set of signs

---

9 This is reproduced in *PP*, p. [1]. Further citations from this edition are given in the text in parentheses.
10 Sigmund Freud, *The Interpretation of Dreams* (1953; Harmondsworth: Penguin, 1978), p. 58.

and symbols to be decoded and explained; dream analysis, Freud suggests, can illuminate hidden fears and desires, and through interpretation can help to guide and enlighten people about themselves and their lives.

In a sense, when we dream, we are undertaking a journey into unknown territory – into the dark areas of our unconscious. We are entering a world to which the conscious mind does not have direct access. Jung considers that

> We cannot directly explore the unconscious psyche because the unconscious is just unconscious, and we therefore have no relation to it. We can only deal with the conscious products which we suppose have originated in the field called the unconscious, that field of 'dim representations' which the philosopher Kant in his *Anthropology* speaks of as being half a world. [...] One-fifth, or one-third, or even one-half of our human life is spent in an unconscious condition. Our early childhood is unconscious. Every night we sink into the unconscious, and only in phases between waking and sleeping have we a more or less clear consciousness.[11]

Dreams place us in a similar position to Christian in *The Pilgrim's Progress*: we can be faced with our own fears and anxieties, as well as our hidden desires, often in frightening and monstrous forms. We are entering an alien country, full of shadows and symbols; we enter a world of allegory, in which people and objects from the rational world appear, to our consciousness, as distorted, condensed and displaced. If we attempt some kind of rational and/or meaningful explanation of our dreams we are envisioning the dream landscape as a world of symbols and hidden meanings which the conscious mind can, to a greater or lesser degree, understand or make some kind of sense of. Freud recognizes the close relationship between dreams and narratives like Bunyan's when he discusses the symbolism he sees as so prevalent in dreams; 'this symbolism,' he suggests,

> is not peculiar to dreams, but is characteristic of unconscious ideation, in particular among the people, and is to be found in folklore, and in popular myths, legends, linguistic idioms [and] proverbial wisdom.[12]

11 Jung, *Analytic Psychology*, p. 6.
12 Freud, *The Interpretation of Dreams*, p. 408.

One of the important reasons why Bunyan's narrative has spoken so directly to so many is surely because he is taking us to places which are, paradoxically, both familiar and unknown: to what Jung has called the collective unconscious, that we all share, and to that strange and mysterious world of dreams, where we too have encountered our own fears, doubts and heartfelt desires, displaced and defamiliarized into fantastical shapes and images.

Bunyan states a clear purpose for his narrative: '*Mine end*' he writes is '*thy good*' (p. 4). He speaks of 'Truth' often in his 'Apology', and has a strong confidence in his knowledge of this truth, and of the effect the book intends, and 'will' produce:

> *This Book will make a Travailer of thee,*
> *If by its Counsel thou wilt ruled be;*
> *It will direct thee to the Holy land,*
> *If thou wilt its Directions understand:*
> *Yea, it will make the sloathful, active be;*
> *The Blind also, delightful things to see.* (p. 8)

But this effect will only be produced as long as the reader follows the rules and interprets the allegory correctly. Many of his contemporary readers will have been able to follow its direction with a strong understanding of its meaning and its didactic intent. Bunyan could speak about 'Truth' with authority and conviction, and the all-important text, underpinning his narrative, is the Bible. Frye observes that

> in European literature, down to the last couple of centuries, the myths of the Bible have formed a special category, as a body of stories with a distinctive authority. Poets who attached themselves to this central mythical area, like Dante or Milton [and we can add Bunyan here], have been thought of as possessing a special kind of seriousness conferred on them by their subject. Such poems were recognized, in their own day, to be what we should now call imaginative productions, but their content was assumed to be real, if at one remove, and not only real but about what most deeply concerned their readers.[13]

Christian, too, despite his doubts and fears about his own faith and courage, shows a similar conviction about the 'Truth' and authority of

---

13 Frye, *The Secular Scripture*, p. 7.

God's word. The book, its intentions and its strong and sincere conviction, is solidly situated within its own time and context.

* * *

I want now to turn to another version of the quest narrative, but, one which, written as it was in the mid-twentieth century lacks this pervasive reference to an external and unquestionable authority. We are once again, I would suggest, plunged into a dreamlike landscape, but the correspondences between this mysterious world and a comprehensible and explicable overarching 'message' is no longer present. With Bunyan the method is to create a system of equivalences which can be decoded, in a fairly straightforward way, by those with the desire and the knowledge to be ruled by 'its Counsel' and 'understand' 'its Direction'. With Samuel Beckett such a direct form of interpretation is denied to the reader.

Beckett's *Molloy* is separated into two parts. Part One has Molloy as its first person narrator. The goal of his journey is to see his mother: 'I resolved to go and see my mother,' he tells us.[14] This is quest that Freud would understand. It might seem straightforward enough, but isn't. Molloy has forgotten the way. Part Two has Moran as its first person narrator, and his quest is to find Molloy. Again, this could be straightforward, but isn't. He doesn't find him. The basic journey narrative is still present, but not in the traditional and familiar sequence of beginning (setting off), middle (the journey) and end (the achievement of the goal). In many ways *Molloy* is far closer to our real experience of dreams when we awake to consciousness than Bunyan's 'dream'. Actual dreams are not usually remembered with the completeness and plenitude of Bunyan's story. We remember an image here and an image there, perhaps a sequence here and a sequence there, but it is full of gaps (maybe it always was), and soon any details we held at first waking begin to fade into obscurity. The unconscious is an alien territory and that borderline when the two worlds meet at

---

14   Samuel Beckett, *Molloy* (1955) in *The Beckett Trilogy* (London: Picador, 1979), p. 16. Further references are to this edition and are included in parentheses in the text.

waking is fleeting. As soon as the conscious mind begins to try and make sense of the dream all the rationalization, logic and reasonableness of consciousness begins to infect the memory of the dream. The unconscious does not deal with the rational, the logical or the reasonable. Something will come through, but consciousness acts as a censor, and as such distorts our dreams. We will interpret, analyze and seek for explanations of dream materials, but it is like a translation of one language into another, with all the concomitant problems – much is lost, much must be misunderstood, much is rationalized by the conscious mind's overriding need to make sense of things.

There are moments when our expectations concerning journey narratives are met in *Molloy*, but more often these expectations are teasingly denied. There are tantalizing traces of past journey narratives, which are glimpsed for a moment and then disappear. I will pick out some of the allusions to *The Pilgrim's Progress* in *Molloy*, and suggest some ways in which these references could be said to illuminate both texts. What is fascinating is that in many ways *The Pilgrim's Progress* features in *Molloy* like a dream, but one that is only vaguely and intermittently remembered. Part One of *Molloy*, begins, not at the beginning, but at the end of the journey. 'I am in my mother's room,' the narrator announces, 'I don't now how I got there' (p. 9). So right away we have two surprises: we begin at the end, and there is a yawning and unexplained lacuna: how did he get to his mother's room? But this room is the narrative situation. Here Molloy is writing his narrative; a man 'comes every Sunday' to collect what he has written. Bunyan has his own narrative situation – there is the 'Denn' where 'as I slept I dreamed a Dream' (*PP*, p. 10) – and we also hear of the actual experience of writing: '*When at the first I took my Pen in hand*' and '*Thus I set Pen to Paper with delight*' (*PP*, p. 3). Molloy does not speak of delight, nor is able to set out, as Bunyan can, a reason for his writing: 'I don't work for money. For what then? I don't know. The truth is I don't know much' (p. 9). Molloy can mention 'truth' but only, it seems, in relation to what he doesn't know. There is none of Bunyan's appeal to a higher authority; authority here is negated, alongside authorial intention.

Molloy then announces his beginning, and then we have a story, which has an oddly abstract quality, of two figures A and C. Bunyan uses formulations such as 'Now I saw', 'I saw also', 'So I saw' again and again throughout his narrative. Beckett begins this story in the same way: 'So I saw A and C going slowly towards each other' (p. 10). But this isn't allowed to stand without its authority being undermined: 'Perhaps I'm inventing a little, perhaps embellishing' (p. 10). The reader is discouraged from any sense of what Bunyan encourages. Bunyan may be writing 'in the similitude of a dream,' but he wants the reader to engage with his story, and believe it. There is a certainty in 'I saw'; and of course there is also the implication that this story (this dream) that comes upon him *before I was aware* and that he *fell suddenly into* is coming to him from God: *'I pull'd, it came'* (*PP*, p. 3). So Beckett, writing in such a different era, and in such a different context, would seem an enormous distance away from Bunyan. And yet, these characters A and C (or should we call them figures or abstract symbols?) do seem to bear some resemblance to Christian and Pliable. We are told that

> The town was not far. It was two men, unmistakably [...]. They had left the town, first one, then the other, and then the first, weary or remembering a duty, had retraced his steps. [...] They turned [...] and exchanged a few words. Then each went on his way. Each went on his way, A back towards the town, C on by ways he seemed hardly to know, or not at all, but he went with uncertain step and often stopped to look about him [...]. The treacherous hills where fearfully he ventured were no doubt only known to him from afar [...]. He looks old and it is a sorry sight to see him solitary after all these years, so many days and nights unthinkingly given to that rumour rising at birth and even earlier, What shall I do? What shall I do? (pp. 10–11)

So here we have an echo of Christian's 'lamentable cry [...] *what shall I do?*' – the first words we hear him speak in *The Pilgrim's Progress* – but there is no Evangelist to guide Beckett's C and direct him on the way. C is described as 'abroad alone, by unknown ways, in the gathering night', surrounded by 'the innumerable spirits of darkness'. Molloy tells us 'I saw him only darkly'; he disappears 'from time to time, to re-emerge later on' (pp. 11–12). He doesn't have the clarity and constancy of vision of Bunyan's narrator, who sees and recounts all. Molloy can't be sure of important details: he asks, for instance, 'Was he carrying as much as a scrip?' (p. 15). The overwhelming significance of having the roll or certificate of election is stressed many times in *The Pilgrim's Progress*, not least when Ignorance, who does not have one, does not gain admittance at the Gates of the Celestial City (*PP*, p. 154). When Molloy comes to the end of his story of A and C, he undermines any credence the reader may have had in what they have read:

> And I am perhaps confusing several different occasions, and different times, deep down, and deep down is my dwelling, oh not deepest down, somewhere between the mud and the scum. And perhaps it was A one day at one place, then C another at another, then a third the rock and I, and so on for the other components. (p. 15)

There is no certainty, no authority. This is a narrative written in 'the similitude of a dream,' with the failure of memory we associate with trying to recall dreams. With Bunyan's narrative we are aware all the time of the shaping consciousness at work: the reader is given a clear vision of the events, and the interpretation of these events is made as unproblematic as possible. With *Molloy* there is no clarity. There are many questions but no answers: 'And I, what was I doing there, and why come? These are things that we shall try and discover. But these are things we must not take seriously' (p. 15).

We abruptly leave the story of A and C, with some more questions that create further confusion rather than enlightenment:

> A and C I never saw again. But perhaps I shall see them again. But shall I be able to recognize them? And am I sure I never saw them again? And what do I mean by seeing and seeing again? (p. 16)

Now Molloy's quest begins: 'I resolved to go and see my mother' (p. 16). He calls it 'that unreal journey', again evoking the idea of a dream, 'a form fading among fading forms' (p. 17). The description of his journey does have some intriguing echoes of Christian's. We hear of the 'difficult straits' (p. 20) he manages to pass through, his incarceration and later release, the 'slough' which he is convinced he will encounter again (p. 27). He meets a shepherd, but the shepherd doesn't answer his questions. His second incarceration is in the house of a woman (or was it a man?) called Sophie Loy, or was it Lousse?

(he forgets). The house has a garden, and the garden has high walls, but these are unexpectedly 'broken by a wicket-gate giving free access to the road, for it was never locked, of that I was all but convinced, having opened and closed it without the least trouble on more than one occasion' (p. 49). He does eventually leave by this wicket-gate 'one warm airless night, without saying goodbye' (p. 55) and resumes his journey. He is obeying a 'small voice' which says to him: 'Get out of here, Molloy, take your crutches and get out of here' (p. 56).

Molloy's journey is clearly unpropitious from the start: unlike Christian he has no 'Roll with a Seal upon it' (*PP*, p. 37) or 'Certificate' (*PP*, p. 152). 'The only papers,' Molloy tells us, 'that I carry with me are bits of newspapers, to wipe myself, you understand, when I have a stool' (p. 21). He describes his 'progress' as 'slow and painful': 'some days I advanced no more than thirty or forty paces, I give you my oath'. With absurd pedantry he informs us that 'To say I stumbled in impenetrable darkness, no, I cannot. I stumbled, but the darkness was not impenetrable' (p. 76). He often rests (so often a perilous activity for Christian), and finally crawls. As the narrative of Part One reaches its end Molloy hears not the joyous, victorious trumpets and bells which greet Christian at his journey's end, but a gong. We leave him lying in the bottom of a ditch, where he hears 'a voice telling me not to fret, that help was coming' (p. 84).

Molloy, like *The Pilgrim's Progress*, has a second part, the narrative of a second journey. In the *Second Part* of *The Pilgrim's Progress* Christiana and her children set out to retrace Christian's journey. Moran, the narrator of Part Two of *Molloy* is sent out, with his son, to find Molloy, not exactly to retrace his journey, but in a sense that is what he does do. As the journey proceeds Moran begins to resemble Molloy more and more. Moran's story charts a spiritual progression of a kind, presented in a strangely oblique and obscure fashion. At the beginning of Part Two the differences between Molloy and Moran are striking. Molloy has very little in the way of possessions: his crutches, his bicycle (which he leaves behind in Sophie Lousse's garden), and his sucking stones (lost in Sophie Lousse's house). What little he has slips from him, a concretization, it could be suggested, of Christian's metaphorical burden which is 'loosed from off his Shoulders, and fell from off his back' (*PP*, p. 37). Possessions are clearly of great importance to Moran, the narrator and protagonist of Part Two. We hear of 'my desk', 'my lamp' (p. 84), 'my little garden' (p. 85), 'my Beauty of Bath', 'my house' (p. 86). We visualize Moran, sitting peacefully in his garden, smug, self-satisfied and full of pride in ownership of house and garden and all that makes up this little world. The peace is shattered by the entrance of Gaber, 'a messenger' (p. 97). He instructs Moran about his quest to find Molloy, and Moran then begins to prepare himself for his journey. He begins to think about Molloy, the goal of his quest, but the image he conjures up is quite unlike the Molloy we have come to know: 'He did not walk so much as charge'; 'He was massive and hulking'; 'He was forever on the move, I had never seen him rest. Occasionally he stopped and glared furiously around him' (p. 104).

When Moran departs, with his son, they leave by a 'narrow' path, through the 'little wicket-gate.' He is concerned about his son, as he is likely 'to stray from the right road, it of my election' (p. 118). Again there are intriguing echoes of Bunyan's narrative; even the purging of Mathew resonates in Moran's purging of his son (an enema rather than sweet-tasting pill) before they set off (p. 120). As in Part One, there is a wicket-gate and a shepherd and his sheep. In Part Two Moran comments on the lack of dialogue in both parts of *Molloy* when he declares: 'What a restful change it is from time to time, a little dialogue' (p. 130), whereas *The Pilgrim's Progress* is of course written '*Dialogue-wise*' (*PP*, p. 7). But Part Two does include numbered lists, that echo, if parodically, those in *The Pilgrim's Progress*, and at one stage there are numbered 'questions of a theological nature' (p. 153), including: 'Does nature observe the sabbath?' and 'What is one to think of the excommunication of vermin in the sixteenth century?', followed by questions of a more personal nature, including: 'What would become of me?' and 'Would I go to heaven?' (p. 154).

Moran has a strange resistance to telling us those things that traditionally create much of the narrative interest in a story of this kind. 'I have no intention', he tells us, 'of relating the various adventures which befell us, me and my son, together and singly, before we came to the Molloy country. It would be tedious' (p. 121). 'I was saying I would not relate all the vicissitudes of the journey from my country to Molloy's, for the simple reason that I do not intend to' (p. 122). And later we are told:

> I shall not tell of the obstacles we had to surmount, the fiends we had to circumvent, the misdemeanours of the son, the disintegration of the father. It was my intention to tell of these things, almost my desire, to tell of these things, I rejoiced at the thought that the moment would come when I might do so. Now the question is dead, the moment is come and the desire is gone. (p. 145)

And the return journey is treated to the same erasure: 'I shall not dwell upon this journey home, its furies and treacheries. And I shall pass over in silence the fiends in human shape and the phantoms of the dead that tried to prevent me from getting home' (p. 153).

It is exasperating. Moran is leaving out all the events which most delight the reader in a quest narrative. Bunyan recounts Christian's adventures with all the detail and exuberance that satisfies our expectations. Beckett comically deflates our desires, and denies us the joy and vicarious thrill of sharing in the confrontation with dangers and their ultimate defeat. We are revisiting the familiar ground of the quest narrative, but much is erased, subtracted. A possible explanation is that Moran has simply forgotten: again the sense of a dream comes to mind, and the way dream elements fade and disappear on waking. These two quests are failed quests, and the failure on the diegetic level, it seems, is in reflected in the telling.

Christiana's journey in the *Second Part* of *The Pilgrim's Progress* retraces Christian's journey, so there are many echoes, many stages of the original journey are revisited, and Christian's success is celebrated. Part Two of *Molloy* also has many echoes of Part One, but they feature in a quite different way. For instance, there is the bicycle. When Molloy sets off on his journey he has a bicycle: 'So I got up, adjusted my crutches and went down the road, where I found my bicycle (I didn't know I had one) in the same place I must have left it' (pp. 16–17).

> It was a chainless bicycle, with a free wheel, if such a bicycle exists. Dear bicycle, I shall not call you bike, you were green, like so many of your generation. I don't know why. It is a pleasure to meet it again. To describe it at length would be a pleasure. (p. 17)

Moran sends his son to buy a bicycle, and describes his return:

> He was pushing a bicycle which, when he had joined me, he let fall with a gesture signifying he could bear no more. Pick it up, I said, till I look at it. I had to admit it must once have been quite a good bicycle. I would gladly describe it, I would gladly write four thousand words on it alone. (p. 143)

He, however, doesn't describe it, but both narrators express the pleasure or gladness such a description would involve.

Similarly, the 'distant gong' (p. 82) Molloy hears towards the end of his narrative also sounds in Moran's story, but here it is the dinner gong summoning him to his meal. What appears as inexplicable in Molloy's story is thus given a rational, even banal place in Moran's. The same applies to a 'little object' that Molloy discusses and gives a long description of: 'it resembled a tiny sawing-horse, with the difference however, that the crosses of the true sawing-horse are not perfect crosses, but truncated at the top, whereas the crosses of the little object I am referring to were perfect' (p. 59). The description continues, with the object never named, and its purpose remains a mystery to Molloy, and 'haunts' him:

> For a certain time I think it inspired me with a kind of veneration, for there was no doubt in my mind that it was not an object of virtue, but that it had a most specific function always hidden from me. I could therefore puzzle over it endlessly without the least risk. For to know nothing is nothing, not to want to know anything likewise, but to be beyond knowing anything, to know you are beyond knowing anything, that is when peace enters in, to the soul of the incurious seeker. (p. 59)

This is certainly a 'peace' that Christian would not have understood, nor would Moran at the beginning of his narrative. Here there is no endless puzzling over the little object. Moran simply describes 'playing with the knife rest' on the dining table while 'waiting to be served' (p. 106) – and this is what Molloy's object of mystery is: a knife rest.

But although Moran's narrative begins in what appears to be a rational, conscious world, where gongs and knife rests have a clear and utilitarian purpose, during his journey he does begin to inhabit a dream-like world of symbols and hidden meanings very like the one that Molloy traverses. He begins to resemble Molloy more and more 'with his feral aspect and crutches',[15] his physical deterioration, and the gradual dispossession he experiences. On returning home he discovers that his bees and hens are dead (p. 161), but intriguingly he speaks about his bees and their system of communication through different dances and hums in a way not dissimilar to Molloy's meditation on the knife rest: 'And I said, with rapture, Here is something I can study all my life, and never understand' (p. 156). Just as Molloy, at the end of his narrative, hears a 'voice' (p. 84), Moran, too, hears 'a voice telling [him] things' (p. 162). You do get a sense of an interpenetration of the two characters,[16] and a suggestion of some kind of spiritual pilgrimage on Moran's part. It does seem that the materialism, with the obsessive stress on possessions, has gone, and has been replaced by a more spiritual outlook.

* * *

In a sense Moran has found Molloy, in that he becomes like Molloy, someone who can find peace in the contemplation of something he can 'never understand'. Maybe what has happened is that Moran has become more in touch with his unconscious, where, Jung suggests, 'we are all the same'.[17] Jung speaks of the 'precious connection with the unconscious' which is only possible 'through our feebleness and incapacity' (p. 109). Moran's physical deterioration during his journey could be what has allowed him to be 'linked up with the unconscious,' which for Jung is a 'precious' and positive gain (p. 109).

Jung's ideas about how important it is for us to keep in touch with the collective unconscious and the need to regulate our experience of archetypal images are significant in terms of both the texts I am discussing. Jung contends that there have always been religions as they offer a ritualized way of dealing with the power and the

---

15   David Houston Jones, 'Que Foutait dieu avant la creation: Disabling sources in Beckett and Augustine', in *Beckett and Religion*, eds Marius Buning, Mattijs Engelberts and Onno Kosters (Amsterdam: Rodopi, 2000), pp. 185–98.
16   Ibid.
17   Jung, *Analytic Psychology*, p. 46.

fascination of the collective unconscious. Religion is, for Jung, 'a psychotherapeutic system. It is the most elaborate system, and there is a great practical truth behind it'. It provides 'a suitable form for [the] projection' of archetypal images, which otherwise could be 'very destructive' to the human psyche.[18] Jung also recognized artistic creativity and the 'active imagination' as psychotherapeutic, as art is also a 'suitable form' or 'method' for the projection of archetypal elements.[19] Art can achieve an externalization of unconscious elements, and can give both creator and the reader or spectator some sense of conscious control over these powerful forces. Frye has made a useful observation concerning systems which follows on from Jung's ideas, and I think is also useful in that it points to the very different perspectives of the two authors under discussion.

> There is a line of Pope's which exists in two versions: 'A mighty maze of walks without a plan,' and 'A mighty maze of walks, but not without a plan'. The first version recognizes the human situation; the second refers to the constructs of religion, art, and science that man throws up because he finds the recognition intolerable. Literature is an aspect of the human compulsion to create in the face of chaos.[20]

Bunyan depicts the maze – this is the terrain Christian journeys through – but he also depicts a plan: there is salvation if we live our lives according to God's word. Bunyan has faith in his system – his religion – and alongside this he employs another very formulaic and regulated system – the quest narrative – to provide yet another pattern or construct 'in the face of chaos'.

But what if such consoling patterns no longer hold validity? Colin Duckworth reports that Beckett told him 'I see no evidence of any pattern in the universe'.[21] Beckett has also stated: 'I can see no trace of any system anywhere'.[22] But there are traces of patterns and

---

18   Ibid., pp. 181–2.
19   Ibid., p. 190.
20   Frye, *The Secular Scripture*, pp. 30–1.
21   Colin Duckworth, 'Beckett and the Missing Sharer', in *Beckett and Religion*, eds Buning, Engelberts and Kosters, pp. 133–43 (p. 135).
22   I. Shenker, 'Moody Man of Letters', *New York Times*, 6 May 1956, quoted in Duckworth, 'Beckett and the Missing Sharer', p. 137.

systems in his work. Duckworth asked Beckett about allusions to Christianity in his work, and Beckett replied: 'Christianity is a mythology with which I am perfectly familiar. So naturally I use it'.[23] He is also familiar with the quest narrative, and uses elements from this literary form in his work. The essential point is, of course, the way they are used. Beckett famously spoke about the need for a 'form to accommodate the mess,' which 'will be of such a type that it admits the chaos and does not say that the chaos is really something else'.[24] He recognizes that constructs that are used to evade the human condition, to shield us from the chaos, are not for him. He is facing the chaos. He sees, and is encouraging us to see, the 'maze [...] without a plan.' Bunyan sees the 'maze [...] but not without a plan.'

Jung regards religion in a very positive light: religion 'deals with the troubles of the soul'.[25] He also writes about 'the fascination which the archetypes always have upon consciousness',[26] and Bunyan is able to make good use of this fascination in his narrative. He draws the reader in by accessing elements from our collective unconscious, and at the same time makes them safe: there is a plan; there are rules to follow; there is incarceration followed by release; a battle to emerge from victoriously, and finally the fears of failure are defeated at last, with the reward of eternal salvation. The reader will of course identify with Christian and his success. This is the pattern, the familiar pattern: all the failures, the characters such as Pliable, Talkative and Ignorance are projections, from the point of view of Bunyan, Christian and the reader. They are externalized in order to guarantee the success we all desire, and Jung applauds such a procedure.

However, Bunyan had not read Jung. It is possible to interpret his wish-fulfilment narrative in terms of Jung's theories, but we still need to recognize the gap between such an interpretation and that which Bunyan would have expected from his contemporary readers. By con-

---

23   Duckworth, 'Beckett and the Missing Sharer', p. 133.
24   Tom Driver, 'Beckett by the Madeleine', in *Samuel Beckett: The Critical Heritage*, eds Raymond Federman and Lawrence Graver (London: Routledge & Kegan Paul, 1979), p. 219.
25   Jung, *Analytic Psychology*, p. 181.
26   Ibid., p. 198.

trast, Beckett was present at the third of Jung's Tavistock Lectures that I am referring to in this paper. At the same time he was also undergoing psychoanalysis. He was searching for a way of dealing with 'troubles of the soul', but did not have access to the consolations and defences that religious faith can provide: there is no plan to help him through the 'mighty maze'. He had no faith in systems of any kind. This is clear in *Molloy*. There are traces of systems, religious and literary, but they fail to adhere into a unified pattern. The external goals of each protagonist are not accomplished; the full story is never told; the reader's expectations are thwarted. But there is a passage of Jung's which might approach explaining what has perhaps been achieved, which Jung describes as 'an essential part of individuation':

> Its goal is to detach consciousness from the object so that the individual no longer places the guarantee of his happiness, or of his life even, in factors outside himself, whether they be persons, ideas, or circumstances, but comes to realize that everything depends on whether he holds the treasure or not.[27]

What is this treasure? Jung tells us that we should not seek perfection, but aim instead for a sense of completeness.[28] I think that the treasure he speaks of is life. I think that he means that we need to find a sense of completeness in ourselves, and not in external things, not in our mother (like Molloy), or in our material possessions (like Moran). Religions of all kinds teach this doctrine, but in our secular age such teachings hold less force. Beckett was very aware of the suffering the human condition entails: 'a mighty maze [...] without a plan.' He gives us no plan, no system, no rules to follow, but encourages us instead to face the chaos. Jung advocates a 'condition of detachment',[29] and Moran, in his garden at the end of his story seems to be on in his way to achieving this. In a sense Molloy does seem to have attained this state with the final words of his narrative: 'Molloy could stay, where he happened to be' (p. 84). The quest is over.

---

27   Ibid., p. 186.
28   'My principle is: for heaven's sake do not be perfect, but by all means try to be complete – whatever that means.' When asked to explain what it means, Jung replies: 'I must leave something to your own mental efforts'; ibid., p. 110.
29   Ibid., p. 187.

But surely this is too trite, too simple. Jung's psychotherapeutic theories and practice are a system, and I think we need to hold fast to Beckett's distrust and denial of systems. Suggesting that Beckett is following Jung here is to miss the irony with which the endings of the two parts of *Molloy* are charged. Molloy is left in a ditch; Moran is left in his empty house with the electricity cut off. These are not the consoling and triumphant endings of the traditional quest narrative. Beckett faces the human condition 'without a plan', but is still exploring the 'mighty maze' yet without the conviction that there will be a way out, a satisfactory conclusion. His is a bleak vision, but not without humour to lighten the way. Bunyan's exploration is far more earnest. He has faith, he has a plan, but there are also doubts, despair and fear of failure, all given shape in the dream landscape he has Christian traverse. The faith and hope he transmits to Christian he was also transmitting to his readers, and this is a great thing. The fact that so many of us today are facing the 'mighty maze [...] without a plan' perhaps gives Beckett's version of the quest a greater validity for contemporary readers. Many of us have lost the faith Bunyan advocates, and this is a great loss, but Beckett's ability to face the chaos without any of the systems that we erect to shield us from sufferings and anxieties of life shows courage, and I think demands our admiration.

MICHAEL DAVIES

9 The Relevant Pilgrim: John Bunyan in *A Matter of Life and Death*

Among the more spectacular instances of John Bunyan's 'afterlife' in the twentieth century must be his brief appearance in one of British cinema's now most popular and best-loved films: Michael Powell and Emeric Pressburger's Second World War 'classic', *A Matter of Life and Death* (released in Britain in 1946, and in the USA in 1947 as *Stairway to Heaven*).[1] The circumstances of Bunyan's career as a film star should be explained first, though, in the context of the plot of *A Matter of Life and Death* itself. RAF Squadron Leader, Peter D. Carter (David Niven), somehow survives bailing out of a burning Lancaster, without a parachute, when returning to England after 'a thousand bomber raid' over Germany on the night of 2 May 1945 (that is, just before the end of war in Europe). His miraculous survival is not the result of divine intervention, however, but of empyrean error: the heavenly guide responsible for collecting and escorting him to the afterlife, a French aristocrat guillotined during the French Revolution, known only as Conductor 71 (Marius Goring), was unable to locate him that night, due to a terrible English fog ('a ruddy pea-souper', in fact). Peter remains alive, then, but only as something of a cosmic anomaly. Moreover, having fallen in love during this brief extra time on Earth with June (Kim Hunter), an American WAC with whom he

---

1   On the status and popularity of *A Matter of Life and Death* as a 'classic' film, see esp. Ian Christie, *A Matter of Life and Death* (London: BFI Publishing, 2000), pp. 9–12, and *The Cinema of Michael Powell: International Perspectives on an English Film-Maker*, eds Ian Christie and Andrew Moor (London: BFI Publishing, 2005), pp. 2–3. On the alteration of the film's title for audiences in the USA see Michael Powell, *A Life in Movies: An Autobiography* (London: Heinemann, 1986), pp. 486–8. I would like here to thank David Salter, who pointed me towards *A Matter of Life and Death*.

had had final radio contact before jumping to what seemed certain death, Peter subsequently refuses to take up his awaiting place in the next world, despite the attempts of Conductor 71 to persuade him otherwise. On the basis of his significantly changed circumstances (i.e. the love he and June now hold for one another), Peter successfully launches an appeal in the 'Other World', the film climaxing in a celestial courtroom drama to decide whether the young airman now has the right to remain on Earth or not: his 'case' is thus, quite literally, a matter of life and death.

It is just prior to this final trial sequence (taking place simultaneously with a surgical operation on Peter's brain, a medical problem having been diagnosed as the source of his 'highly organized hallucinations'), that John Bunyan appears, shepherding Peter's advocate for the forthcoming trial, his recently deceased friend and doctor, Frank Reeves (Roger Livesey), into the heavenly arena. Looking exactly as though he has just stepped out of any one of his seventeenth-century portraits or engravings and onto the silver screen, Bunyan carries a weighty ledger with which he signs his ward, Reeves, over to the French Conductor to be escorted to the 'court of appeal'. Putting his hand supportively on the doctor's shoulder, Bunyan says warmly, 'Be of good cheer, friend', and then exits, leaving Conductor 71 to remark approvingly, in Goring's dandified French accent: 'One of the best men in the service. A compatriot of yours.' 'What's his name?' asks Reeves. 'Oh, John – uhh…' replies the Conductor airily, the name having escaped him momentarily: 'Bunyan!', Reeves proclaims, 'Yes, of course'.

The question remains, however, 'Why Bunyan?', and certainly why: 'Bunyan! Yes, of course'? For in a film which draws attention, in various ways, to a rich English literary tradition, from Peter's fragmentary citation of Marvell's and Raleigh's poetry in the burning bomber at the beginning of the film to Reeves's equally explicit roll-call of great English authors ('John Donne, Dryden, Pope, Wordsworth and Coleridge, Shelley and Keats, Tennyson', and not forgetting 'Milton and Shakespeare', of course) in the trial scene, one might wonder why it is not a more prominent, or a more centrally 'canonical', or even a more readily recognizable English writer, such as Shakespeare, who would be given this walk-on role. In a film abounding too in resurrected historical personae (from the aristocratic Conductor 71 to Peter's 'prosecutor' in the final trial, Abraham Farlan, the first Bostonian to be killed by a British bullet in the American Revolution), Bunyan stands singularly as the only identifiable English historical individual in the entire film. So why is Bunyan given this privileged position, rather than Shakespeare or Milton, or anyone else for that matter? The purpose of this essay is to address these simple questions in order to explore some of the more complex issues raised by Bunyan's appearance in and broader influence upon *A Matter of Life and Death*. Considering the question 'Why Bunyan?' offers some useful ways of understanding and appreciating this film's central concerns, thematic and conceptual, as well as narrative and political. Equally, Powell and Pressburger's unique inclusion of Bunyan within one of the most sensational and highly publicized films of its time (despite some of the baffled reviews it may have at first received) indicates something noteworthy too about Bunyan's place in the popular imagination of mid-twentieth-century Britain, and especially about his cultural value for the re-examination and re-establishment of England's identity in the years immediately following the end of the Second World War.[2] Bunyan's cameo appearance in *A Matter of Life and Death* has, in other words, a much greater significance than his mere 30 seconds of on-screen fame might at first suggest.

* * *

While Powell and Pressburger's presentation of a cinematic Bunyan might be seen as typical of their idiosyncratic style of film making, being the 'erratic *enfants terribles* of the forties', there are a number of reasons why Bunyan's arrival in *A Matter of Life and Death* should not surprise us.[3] At the most basic level, Bunyan's role is explicable,

2   *A Matter of Life and Death* was premièred at a Royal Command Film Performance, 1 November 1946, the first to be held since before the war. For accounts of this occasion, and of the film's initial reception in the press, see Christie, *A Matter of Life and Death*, pp. 57–62; Powell, *A Life in Movies*, pp. 585–92.

3   Ian Christie, *Arrows of Desire: The Films of Michael Powell and Emeric Pressburger* (London: Faber and Faber, 1994), p. 94.

as Ian Christie notes, in offering 'a visual epigraph' which 'serves to trigger a series of associations', particularly 'recalling that Peter identifies himself as a pilgrim in the opening scene by quoting Raleigh: "Give me my scallop shell of quiet [...] / And thus I'll take my pilgrimage."'[4] But the terms surrounding Bunyan's on-screen introduction also provide an important clue. Given that it is the job of a Conductor to guide souls between the two worlds of Earth and the afterlife (in Peter's case, he was destined for an 'Other World' which, despite a monochrome coldness reinforced by Alfred Junge's futuristic set designs, nevertheless is clearly a version of Heaven), then Bunyan – who brings Frank Reeves into this afterlife – could indeed be considered 'one of the best men in the service'. As one of English literature's most enduring and popular religious writers, whose most famous book, *The Pilgrim's Progress*, is entirely concerned with making the journey successfully 'From this World to the Next' (a key theme of the film, quite obviously), Bunyan could confidently be hailed as one whose life and works were dedicated entirely to the safe conduct of earthly souls in 'the service' of a Christian 'Heaven'. Even in such basic terms, Bunyan – like Evangelist or Greatheart in *The Pilgrim's Progress* itself – becomes a prime candidate for such a role.

But we might also hear something distinctly military in the phrase 'One of the best men in the service', and for good reason too. For Bunyan's appearance in a 'war' film (albeit one as unusual as *A Matter of Life and Death*) should not really surprise us either, given that Bunyan's cultural importance had nowhere been more secure in twentieth-century Britain (beyond, perhaps, the specialist interests of an evangelical or an academic readership) than in the memory and literature of modern war. It may well be the case that, as Q. D. Leavis noted in the early 1930s, readers of *The Pilgrim's Progress* had been shrinking in number as 'the Puritan conscience [...] decayed' and as the twentieth century progressed, particularly in comparison to its famously firm place in the hearts and homes of the British people during previous eras.[5] Yet, at the same time, the enduring significance

---

4   Christie, *A Matter of Life and Death*, p. 24.
5   'It is impossible now to count on even an educated person's knowing his Bunyan', Leavis posits; see Q. D. Leavis, *Fiction and the Reading Public*

of *The Pilgrim's Progress* was being signalled nevertheless, and no more so than during the 1930s, by the widespread allusions to it among numerous war-writings published since 1918.

Paul Fussell's *The Great War and Modern Memory* is an especially important study in this respect, for it reminds us just how and why the language and imagery of *The Pilgrim's Progress*, perhaps more than any other literary work, infused the minds and writings of so many British soldiers and officers of the twentieth century. Drawing on Christian's 'Dangerous Journey' through the 'Slough of Despond' and the 'Valley of the Shadow of Death' to explain what it was like to be mobilized, or to slog through No Man's Land, enabled soldiers to 'describe the indescribable', as Fussell argues, and thus to overcome the 'incommunicability' of war, and its 'utter incredibility'.[6] On the basis that 'when an English sensibility looks for traditional images of waste and horror and loss and fear, it turns not to the *Inferno* but to *Pilgrim's Progress*', Fussell's account thus helps to explain why allusions to Bunyan abound in so many works about war (poetic, autobiographical and fictional) produced between 1914–39, from John Buchan's wholesale appropriation of Bunyan's allegory in his Richard Hannay war novel, *Mr Standfast* (1919), to the more complex allusive structures of E. E. Cummings' *The Enormous Room* (1922), Henry Williamson's *The Patriot's Progress* (1930), or the

---

(London: Chatto & Windus, 1932), p. 97, n. 57 (p. 294). On the place of *The Pilgrim's Progress* among the popular books read by the British during the nineteenth and twentieth centuries see also Jonathan Rose, *The Intellectual Life of the British Working Classes* (New Haven and London: Yale University Press, 2001) and, though with a different emphasis, Barbara Johnson, *Reading 'Piers Plowman' and 'The Pilgrim's Progress': Reception and the Protestant Reader* (Carbondale and Edwardsville, Ill.: Southern Illinois University Press, 1992). See also Christopher Hill, *A Turbulent, Seditious, and Factious People: John Bunyan and his Church 1628–1688* (Oxford: Oxford University Press, 1988), pp. 373–80, and Richard L. Greaves, *Glimpses of Glory: John Bunyan and English Dissent* (Stanford, CA: Stanford University Press, 2002), pp. 601–34.

6   Paul Fussell, *The Great War and Modern Memory* (Oxford: Oxford University Press, 1975), pp. 137–44.

final volume of Siegfried Sassoon's autobiographical *Memoirs of George Sherston, Sherston's Progress* (1936).[7]

Michael Powell and Emeric Pressburger may have had this connection between Bunyan and war in mind, then, along with the kind of 'English Spirit' celebrated in Sassoon's *Pilgrim's Progress*-based 1940 poem of the same title, when deciding to place Bunyan squarely in the frame of their 'final war picture'.[8] But it is also clear that they had other reasons for including Bunyan – rather than anyone else – in this particular film. Most significant, for instance, is that in 1943 Powell and Pressburger had considered filming a version of *The Pilgrim's Progress*. Having established in 1941–2 their own independent production company, The Archers, with the financial and distributive support of J. Arthur Rank, owner of the Rank film organization and commander of the nation's Odeon theatres, Powell and Pressburger may have discussed a cinematic adaptation of *The Pilgrim's Progress* largely as 'an intended favour to their main sponsor': a Methodist who 'had started in films by funding religious shorts', the evangelically-minded Rank naturally 'gave enthusiastic support to the project'.[9] Equally, *The Pilgrim's Progress* also pre-

[7] Fussell, *The Great War and Modern Memory*, p. 139. See also George Parfitt, *Fiction of the First World War* (London: Faber and Faber, 1988), pp. 12–25. The coincidence in 1928 of the tercentenary celebrations of Bunyan's birth with the ten-year anniversary of Armistice may also have helped to cement the association between Bunyan and war.

[8] Sassoon's 'duty' poems, 'The English Spirit' and 'Silent Service' were published by the *Observer* newspaper, in May and June 1940, 'when the war was entering its second, more aggressive phase'; see Jean Moorcroft Wilson, *Siegfried Sassoon: The Journey from the Trenches – A Biography 1918–1967* (London: Duckworth, 2003), pp. 313–14, 316; *Michael Powell: Interviews*, ed. David Lazar (Jackson, Miss.: University Press of Mississippi, 2003), p. 108.

[9] Christie, *A Matter of Life and Death*, p. 24; Kevin Macdonald, *Emeric Pressburger: The Life and Death of a Screenwriter* (London: Faber and Faber, 1994), p. 234. Powell would later refer to Arthur Rank as 'the sole architect of the British film industry during the war': *Michael Powell: Interviews*, ed. Lazar, p. 110. On The Archers' relationship to Rank see also Christie, *Arrows of Desire*, pp. 41–2, and Andrew Moor, *Powell & Pressburger: A Cinema of Magic Spaces* (London and New York: I. B. Tauris, 2005), pp. 18–21, 128–9. See also Geoffrey Macnab, *J. Arthur Rank and the British Film Industry* (London: Routledge, 1993).

sented Powell and Pressburger with an option when reconsidering the direction they wanted their later wartime films to take. Having released a number of successful propaganda films (including *49th Parallel* in 1941, and *One of Our Aircraft is Missing* in 1942), as well as a controversial war film, *The Life and Death of Colonel Blimp* (1943), which Winston Churchill himself had attempted to prevent being made or shown, nevertheless with 'an American-aided victory assured sooner or later' by 1943, they turned their cinematic attention away from the issue of 'how to win the war' and towards 'the moral health of the country'.[10] Powell and Pressburger's films now aimed to address 'the reasons why we had thrown ourselves in combat' and 'to examine the values for which we were fighting', as Powell would later put it: 'reasons' which had less to do with the political or material causes of the war than with the '[i]mmaterial values' Britain had been defending, the purpose being to explain 'to the Americans, and to our own people, the spiritual values and traditions we were fighting for'.[11]

With Powell also giving lectures on the subject of 'religion and films' around 1942–3, *The Pilgrim's Progress* might have seemed an obvious choice for the kind of film The Archers now intended to make.[12] Yet, despite the fact that no *Pilgrim's Progress* ever appeared (according to Macdonald, Pressburger 'was dubious about Bunyan's filmic potential'), the project seems not to have been abandoned as much as absorbed into their subsequent wartime films, all of which focus on 'immaterial values' and invoke a central motif of 'pilgrimage'.[13] *A Canterbury Tale* (1944), the first film in Powell and Pressburger's 'crusade against materialism', thus opens with a depiction of medieval pilgrimage, the 'nod' here being towards Chaucer rather than

---

10　Macdonald, *Emeric Pressburger*, p. 233. On Churchill's opposition to *The Life and Death of Colonel Blimp* see esp. Ian Christie, 'Blimp, Churchill and the State', in *Powell, Pressburger and Others*, ed. Ian Christie (London: BFI Publishing, 1978), pp. 105–24, and also 'The Colonel Blimp File', *Sight and Sound*, 48 (1978/79), pp. 13–14.

11　*Michael Powell: Interviews*, ed. Lazar, pp. 51–2, and see also pp. 69, 150; David Badder, 'Powell and Pressburger: The War Years', *Sight and Sound*, 48 (1978/79), 8–12 (p. 11); Powell, *A Life in Movies*, p. 437.

12　Macdonald, *Emeric Pressburger*, p. 234.

13　Ibid.

Bunyan (as the film's title also indicates). But the shadow of the unmade *Pilgrim's Progress* still seems discernible, not only in the strange episodic journeying undertaken by this film's odd assortment of modern-day pilgrims, but also in their experience of something approaching mystical revelation as they eventually reach Canterbury.[14] In this sense, the referential frame of *A Canterbury Tale*'s title and opening *mise en scène* may belong to Chaucer, as well as to Powell's own 'semi-mystical feeling' for his childhood landscape of East Kent, but its narrative movement – particularly with Canterbury becoming a 'Celestial City' of sorts – owes more to *The Pilgrim's Progress*, as well as to its American cinematic counterpart, *The Wizard of Oz* (Victor Fleming, 1939, US), than anything else.[15] Likewise, *I Know Where I'm Going!* (1945) – the next Archers' production – also seems to have *The Pilgrim's Progress* firmly in mind, though again largely in terms of its structure as a 'travel' narrative, being a romantic comedy about an ambitious young woman, Joan Webster (Wendy Hiller) whose dangerous journey to a remote Scottish island, in order to marry a wealthy industrialist whom she does not actually love, leads to her casting off the burden of materialism for the more wholesome values

---

14   Ibid., p. 233; *Michael Powell: In Collaboration with Emeric Pressburger*, ed. Kevin Gough-Yates (London: National Film Theatre, 1970), p. [9]; Powell, *A Life in Movies*, p. 437. For an exploration of *A Canterbury Tale*'s relationship to 'propaganda', and of its rootedness not just in a Chaucerian but also in a 'Chestertonian' vision of Englishness, see Ian Christie's essays in *The Cinema of Michael Powell*, eds Christie and Moor: '"History is Now and England": *A Canterbury Tale* in its Contexts', pp. 75–93, and 'Another Life in Movies: Pressburger and Powell', pp. 171–86. See also Christie, *Arrows of Desire*, pp. 48–51; Macdonald, *Emeric Pressburger*, pp. 236–9; and Moor, *Powell & Pressburger*, pp. 87–118.

15   Badder, 'Powell and Pressburger: The War Years', p. 11, and Powell, *A Life in Movies*, p. 437. On how Canterbury becomes the locus for 'a healing process in the film [...] given in mystical dimensions' and which 'culminates in a surge of optimistic idealism', see Moor, *Powell & Pressburger*, pp. 88, 94. Moor also sees *A Canterbury Tale* as 'an Anglicization of *The Wizard of Oz*' (pp. 116–18), this film being alluded to also in the refrain, 'We're off to see the wizard' sung by Spud (James McKechnie) in *The Life and Death of Colonel Blimp*, and implicitly again in *A Matter of Life and Death*'s similar juxtaposition of colour and monochrome 'worlds'.

of more traditional (in this film, Gaelic) ways of love and life, as represented by the penniless but aristocratic, Torquil MacNeil (Roger Livesey). *I Know Where I'm Going!* thus gives us a version of *The Pilgrim's Progress* with a distinct twist: typical of Emeric Pressburger's canny ability to turn narrative conventions 'inside out', this film's happy ending rests, paradoxically, on the protagonist's failure to reach her intended destination.[16]

As 'intimate films, stories of self-discovery, about individuals finding the correct values to live by', both *A Canterbury Tale* and *I Know Where I'm Going!* illustrate the extent to which, by 'asking the population to remember the values they had fought for, and to think about what sort of brave new world they would like post-war Britain to be', Powell and Pressburger had turned 'from propagandists to preachers'.[17] While demonstrating Powell's 'poetic approach' as a director to telling 'the truth' through his 'own brand of visual and dramatic romanticism', as Andrew Moor describes it, these films also confirm 'the imprint of Pressburger's authorial presence', especially in his ongoing design, as a screenwriter with a penchant for episodic stories about fugitives and exiles, 'to write his own pilgrim's progress', *A Canterbury Tale* and *I Know Where I'm Going!*, each being, as Kevin Macdonald notes, precisely that: 'a modern parable about modern problems'.[18]

16 As Moor points out, both *A Canterbury Tale* and its 'sister-film', *I Know Where I'm Going!*, present 'frustrated' journeys, in the 'stoppages' of which 'their protagonists are re-educated and taught to reprioritize their lives': *Powell & Pressburger*, pp. 17, 120. Powell evidently admired Pressburger's 'typically Hungarian' ability to turn narratives 'inside out' and 'to deal in paradoxes' and 'reverse jokes': see Badder, 'Powell and Pressburger: The War Years', p. 10; *Michael Powell: In Collaboration*, ed. Gough-Yates p. [6]; Powell, *A Life in Movies*, p. 458. On this 'paradoxical' aspect of Pressburger's 'narrative imagination', see also Christie, 'Another Life in Movies', pp. 175–7.

17 Macdonald, *Emeric Pressburger*, p. 234. According to Powell, Jack Beddington, head of the Films Division at the Ministry of Information in 1943–4, commented: 'You fellows don't make ordinary films, after all. In a way, they're sort of sermons'; *A Life In Movies*, p. 456.

18 Macdonald, *Emeric Pressburger*, p. 234; Gough-Yates, ed., *Michael Powell: In Collaboration*, p. [5]; Moor, *Powell & Pressburger*, p. 12. For Powell's lifelong distrust of 'documentary' and his rejection of 'neo-realism and 'naturalism' in

With *The Pilgrim's Progress* standing as something of an *ur*-text for the narrative and thematic structures of Powell and Pressburger's later wartime films, it becomes clear to see just how and why *A Matter of Life and Death*, originally planned for production immediately after *A Canterbury Tale* in 1944, stands as another cinematic reshaping of *The Pilgrim's Progress*.[19] In fact, more than either *A Canterbury Tale* or *I Know Where I'm Going!*, *A Matter of Life and Death* invites direct comparison with Bunyan's book, beyond Peter Carter's identification with Raleigh's 'passionate pilgrim' at the beginning of the film or the appearance of Bunyan himself just before the closing trial sequence (and beyond too Ian Christie's ingenious suggestion that the film's most striking visual motif, the celestial escalator between Earth and the Other World, may well have been drawn from the vision of a stairway to heaven shown to Christiana in *The Pilgrim's Progress, Part II*).[20] Indeed, as 'a story of two worlds', about a man caught at a crucial point in his final 'pilgrimage' from this life to the next, Bunyan's allegory appears to be evoked by Powell and Pressburger primarily to underscore the film's 'construction' of Peter Carter as 'a modern hero' whose trials and tribulations might seem comparable to

---

the presentation of 'truth' see also *Michael Powell: Interviews*, ed. Lazar, pp. 13–15, 43, 70, and Powell, *A Life in Movies*, pp. 457, 591–2. For other examples of Pressburger's interest in 'journey' and 'exile' stories, we need only consider the 'picaresque' plot of *49th Parallel* and its inversion in *One of Our Aircraft is Missing*, as well as the 'figurative' journeys through the lives of Blimp and his German friend, Theo, in *The Life and Death of Colonel Blimp*: see Moor, pp. 17, 47–8, and Macdonald, *Emeric Pressburger*, pp. 166–7, 190–1. In 1941, Pressburger also wrote the story for a film entitled *Squadron Leader X*, eventually directed by Lance Comfort and released in 1943, about a German agent fugitive in wartime Britain, of which one reviewer noted a thematic connection with Pressburger's other films: 'His speciality is escape' (see Macdonald, *Emeric Pressburger*, pp. 195–6). On the significance of exile as a narrative motif centred in Pressburger's biographical circumstances, see Kevin Gough-Yates, 'Pressburger, England and Exile', *Sight and Sound*, 12 (1995), 30–5; Moor, *Powell & Pressburger*, pp. 2–3, 6–7, 11–18.

19 Filming *A Matter of Life and Death* was delayed, owing to the unavailability of Technicolor film stock in Britain in 1944 – hence *I Know Where I'm Going!* was made in the interim: Powell, *A Life in Movies*, p. 459.

20 Christie, *A Matter of Life and Death*, pp. 24–5.

those of Bunyan's own allegorical hero. For, as Christie comments, by the end of the film:

> Like Bunyan's pilgrim, Christian, he [i.e. Peter] has suffered yet persevered in his search for 'salvation'. He has been tempted to give in – though it is a heavenly messenger who has tempted him – but thanks to his advocate Dr Reeves, endorsed by Bunyan himself – he wins through.[21]

This concern with spiritual journeying and persevering, with 'pilgrimage' from one world to another, and with the idea (implicit in the allegorical form of *The Pilgrim's Progress* itself) that life, as Powell observed, is 'not everything you see but many layers underneath', with much more going on 'below the surface than people realise', confirms for Christie the extent to which Powell and Pressburger were 'imbued with the same sturdy mysticism as Bunyan, which saw no discontinuity between this world and the next'.[22] On this basis, one might be tempted to suggest further that the film's striking ability to disturb 'the habitual assumptions' of both 'narrative' and 'representation' through its projection of 'two realities, two truths, two worlds' throughout, are rooted in precisely the kind of 'dislocations' effected by Bunyan's use of allegorical dream-narrative in *The Pilgrim's Progress*.[23] John Ellis reads *A Matter of Life and Death* as a work that disrupts 'the process of subject positioning by providing [...] two regimes of coherence for the subject', making it difficult to distinguish between 'realities' in the film (between the documentary and the fictional, the actual or the hallucinated, the medical or the supernatural) in order to inculcate an awareness in the audience about 'the problems of representation' and to produce 'a scepticism about notions of realism'.[24] There would seem to be an affinity here to *The Pilgrim's Progress*'s own concerns with representing spiritual 'Truth', in this-worldly as well as in fictive terms, and with making visible

---

21   Christie, *Arrows of Desire*, p. 57; *A Matter of Life and Death*, p. 25.
22   Badder, 'Powell and Pressburger: The War Years', p. 12; Christie, *Arrows of Desire*, p. 116.
23   John Ellis, 'Watching Death at Work: An Analysis of *A Matter of Life and Death*', in *Powell, Pressburger and Others*, ed. Christie, pp. 79–104 (79, 99).
24   Ibid., pp. 91, 99, 101, 103.

'unseen things'. Indeed, the collision of worlds, of different realities that no longer remain distinct but, rather, invade one another in *A Matter of Life and Death*, is a form of ontological and narrative 'disruption' familiar to any reader of *The Pilgrim's Progress*, a book which teaches us about 'how to read' as much as *A Matter of Life and Death* teaches us, as Ellis puts it, about 'how you see'.[25]

* * *

Viewing *A Matter of Life and Death* in these terms might help to confirm it, then, as Powell and Pressburger's final attempt at a modern-day *Pilgrim's Progress*. It might also go some way towards suggesting why it is Bunyan – 'Bunyan! Yes, of course' – who walks onto the screen so prominently, later in the film. But does reading *A Matter of Life and Death* in this way really explain Bunyan's appearance, either fully or satisfactorily? Perhaps not. Despite the various signals given, and despite too Ian Christie's persuasive arguments, it is actually quite difficult to read onto *A Matter of Life and Death* any straightforward correlation with *The Pilgrim's Progress*. Although Peter Carter's is 'a story of two worlds', the film seems to frustrate such a correspondence as much as it invites it. Not only does a distinctly un-burdened (because parachute-less) Peter first appear in flight from an unnamed 'burning' city that he has himself been bombing into oblivion, offering an odd inversion of Bunyan's guilt-laden Christian escaping from his City of Destruction, but he becomes a 'pilgrim' reluctant to make his final journey heavenward and who, refusing to leave his beloved behind, ultimately prefers to remain on Earth. With Pressburger once again turning the *telos* of Bunyan's narrative 'inside out', *A Matter of Life and Death* is a *Pilgrim's Progress* riddled with paradoxes: as Ian Christie's own hesitations indicate, Peter Carter might 'persevere' through obstacles and temptations, like Bunyan's pilgrim, but these are, paradoxically, set by 'a heavenly messenger', with the 'modernized Jacob's Ladder' of the 'stairway' to heaven thus becoming not 'a symbol of transcendence' in the film 'but a trap' in what is, finally, a 'quite secular allegory'. It would take a

25 Ibid., p. 101.

strained interpretation of *The Pilgrim's Progress* indeed to equate its message with that of Powell and Pressburger's film too, given that life on Earth in *A Matter of Life and Death* is famously presented in Technicolor, colour representing 'the freshness and tangibility of the everyday', and thus 'everything that Peter will lose if he submits to death', in contrast to the colder, 'pearly' black-and-white of the film's afterlife.[26]

With 'this world' being something to be returned to (rather than fled from) in *A Matter of Life and Death*, it might seem more sensible to follow Andrew Moor, among others, in seeking more secure correspondences between *A Matter of Life and Death* and its other key literary intertext, Shakespeare's *A Midsummer Night's Dream* (rehearsals and preparations for a performance of which form an important backdrop in the film itself). Not only does Shakespeare's comedy offer a 'ludic space' for the collision of realities – the fairy kingdom of Oberon, Titania, and Puck intruding in various ways the lives of the play's earthly lovers – but being a work in which 'dream' and 'reality' become indistinguishable, it also offers Powell and Pressburger an opportunity to signal 'their own recurring fascination with opposed worlds, dream states, alien territories and magical spaces'.[27] With *A Matter of Life and Death* self-consciously addressing the business of interpreting films, as John Ellis has argued, Powell and Pressburger may well have had Shakespeare's self-reflexive art in *A Midsummer Night's Dream* more firmly in mind than *The Pilgrim's Progress* when framing their own dream-like fantasy of Peter Carter's colliding worlds. The fact that we are shown not just preparations for a performance of *A Midsummer Night's Dream* in the film, but a scene in which amateur actors (American servicemen) are rehearsing the parts of amateur actors (rude mechanicals) who are, of course, rehearsing parts for their own play-within-a-play, offers a dizzying '*mis en abyme*', as Christie notes, serving to illustrate the

26   Christie, *A Matter of Life and Death*, pp. 24, 79, 43. See also Powell, *A Life in Movies*, pp. 457–9, 495–9 on the use of monochrome and colour in the film.
27   Moor, *Powell & Pressburger*, pp. 4, 96, 146. See also Christie's discussion of the film's relation to *A Midsummer Night's Dream* as a 'modern masque' in *Matter of Life and Death*, pp. 14–20.

way Powell and Pressburger, following Shakespeare, are consciously conjuring worlds-within-worlds in their own cinematic 'dream', and drawing their audience's attention to the sheer pleasure of doing so.[28]

But if *A Midsummer Night's Dream* provides the central English 'model' for *A Matter of Life and Death*, being 'the chief other work to which it alludes', as Philip Horne has also recently noted, then we might ask again why Shakespeare does not appear as the key 'visual epigraph' in the film?[29] Why, in other words, is it still Bunyan? The answer to this question lies, finally perhaps, beyond the issues addressed so far in this essay, and instead in the well-documented origins of *A Matter of Life and Death* as pro-American propaganda. While finishing *A Canterbury Tale* early in 1944, Powell and Pressburger were approached (or rather ordered, 'an official order', as Powell elsewhere puts it) by Jack Beddington of the Ministry of Information 'to film a movie exalting Anglo-American relations' which were deteriorating, possibly due to 'resentment over American claims of leadership and Britain's growing economic and material dependence on its ally', but also due to uncertainty over Britain's position within any post-war global balance of power.[30] Having addressed the matter of Anglo-American relations already in a number of their wartime films (from *49th Parallel* to *A Canterbury Tale*), Powell and Pressburger were perhaps the obvious pair for the British government to approach, their brief being (as Powell recalls) to make

---

28   Christie, *A Matter of Life and Death*, p. 19. See also Moor on this point: *Powell & Pressburger*, pp. 151–2.

29   Philip Horne, 'Life and Death in *A Matter of Life and Death*', in *The Cinema of Michael Powell*, eds Christie and Moor, pp. 117–31 (119). The film has, of course, many other sources and parallels beyond *The Pilgrim's Progress* and *A Midsummer Night's Dream*, from a newspaper report 'about that English pilot who jumped from his aircraft and the parachute failed to open and he survived' (Powell, *A Life in Movies*, p. 458, and see also Macdonald, *Emeric Pressburger*, p. 251) to the Hungarian writer, Frigyes Karinthy's book *A Journey Round My Skull* (1938): see esp. Christie, *A Matter of Life and Death*, pp. 9–28.

30   *Michael Powell: Interviews*, ed. Lazar, p. 40; Powell, *A Life in Movies*, pp. 455–8; Christie, *A Matter of Life and Death*, pp. 12–13, and 80, ns. 6 and 7; Moor, *Powell & Pressburger*, pp. 126–9, 148–9; Badder, 'Powell and Pressburger: The War Years', pp. 11–12; Macdonald, *Emeric Pressburger*, pp. 250–1.

'a big film' that would 'appeal to the Yanks as much as the British', and which would 'make the English and Americans love each other' at a time when, with Europe falling apart, 'old jealousies, misunderstandings and distrusts will return' in the resulting 'bickering and skulduggery'.[31]

While *A Matter of Life and Death* may not have been exactly what the Ministry of Information had expected of such official end-of-war propaganda (as a surrealist 'fantasy', it was, by Powell's own confession, something of a 'tilting match' at the wartime 'documentary boys'), nevertheless the extent to which it fulfils Beddington's commission is clear: it is 'to prove to the Americans and the British how much they love each other' that *A Matter of Life and Death* centres on the star-crossed love story of 'a good Englishman' and 'a young lady of good American stock', and also why Peter's trial at the hands of an anti-British American prosecutor, Abraham Farlan (Raymond Massey), becomes a vehicle for underscoring the shared traditions that form (according to the film, at least) the natural basis of a continuing Anglo-American alliance.[32] The film's propaganda message is thus reflected, quite clearly, in the final trial sequence, which highlights Anglo-American sources of friction before cementing the two countries' shared commitment to justice and freedom, summarized by Reeves's extended debate with Farlan about 'the rights of the individual' during Peter's trial. 'Where else in the world have the rights of the individual been held so high?', other than in England, asks the Englishman Reeves, to which the American Revolutionary, Farlan, answers resoundingly: 'In America, sir. Where these rights are held to be inalienable.'

While for some (including Powell himself, it seems) the propaganda aspect of *A Matter of Life and Death*, exemplified by the debates held during the trial sequence, marks a point of weakness in the film, it nevertheless helps to explain why it is Bunyan, and no one else, who escorts the freshly-deceased Reeves on-screen, just before Peter's trial takes place. With Bunyan having such a firm foothold in

31   Powell, *A Life in Movies*, p. 456.
32   *Michael Powell: In Collaboration*, ed. Gough-Yates, p. 10; Powell, *A Life in Movies*, pp. 455–9.

the popular literary and imaginative traditions of both the United States and Britain, who else could be projected in this film as a solid symbol of Anglo-American heritage, one might wonder? Bunyan! Yes, of course. It is thus Bunyan's status as a formidably transatlantic figure – typically English, yet practically native to New England too – that guarantees his place in *A Matter of Life and Death*.[33] Why it is Bunyan rather than Shakespeare who is conjured before our eyes thus becomes clear too, on this basis. Aside from the problem of Shakespeare's status as Nazi Germany's favourite playwright, even during wartime, the fact that the Americans are depicted as unable even to spell Shakespeare's name in *A Matter of Life and Death*, when preparing an advertisement for their production of *A Midsummer Night's Dream*, or to speak Shakespeare's language without sounding like 'a gangster', as the film's exasperated Rev. D'Arcy Pomfret (Robert Atkins) comments, all serves to underscore 'a history of Anglo-American cultural unease over Shakespeare', which, in anticipation of Peter's trial, 'amplifies the general theme of how *mis*understanding can arise between England and America'.[34] With the film offering a carefully co-ordinated accumulation of such cultural canyons throughout (a favourite subject of Powell's, it seems), Bunyan's later on-screen arrival has all the more impact by providing, at last, a

---

[33] See esp. David E. Smith, *John Bunyan in America* (Bloomington and London: Indiana University Press, 1966), and Greaves, *Glimpses of Glory*, pp. 601–34.

[34] Christie, *A Matter of Life and Death*, pp. 15–16. On Shakespeare's position in Britain and Germany, during both the First and Second World Wars, see esp. Werner Habicht, 'Shakespeare and Theatre Politics in the Third Reich', in *The Play Out of Context: Transferring Plays from Culture to Culture*, eds Hanna Scolnicov and Peter Holland (Cambridge: Cambridge University Press, 1989), pp. 110–20; Balz Engler, 'Shakespeare in the Trenches', *Shakespeare Survey*, 44 (1992), 105–11; and esp. Gerwin Strobl, 'Shakespeare and the Nazis', *History Today*, 47 (1997), 16–21. Strobl reports how early in the war, and much like Powell and Pressburger's American servicemen and women in *A Matter of Life and Death*, 'members of a Berlin FLAK regiment took time off from guarding the skies over Hitler's capital' in order to stage *A Midsummer Night's Dream* (p. 16).

much-needed point of cultural affinity: a bridge between the film's 'two worlds' indeed.[35]

* * *

Yet Bunyan's role is more than just to serve as an agent ('One of the best men in the service') for 'official' Anglo-American propaganda, even in a film which, following hard on Churchill's 'iron curtain' speech at Fulton, Missouri, in March 1946, seems firmly to anticipate Britain's anti-Soviet position in the subsequent 'Cold War'.[36] Rather, Bunyan's appearance offers a deeper resonance in *A Matter of Life and Death*, though again in terms of Powell and Pressburger's commitment to the 'immaterial values' and 'traditions' for which Britain had gone to war, more than anything else. In *A Matter of Life and Death* these 'values' revolve primarily, of course, around the individual's 'liberty'. For this reason, one might object to the final trial sequence on the grounds that, as 'propaganda', it 'fails' cinemat-

---

[35] Consider, for example, the second short sequence of shots set inside Lee Wood Hall, the country house where June and the other Americans are stationed and where Peter and Frank meet for the first time: here, a glamorous and red-haired American servicewoman looks blankly up at a Tudor portrait of an old English noblewoman, who appears also to be staring uncomprehendingly back, thus signalling the film's divisions: ancient versus modern, American versus English. Consider also the film's visual 'gag' in having a Coca Cola machine waiting in the 'Other World' for the dead American servicemen at the beginning of the film. Such scenes can be compared to others from earlier Archers films too, such as Sgt. Bob Johnson's awe and estrangement when awaking in the grand chamber of an ancient English house in *A Canterbury Tale*, or Colonel Blimp's semantic difficulties when trying (and failing) to communicate with American soldiers towards the end of *Blimp*'s First World War sequence. For as much as *A Matter of Life and Death* argues for Anglo-American unity, Powell himself continued to have been exasperated by transatlantic differences, not least over the film's American change of title to *Stairway to Heaven*; see Powell, *A Life in Movies*, pp. 486–7, 543, 591.

[36] On this 'Cold War' context see esp. Christie, *A Matter of Life and Death*, pp. 65–9. See also Sue Harper and Vincent Porter, '"*A Matter of Life and Death*": The View from Moscow', *Historical Journal of Film, Radio and Television*, 9 (1989), 181–8, which documents and discusses a Soviet review of the film and its politics published in Russia in 1947.

ically, overwhelming us with 'dialogue and ideology', as Scott Salwolke complains.[37] But it is not just in Peter's trial that the 'immaterial values' of liberty and justice, freedom and conscience are highlighted in this film, nor for propaganda purposes alone, it seems. Indeed, only by recognizing how the matter of 'rights' and 'liberties' are fundamental to the film's structure and meaning can we begin to see it as something beyond either whimsical fantasy or narrow propaganda. Only in these terms can we finally, and properly, make sense of Bunyan's appearance.

We should, for instance, be alerted to the nature of *A Matter of Life and Death* as a parable about 'inalienable rights', long before the trial sequence begins, by the legal pun (one of Pressburger's 'reverse jokes', it seems) upon which Peter Carter's 'case' seems entirely based: that of *habeas corpus*, arguably 'the most fundamental legal right' of all, the punning significance of which, despite never having been noticed before, becomes obvious given in its literal meaning – 'produce the body'.[38] After all, Peter is only alive because, in all that English fog, Conductor 71 could not locate his 'body' on the night of 2 May 1945, and must subsequently rectify the mistake by 'producing' his still living person as (more correctly) dead in the Other World. But the fact that doing so proves much harder than Conductor 71 expects is not just because Peter is now unreasonably in love. Rather, it is because Peter reasonably argues, precisely on the legal basis of *habeas corpus* – a central tenet in both English and American law for the protection of subjects and citizens from illegal or arbitrary imprisonment – that being returned to and detained in the Other World, without a trial, represents an implicit contravention of his 'liberties' – at least as an Englishman.[39]

---

37 Scott Salwolke, *The Films of Michael Powell and The Archers* (Lanham, MD. & London: Scarecrow Press, 1997), p. 138.
38 See, for example, David J. Clark and Gerard McCoy, *The Most Fundamental Legal Right: Habeas Corpus in the Commonwealth* (Oxford: Oxford University Press, 2000), and Robert J. Sharpe, *The Law of Habeas Corpus*, second edn (Oxford: Clarendon Press, 1989).
39 Christie, taking a different view, places Peter's trial in the context of the Nuremberg trials, taking place during 1945–6: *A Matter of Life and Death*, pp. 69–72.

It is to underscore this point, then, that Powell and Pressburger bookend Peter Carter's story with two all-important debates: between Reeves and Farlan in the trial at the end, in which the 'rights of the individual' are defended 'against the system', but also between Peter and Conductor 71 in their very first encounter near the beginning of the film, the political significance of which is easy to overlook given the cinematic trickery it involves (the Conductor transforming into colour, for example, among cerise rhododendrons, while uttering the witty line, 'Ah, one is starved for Technicolor up there', before making 'time' itself 'stop'). Being informed by Conductor 71 at this point that Peter 'cannot refuse' to return with him to the Other World, Peter's protestation that he is now in love with June is dismissed easily enough: 'But, my friend, what is love? The feeling of the moment', the Frenchman states, whereas 'I represent eternity: the law of this world and the other'. Yet it is precisely because all 'law is based on reason' that Peter manages to re-establish his position on the basis of 'rights'. Because the fault of his continuing existence on Earth lies not on his side, but on the Conductor's, Peter reasonably argues that, unlike anyone else, he actually has a 'right' now to object to and resist any demand to 'return' to death.

The introduction of a language of rights shifts the tenor of the scene, and of the relationship between these two antagonists, significantly too, as it suddenly frees Peter to interrogate the Conductor in directly political terms: 'What kind of government do you represent?' he now demands, and 'what laws govern the place you come from?'. While the Conductor is wrong-footed by Peter's constitutional indignation ('I am not permitted to express any political views', he answers sheepishly), Peter concludes that 'if it's a respectable place there must be a law of appeal', which it will be the Conductor's job 'to find out'. Faced with such resistance, and being left 'in the salad', as he puts, the Conductor's last resort is to threaten Peter: 'Now look here, you don't want me to use force, do you?', flapping a white-gloved fist ineffectually before Peter's face, which Peter merely laughs away – 'Well, you can always try'.

Reminding us, perhaps, of a good-natured (though just as serious) version of Christian's encounter with Apollyon in *The Pilgrim's Progress*, in which the pilgrim's resolve is likewise tested in terms of conscience and coercion, and which too involves the same pattern of reasoned resistance followed by violence, both the initial vanquishing of Conductor 71 and Peter's struggle throughout *A Matter of Life and Death* are rooted in neither sentimentality nor romantic chivalry but, rather, in a discourse about the rule of law and the limits of power. Suspicious of any regime in which 'law' might not be based on 'reason', and which might not guarantee any 'right' of appeal, Peter's trial arises in *A Matter of Life and Death* not simply out of 'love' but from a tenacious sense of his individual and constitutional rights, which seem in danger of violation by this Frenchman in the secret 'service' of an unnamed 'government', a shadowy 'They', as Peter explains to June. By demanding that his 'case' be put before a court, Peter is not simply being wilful, therefore. Rather, he is being shown to invoke his 'most fundamental right' according to English constitutional tradition: that 'Great Writ of Liberty' itself, *habeas corpus*. For it is by writ of *habeas corpus*, dating from at least the fourteenth century but ratified by Act of Parliament for the first time in England during Bunyan's lifetime (in 1679) that English subjects are safeguarded against unlawful arrest and imprisonment, guaranteeing them the right to have any charges against them brought, in person, before a court of law.[40]

Given that the entire narrative of *A Matter of Life and Death* hinges on Peter Carter's 'right' to take his case before a celestial 'court', Powell and Pressburger thus cement an all-important connection between the battles Peter has been engaged in as a 'master bomber' for the RAF and his other, legalistic 'battle' over life and death that takes place in his final trial: both are fought in the name of 'rights'. On this basis, Peter's spirited resistance is rooted in principles traditionally associated with the 'free-born Englishman' on a series of levels: they are Lockean (in Peter's emphasis on 'reason' and 'law' as the means of protecting the individual's life, property and liberty), and also firmly anti-absolutist (in his resistance against any attempted coercion by Conductor 71 in the 'service' of an unnamed, foreign

---

40 See, for example, Sharpe, *The Law of Habeas Corpus*. For the 1679 Habeas Corpus Amendment Act see J. P. Kenyon, *The Stuart Constitution*, second edn (Cambridge: Cambridge University Press, 1986), pp. 391–7, 401–2.

'government'). Indeed, Peter's appeal represents a series of 'traditional' English 'liberties', all of which are summarized in *habeas corpus* – 'freedom from arbitrary arrest, trial by jury, equality before the law', along with 'liberty of thought, of speech, and of conscience', as E. P. Thompson has described them – which the film highlights implicitly as the very things that distinguish Britain, and also America, from the tyrannical, totalitarian regimes of Nazi Germany (as well as, by implication, Soviet Russia).[41] The sharper point of *A Matter of Life and Death*, however, is that even the most 'democratic' of governments can become tyrannical once individual rights and freedoms are overlooked. In this film, even Heaven, in its urgent need to rectify the mistake represented by Peter Carter's survival, is in grave danger of becoming totalitarian, employing 'service' agents who threaten arrest through force, and who are themselves not permitted to hold any 'political views'. Indeed, with 'time' being a mere 'tyranny', as Conductor 71 puts it, the power to arrest 'time' itself becomes a chief instrument in the film through which to invade Peter Carter's life and threaten his liberty.[42]

41 E. P. Thompson, *The Making of the English Working Class* (1963; Harmondsworth: Penguin, 1980), p. 86. See also Linda Colley, *Britons: Forging the Nation 1707–1837*, second edn (New Haven and London: Yale University Press, 2005), esp. pp. 101–45, and Robert Colls, *Identity of England* (Oxford: Oxford University Press, 2002), esp. pp. 13–65. In terms of 'propaganda' the trial thus works to demonstrate that England and America were bound together, 'shoulder to shoulder' no less, in a special relationship based on the same concepts of freedom which had developed over centuries of constitutional reform in Britain, and which had been won for the United States through the American Revolution, for which the same Lockean language of rights had been central. See esp. T. H. Breen, *The Lockean Moment: The Language of Rights on the Eve of the American Revolution* (Oxford: Oxford University Press, 2001), and for broader contexts see also J. C. D. Clark, *The Language of Liberty 1660–1832: Political Discourse and Social Dynamics in the Anglo-American World* (Cambridge: Cambridge University Press, 1994). Having spent time 'in the British Museum reading up on American Revolutionary history' in 1944, Pressburger would certainly have known about such things; Powell, *A Life in Movies*, p. 459.
42 Taking this as a central 'lesson' of the film also offers a context for the unusual setting in which we are first introduced to the film's other hero, Dr. Frank Reeves, shown observing the village and the lives of its inhabitants as if

By seeing Peter Carter's 'case', then, as a defence of traditional English – as well as American – constitutional liberties, we can begin to see, for much clearer political reasons, why Bunyan is indeed afforded such an important place in *A Matter of Life and Death*, beyond the other connections the film may have with *The Pilgrim's Progress*. For who could better serve to represent Britain's historic struggles to establish the rights both of the common and the *un*common man (and woman), other than one of the most famous, and popular, English Dissenters of all, one who lived through the persecution and oppression that led, ultimately, to the Glorious Revolution and the revolutionary 1689 Bill of Rights? Bunyan! Yes, of course. Bunyan's appearance in the film, in other words, serves as a 'visual epigraph' not just for the film's 'pilgrimage' motifs, nor for its origins in Anglo-American propaganda, but, more importantly, for an interest in and commitment to 'liberty' and 'rights' which, for Emeric Pressburger at least, were far from merely academic or propagandist concerns. A Jewish Hungarian who came to Britain as an exile from Nazi Germany in 1935, Pressburger had learned, by November 1944, that most of the Jewish population in his home town of Miskolc 'had been deported to the death camps [...] by the retreating Nazis': among them was his own mother, whom he would never see again.[43]

If nothing else, therefore, the matter of 'rights' in *A Matter of Life and Death* confirms Pressburger's own avowed sense of how in

> omnisciently from a *camera obscura*, which gives him powers of surveillance on an almost Orwellian scale, the ethical ambivalence of which must be resolved in the trial too, by Reeves himself, no less. It is tempting, moreover, to read this dimension of the film in the context of Powell and Pressburger's own experience of government hostility intended to obstruct the production of *The Life and Death of Colonel Blimp* in 1942–3: see Christie, '*Blimp*, Churchill and the State'.

43   Macdonald, *Emeric Pressburger*, pp. 259–60. Macdonald reports that: 'In later life he [Pressburger] felt guilty that he had not taken his mother with him to England when he had the opportunity and that, consequently, she died at the hands of the Nazis' (pp. 132–3), a detail which lends great poignancy to Peter Carter's request that a telegram be sent to his mother, telling her that he loves her, believing that he is about to die.

The Relevant Pilgrim 207

their wartime films, he and Powell 'had always stood for REASON' and for 'fighting for our lives and for everything else' against a Nazi 'jackboot philosophy [...] that was really so'.[44] It is within this context, then, as a prisoner of conscience whose life and works inspired a long tradition of democratic reformers and working-class radicals in the name of English liberty, as E. P. Thompson, Christopher Hill, and Linda Colley have shown, that Bunyan steps forward in *A Matter of Life and Death* in the defence of individual 'rights'. Who else might Powell and Pressburger present to us as the great English example of the 'individual' victorious against 'the system', and thus as the presiding spirit over Peter Carter's final trial?

* * *

Bunyan's position in *A Matter of Life and Death* leaves us, then, with two conclusions. The first concerns Powell and Pressburger's status as 'independent' filmmakers, not just in terms of the way they collaborated in the production of their films according to a 'manifesto' of independence, but also in upholding an intellectual and creative tradition of a particularly 'dissenting' kind.[45] This particular dimension of their craft is especially important to remember when considering that *A Matter of Life and Death* has been received, at one extreme, as 'a basically sensational film about nothing', and as an expression only of narrow, 'High Tory' political values, at the other.[46] While Powell

44 'Interview with Emeric Pressburger', in *Michael Powell: In Collaboration*, ed. Gough-Yates, pp. [14–15]. See also Gough-Yates, 'Pressburger, England and Exile'. Perhaps the greatest testimony to Pressburger's anti-Nazism, though, stands in Theo's characterization, and esp. his monologue when interrogated by the British Aliens Board towards the end of the film: on the basis of this in Pressburger's 'recent personal experience', see Macdonald, *Emeric Pressburger*, pp. 212–14.
45 See Macdonald, *Emeric Pressburger*, pp. 189–90, 337; Moor, *Powell & Pressburger*, pp. 18–21.
46 Dilys Powell, in a review of the film on release in 1946, quoted by Powell, *A Life in Movies*, p. 592: see also Christie, *A Matter of Life and Death*, pp. 57–62, and Ellis, 'Watching Death at Work', pp. 85–8, for other accounts of the film's contemporary reception. For a reading of the film as extolling a 'High Tory moral', esp. in its 'anti-socialist' presentation of Heaven, see Raymond

himself might now be remembered for describing this film as his 'favourite' largely for its 'technical perfection, the fact that it is a wonderful conjuring trick', and who would remain 'unhappy about the ending' as a 'relic of the propaganda period', this is nevertheless the same Powell who, in January 1945, protested against the very idea of a post-war film 'industry' controlled solely either by 'the government' or by 'people [who] think of nothing but money': 'I don't give a damn about money', he stated, 'If I couldn't make what I wanted to make here I would spit in anybody's eye'.[47] As Powell would reiterate over thirty years later: 'If you're prepared to spend your whole life fighting for your art with people who don't like you, don't understand you, don't help you, then you have my respect, and I regard you as a brother'.[48] This same attitude of defiant independence is communicated too in the appearance of that far from 'High Tory' figure, John Bunyan, in *A Matter of Life and Death*, signalling Powell and Pressburger's identification indeed with a 'proud, popular tradition' of visionary 'outsiders', from 'Bunyan and Blake' to 'Kipling, Chesterton, Wells and Shaw'.[49]

Secondly, Bunyan's inclusion in *A Matter of Life and Death* serves to remind us too of something surprising about his cultural importance in Britain just after the Second World War. Far from being a forgotten or an irrelevant figure, Bunyan's appearance in this film confirms his position as a popular icon not just of 'Englishness' and of 'English' values at this time, but of something much broader.[50] For

Durgnat, 'Michael Powell', in *Powell, Pressburger and Others*, ed. Christie, pp. 65–74, and *A Mirror For England: British Movies from Austerity to Affluence* (London: Faber and Faber, 1970), pp. 25–35, 206–18, a view recently countered by Moor, *Powell & Pressburger*, pp. 144–5, and appreciated by Christie for taking the film as a serious expression of an 'explicit ideological position'; Christie, *A Matter of Life and Death*, pp. 62–3.
47 *Michael Powell: In Collaboration*, ed. Gough-Yates, p. 10; *Michael Powell: Interviews*, ed. Lazar, pp. 16–17.
48 *Michael Powell: Interviews*, ed. Lazar, p. 142.
49 Christie, *Arrows of Desire*, p. 6, and see also p. 98.
50 See also, for example, *The Character of England* (Oxford: Clarendon Press, 1947), a collection of scholarly essays addressing the 'spirit of England' after the war, and esp. James Sutherland's chapter on 'Literature', pp. 303–20, in which Bunyan is praised for epitomizing the 'self-reliance of the Englishman'

example, Vera Brittain's post-war biography, *In the Steps of John Bunyan* (begun in 1946-7, and first published in 1950) locates its origins too in an explicit recognition of Bunyan's ability to speak to a contemporary world ravaged by war on an 'apocalyptic' scale. In terms echoing exactly those of *A Matter of Life and Death*, in fact, Brittain sees in *The Pilgrim's Progress* 'a special relevance for our own epoch' in that it 'brings the challenge of hope and courage to all those who are fighting for the integrity of the human soul against totalitarian philosophies and spiritual demoralization'.[51] Indeed, by placing Bunyan's 'peculiar relevance for this present century' in the context of 'international conflicts' that had resulted in 'the descent of civilization into a deepening inhumanity', and in 'the modern struggle of democracy against totalitarianism', Bunyan stands in Brittain's account as someone who exemplifies not just an English or an Anglo-American history of 'liberty' alone.[52] Rather, Bunyan's visible re-emergence after the war in both *A Matter of Life and Death* and in Brittain's book, as a figure representative of the individual's 'rights' in the face of tyranny and oppression, mirrors an altogether more fundamental development occurring at this time: the formulation and issuing, in 1948, of the Universal Declaration of Human Rights by the United Nations.[53] The Bunyan of Brittain's biography and of Powell

---

and the same 'determined individuality', as well as 'tolerance' in one form or another, characteristic of the English literary tradition as a whole (pp. 307-9). *The Pilgrim's Progress* is still lauded in this volume as one of the 'permanent channels of English reading' (p. 573).

51 Vera Brittain, *In the Steps of John Bunyan: An Excursion into Puritan England* (London: Rich and Cowan, 1950), pp. 416, 15.
52 Ibid., pp. 415-18.
53 For the development of the concept and language of 'human rights' as a response to events both leading up to and occurring throughout the Second World War, and as a protection against 'totalitarianism', see esp. Richard Primus, *The American Language of Rights* (Cambridge: Cambridge University Press, 1999), esp. pp. 177-233, and *The Human Rights Reader: Major Political Essays, Speeches, and Documents: From the Bible to the Present*, ed. Micheline R. Ishay (London and New York: Routledge, 1997), and which reprints the 1948 Declaration, pp. 407-12. See also *Human Rights: From Rhetoric to Reality*, eds Tom Campbell, David Goldberg, Sheila Maclean and Tom Mullen (Oxford: Blackwell, 1986), esp. pp. 1-59.

and Pressburger's film thus emerges as 'The Relevant Pilgrim' (to borrow Brittain's phrase) precisely because of his capacity, as they see it, to conduct his readers into a post-war, post-Holocaust, nuclear world, not just as a reminder of past struggles for constitutional rights and individual freedoms, but also as a guiding spirit in the ongoing and future battle for 'human rights'.

The near-miraculous story of the postcard of John Bunyan, received by Terry Waite when held captive in Beirut during the late 1980s, certainly suggests that a popular association between Bunyan and the 'human rights' of hostages and other prisoners of conscience may have survived in and for more recent times too.[54] But despite the exceptional example of Terry Waite's postcard, sent to him by Joy Brodier, a well-wishing woman from Bedfordshire, it is difficult to imagine, today, many Britons turning to Bunyan as 'The Relevant Pilgrim', in the ways that Powell and Pressburger, Vera Brittain, and Ralph Vaughan Williams did with such urgency in the aftermath of the Second World War (the latter's triumphant musical celebration of *The Pilgrim's Progress* being presented for the first time, of course, at the Festival of Britain in 1951).[55] However, given the increasing concern being voiced at the beginning of the twenty-first century, over what seems to many to be the erosion of traditional, democratic freedoms within a global political climate increasingly defined by terrorism, there can hardly be more pressing circumstances in which to examine, once again, the significance of Anglo-American constitu-

---

54 Waite's story of the postcard of Bunyan was widely publicized in the British press at the time of his return to Britain, in November 1991, and is also recounted in his *Taken On Trust: Recollections from Captivity* (London: Hodder & Stoughton, 1993). For comments on the appropriation of Bunyan in this context, see Tamsin Spargo, 'The Purloined Postcard: Waiting for Bunyan', *Textual Practice*, 8 (1994), 79–96, and *The Writing of John Bunyan* (Aldershot: Ashgate, 1997), pp. 96–9.

55 Brittain too reports a performance of *The Pilgrim's Progress* being staged at Covent Garden in 1948; *In the Steps of John Bunyan*, p. 415. For Vaughan Williams see esp. Arleane Ralph, '"They Do Such Musick Make": *The Pilgrim's Progress* and Textually Inspired Music', *Bunyan Studies*, 5 (1994), 58–67, and Robert Manning, '*The Pilgrim's Progress*: A Vindication and Celebration of Vaughan Williams's Neglected Masterpiece', *Bunyan Studies*, 6 (1995–6), 70–7.

tional history for the upholding of civil liberties, and indeed of human rights. To whom might we look, then, when arguing still for the right to think and to act freely 'in religion and politics', as Reeves puts it in *A Matter of Life and Death*, and to defend 'the rights of the uncommon man', or woman, 'against the system'? Given the many examples from which to choose, not least from the twentieth-century's great defenders of civil liberties and human rights, could John Bunyan still be considered among them? Our answer might well be, yet once more: Yes, of course.

STUART SIM

10 Bunyan and his Fundamentalist Readers

Bunyan's appeal has been all but universal, with *The Pilgrim's Progress* seeming to transcend cultural barriers consistently down through the centuries. The notion of 'International Bunyan' is now well established in the critical community, which has a rich and varied history of reception on which to draw for textual and socio-historical analysis.[1] Bunyan is a genuinely popular writer, but he has always had a particular appeal to radicals – whether of the religious or political variety. In his own time his message had radical political connotations for the nonconformist community suffering persecution under the Restoration regime. For the Chartist movement in the mid-nineteenth century Bunyan was a cultural hero of subversive intent, as he was also for many twentieth-century Marxists, such as Jack Lindsay, Alick West, Arnold Kettle, and Christopher Hill.[2] Thus we have Hill's claim in *A Turbulent, Seditious, and Factious People: John Bunyan and his Church* that Bunyan's

> deep roots in his own popular culture, and in the social realities from which that culture grew, together with his millenarian Puritanism, tenacious especially in

[1] For an excellent study of Bunyan's appropriation in the African context, for example, see Isabel Hofmeyr, *Portable Bunyan: A Transnational History of The Pilgrim's Progress* (Princeton, NJ: Princeton University Press, 2003).

[2] See Jack Lindsay, *John Bunyan: Maker of Myths* (London: Methuen, 1937); Alick West, *The Mountain in the Sunlight* (London: Lawrence and Wishart, 1958); Arnold Kettle, *An Introduction to the English Novel* (London: Hutchinson, 1951); Christopher Hill, *A Turbulent, Seditious, and Factious People: John Bunyan and his Church* (Oxford: Oxford University Press, 1988). For a survey of Marxist approaches to Bunyan, see Robert G. Collmer, 'Bunyan and the Marxists', *Christianity and Literature*, 28 (1978), 14–16, and David Herreshoff, 'Marxist Perspectives on Bunyan', in *Bunyan in Our Time*, ed. Robert G. Collmer (Kent, OH and London: Kent State University Press, 1989), pp. 159–85.

defeat, combined to make *The Pilgrim's Progress* not only a foundation document of the English working-class movement but also a text which spoke to millions of those poor oppressed people whom Bunyan, like Winstanley, wished to address.[3]

In similar vein, West sees Bunyan as instinctively anti-capitalist in outlook, arguing that the Vanity Fair episode of *The Pilgrim's Progress* shows us that 'pilgrims must stand firm against the unjust and inhuman power of the market, which takes no account of the human soul; they must stand firm even unto death'.[4] Bunyan's diatribe against a society where absolutely everything is for sale, down to 'Lusts, Pleasures, and Delights of all sorts, as Whores, Bauds, Wives, Husbands, Children, Masters, Servants, Lives, Blood, Bodies, Souls' (*PP*, p. 86), is held to prefigure communist ideals. For Chartists and Marxists alike, Bunyan was an anti-establishment figure who in both his life and his fiction refused to compromise his beliefs, no matter what pressure was applied to him to conform. He has retained the same ability to inspire radical Protestant believers that he did in his own lifetime, with *The Pilgrim's Progress* continuing to be for many of the latter, as it was for the Chartist movement, the 'book of books'.[5]

---

3   Hill, *A Turbulent, Seditious, and Factious People*, p. 380.
4   West, *The Mountain in the Sunlight*, p. 162. It is worth noting that Bunyan's economic beliefs are a matter of some dispute amongst critics. For John McVeagh, for example, Bunyan's anti-capitalist bias is reactionary rather than revolutionary, the views of 'a throwback' harking back to medieval times; see his *Tradefull Merchants: The Portrayal of the Capitalist in Literature* (London: Routledge and Kegan Paul, 1981), p. 49. Michael McKeon, on the other hand, argues that in *The Pilgrim's Progress* Christian's career demonstrates how nonconformists can come to an accommodation with the new capitalist order, 'somewhere within the antithetical extremes of utter selfishness and utter selflessness'; see *The Origins of the English Novel, 1600–1740* (Baltimore: Johns Hopkins University Press, 1987), pp. 311–12.
5   Thomas Cooper; quoted in E. P. Thompson, *The Making of the English Working Class* (Harmondsworth: Penguin, 1968), p. 34. Thompson deals with Bunyan's influence on eighteenth- and nineteenth-century political radicalism in chapter 2, 'Christian and Apollyon', arguing that '*Pilgrim's Progress* is, with *Rights of Man*, one of the two foundation texts of the English working-class movement' (ibid.).

It is worth exploring why Bunyan's work has met with such a sympathetic reception in radical circles. In large part this is most probably because of the unyielding quality of his primary fictional hero, Christian, whose steadfast commitment to his belief system appeals to those of like temperament. Christian's agonistic relationship to the majority of those travellers he encounters on the road to the Celestial City, certainly to any who question his convictions or the necessity of his journey (Worldly-Wiseman, Formalist and Hypocrisy, Atheist, etc.), reveals a character prepared to defend his cause to the last. He becomes a role model for future generations of Dissenters in this respect: the man, who despite meeting repeated obstacles never loses faith, never surrenders. Once through the conversion experience, and the receipt of the all-important roll to hand in on arrival at the Celestial City, Christian is utterly convinced that he is in possession of the truth and can only treat anyone who chooses to dispute the point as an enemy – even the apparently innocuous Ignorance and the painfully eager-to-please Talkative. Similar traits can be identified in Bunyan's other fictional heroes: Mansoul (despite several lapses from grace), Wiseman and Attentive. Conviction of one's rightness acts as a signal of elect status to the audience in each case.

It could be argued that Bunyan seems to speak most powerfully to those who have a fundamentalist streak in their character, whose belief system regards compromise with other systems as weakness and who also feel themselves to be in possession of the ultimate truth.[6] Add to those characteristics an intolerance of other viewpoints and a distinct bias towards authoritarianism, and we have the basis of the fundamentalist temperament – a temperament which can thrive just as well outside as inside the religious domain, amongst political no less than religious zealots (not to mention nationalists, eco-warriors, and cultists of various exotic kinds). Through an analysis of *The Pilgrim's*

---

6   Certainly, Michael Davies implies that Bunyan's fictions speak more fully to believers (admittedly, not necessarily fundamentalist in outlook), arguing 'that non-doctrinal readings can sometimes be inappropriate (if not pernicious, on occasion) and often for distinct historical and polemical reasons'; see *Graceful Reading: Theology and Narrative in the Works of John Bunyan* (Oxford: Oxford University Press, 2002), p. 13.

Progress, *The Holy War*, and *The Life and Death of Mr Badman*, this essay will explore the extent to which Bunyan himself could be said to fit a fundamentalist character specification, and whether this is indeed to be considered the main source of his appeal to radicals: a fundamentalist speaking to fellow fundamentalists. Perhaps such an enquiry will cast Bunyan's legacy in a new, and possibly more problematical, light.

Admittedly, Bunyan can present a less harsh side to us on occasion, as he does in Part Two of *The Pilgrim's Progress*, for example. Critics have remarked on the less aggressive or anxiety-ridden tone of this work compared to Part One, even suggesting that it represents a feminization of the author's vision. While it would not as such undermine the argument being pursued in this essay to concede this – one text by an author does not necessarily cancel out another – what is more relevant to note is that it is Part One that has come to define Bunyan for future generations. Part Two has never exerted anything like the same appeal as its predecessor, and exists in cultural history as a somewhat shadowy, little-read afterthought. Perhaps this does the author an injustice, but if a more mellow Bunyan appears in his later years that does not materially affect the legacy left by his other major works of fiction – in particular, of course, his undisputed masterpiece, *The Pilgrim's Progress*, Part One. It is to that latter work above all that radicals are ineluctably drawn; *that* Bunyan who is the subject of such widespread appropriation.

Fundamentalism: The Phenomenon

Before moving on to Bunyan's fiction, I will briefly consider the phenomenon of fundamentalism – a topic I cover at length in my book *Fundamentalist World: The New Dark Age of Dogma*.[7] Fundamental-

---

7 *Fundamentalist World: The New Dark Age of Dogma* (Cambridge: Icon Press, 2004). For more on fundamentalism and its history, see Malise Ruthven,

ism is a recent phenomenon as far as the term itself goes: it was only coined in 1920 to describe those who accepted the tenets of *The Fundamentals*, a series of short works published in America from 1910–15 by evangelical Christian theologians concerned at the inroads they felt secularism was making into religious belief in their society.[8] America had seen a series of religious revivals over the course of its history (from the 'Great Awakening' of the eighteenth century onwards), and this particular project was to herald one of the most successful and long-lasting in terms of its effects – effects which can still be felt to this day.[9] *The Fundamentals* were designed to establish core concepts for Christian belief that could not be contested: beliefs that had to be considered 'fundamental' to the Christian faith and that lay beyond question or the need for debate or interpretation. There were five of these:

(1) the inerrancy of Scripture;
(2) the Virgin Birth of Christ;
(3) Christ's substitutionary atonement;
(4) Christ's bodily resurrection;
(5) the authenticity of Christ's miracles.[10]

Later, dispensationalism was added to this list, with its theory of world history as divided up by God into a series of seven eras, or 'dispensations', set to end with the Second Coming and the millennium of Christ's personal reign over earth. According to this theory, we were on the verge of the latter event; all the more reason exactly to clarify

Fundamentalism: The Search for Meaning (Oxford: Oxford University Press, 2004).

8 *The Fundamentals*, ed. A. C. Dixon (1910–15; New York and London: Garland, 1988).

9 Fundamentalist Christianity has taken root in the Republican Party in America in recent years, for example, and was much in evidence in the 2004 presidential election when its cohorts were deeply involved in the Bush campaign, particularly in getting the vote out for their candidate on the day. At the very least, President Bush has fundamentalist sympathies. For more on the history of religious revivals in America, see Malise Ruthven, *The Divine Supermarket: Travels in Search of the Soul of America* (London: Chatto and Windus, 1989).

10 For more on this, see George M. Marsden, *Fundamentalism and American Culture: The Shaping of Twentieth-Century Evangelism: 1870–1925* (New York and Oxford: Oxford University Press, 1980).

those doctrinal fundamentals for the expectant faithful. (We are still on the verge of the millennium apparently, and a thriving publishing industry in America does its best to make it seem very imminent.)[11]

A fundamentalist was someone willing, as one supporter put it, 'to do battle royal for the Fundamentals', and that combative attitude has marked out Christian fundamentalism ever since.[12] The editor of *The Fundamentals*, A. C. Dixon, once notoriously remarked that 'the next best thing to peace is a theological fight', which gives a revealing glimpse into the fundamentalist mentality.[13] Fundamentalists are in almost constant battle with the various liberalizing forces within Western culture, and are prepared to reverse any of the gains these forces may have made (on issues such as abortion and the teaching of evolution, for example). For those actively seeking them, theological fights can always be found.

Fundamentalism can be summed up as displaying the following features:
- intolerance of all other viewpoints;
- repression of dissent;
- authoritarianism (often of an extreme form);
- strict adherence to a sacred text or set of principles to be accepted without question (literalism with regard to these being one of the cornerstones of the fundamentalist ethos).

I would see these features as holding across all kinds of fundamentalism, as I argue in *Fundamentalist World*, although I am concentrating on the religious and political varieties here.

If fundamentalism is recent in terms of its conceptualization, it has a much longer history as a practice, and all monotheistic religions have a fundamentalist aspect to them at some stage in their development. It is entirely possible to see radical sectarian Protestantism in the seventeenth century as fundamentalist in character, for example; espe-

---

11 Witness the massive success of the *Left Behind* series by Tim LaHaye and Jerry B. Jenkins (Wheaton, IL: Tyndale House, 1995–). The eleven volumes of this story of post-Rapture existence have sold over fifty million copies to date.
12 Curtis Lee Laws; quoted in Marsden, *Fundamentalism and American Culture*, p. 159.
13 Quoted in ibid., p. 101.

cially given its fixation with the biblical 'Word', not to mention its eagerness 'to do battle royal' over its understanding of that 'Word'. (It should be noted that this battle was as much with other Protestants as with 'enemy' Catholics, divisiveness being built into the very soul of Protestant sectarianism.) That sense of having found the real religious truth and of being able to prove this comprehensively from the Scriptures is very much the seventeenth-century English sectarian experience.[14] And Protestantism is very much the heartland of Christian fundamentalism.

Bunyan's Fiction: Dogmatism or Debate?

We move on now to Bunyan's fiction, to consider whether it communicates primarily the spirit of dogmatism or debate. A characteristic feature of that fiction is the image of the embattled individual fending off hostile forces: sometimes successfully, as in both parts of *The Pilgrim's Progress* (Christian, and then Christiana and her circle); sometimes more problematically, as in *The Holy War*, with its ebb and flow of defeat and triumph that is still unresolved at the end of the narrative. It is small wonder that the besieged Christian and Mansoul come to develop dogmatic personalities under the circumstances, as a self-defence mechanism as much as anything else: but does that mean their author's outlook is also dogmatic? Let us investigate how opponents of the heroes are viewed in these works to see what this may reveal about Bunyan's value-system.

On the face of it, *The Pilgrim's Progress* is debate-oriented. Figure after figure accosts Christian on the road and enters into animated discussion with him over a variety of topics: religious,

---

14   For a discussion of the socio-political implications of there being so many competing 'true' interpretations of Scripture in the period, see Stuart Sim and David Walker, *Bunyan and Authority: The Rhetoric of Dissent and the Legitimation Crisis in Seventeenth-Century England* (Bern and New York: Peter Lang, 2000).

moral, social, political. With the exception of Faithful and Hopeful (and of course his mentor Evangelist), Christian falls out with everyone else he meets. There is little pragmatism in his character; instead he is programmed to follow his allotted path in order to achieve his final reward of acceptance into the Celestial City. This reward is oriented towards an elite, we might say, since only a small 'elect' will ever be successful in gaining acceptance. Any deviations from that path prove dangerous, as Evangelist is always on hand to remind him: '*Cursed is every one that continueth not in all things which are written in the Book of the Law to do them*' (*PP*, p. 24). No concessions are made to those holding different views (Dissenters are definitely not pluralists). True, Christian can show weakness at times, and is prone to debilitating attacks of anxiety revealing deep-seated fears as to his ultimate soteriological fate, but we observe a steady strengthening of his character as the narrative unfolds. There really is 'progress' to be noted in this respect; the development of inner conviction, which can be shaken but never completely eradicated once it takes root. After a shaky start, graphically illustrated by his trials in traversing the Slough of Despond, 'whither the scum and filth that attends conviction for sin doth continually run' (*PP*, p. 17), Christian comes to realise that he is in possession of the truth and that all who question his conduct are to be treated with deep suspicion. Nothing less than the wholehearted agreement he receives from the theologically like-minded Faithful and Hopeful will suffice:

> Now I saw in my Dream, that *Christian* went not forth alone, for there was one whose name was *Hopeful*, (being made so by the beholding of *Christian* and *Faithful* in their words and behaviour, in their sufferings at the *fair*) who joyned himself unto him, and entring into a brotherly covenant, told him that he would be his Companion. Thus one died to make Testimony to the Truth, and another rises out of his Ashes to be a Companion with *Christian*. (*PP*, pp. 96–7)

Christian's exchanges with others eventually become mere excuses to assert his own belief as the ultimate truth – exercises in self-justification and morale-boosting, in effect, rather than genuine explorations of the virtues or otherwise of different value-systems. Talkative's complaint to Christian and Faithful that 'you lie at the catch, I perceive' to confuse him, is only too heartfelt (*PP*, p. 80).

There is no real dialogue taking place in these situations; instead, confrontation is the order of the day, as Christian and his associates seek to find gaps in their fellow travellers' doctrinal understanding. If contested in any way by his opponents Christian can always take refuge in a string of biblical quotations and references. Like all good fundamentalists Christian has his sacred text to fall back on when trouble looms, and his uncritical use of it suggests that he shares the modern-day fundamentalist's belief in its inerrancy. *'Except the word of God beareth witness in this matter, other Testimony is of no value'* (*PP*, p. 138): debate over as far as this believer is concerned. To argue with Christian is to argue with the Bible, and that is an argument no-one can win in a society which takes biblical inerrancy for granted. It will never save you to protest that, 'this kind of discourse I did not expect' (*PP*, p. 82): you must not just expect but positively welcome theological discussion, and be ready to set aside all your own desires and emotions to become a champion of 'the Word'. To shy away from this duty is to take on the aura of the reprobate, and Talkative, like the majority who debate with Christian, is duly 'caught'.

The Holy War is an altogether more violent work than *The Pilgrim's Progress*, with large-scale pitched battles punctuating the action at regular intervals, and an ending which is pictured as a mere temporary respite in an epic conflict between good and evil which has by no means run its course yet. Despite three rescues in a row by Emmanuel, Mansoul is warned that he must be prepared to *'watch and fight'* on into the future as the still-at-large forces of the unrepentant Diabolus renew their efforts at conquest.[15] There are no grey areas in this struggle: either you are for Emmanuel or you are for Diabolus, and both sides are totally convinced of the justice of their cause. Each claims full sovereignty over Mansoul, with Emmanuel proclaiming, *'Let all men know who are concerned, That the Son of* Shaddai *the great King, is ingaged by Covenant to his Father, to bring his* Mansoul *to him again'*;[16] whereas Diabolus warns the town's inhabitants that, *'they should never desert him, nor his Government, nor*

---

15 *The Holy War*, eds Roger Sharrock and James F. Forrest (Oxford: Clarendon Press, 1980), p. 249.
16 Ibid., p. 29.

yet betray him, nor seek to alter his Laws; but that they should own, confess, stand by, and acknowledge him for their rightful King'.[17] Neither statement is exactly a basis for talks towards a negotiated settlement: the other is accorded no credibility whatsoever and nothing less than total domination will be countenanced by either party to the dispute. We have what Jean-François Lyotard calls a 'differend': mutually exclusive claims, the continued pursuit of which can only end badly – the kind of situation in which fundamentalism traditionally thrives.[18] As we have seen, there is nothing more calculated to inspire a fundamentalist than a fight over principles.

Mansoul must display its integrity by rising up from repeated defeat by the Diabolonians and re-embracing Christian virtue: again, any move towards accommodation with one's opponent can only be treated as weakness. There is one true way to behave, and you must adhere to it despite all the attempts being made to deflect you: '*and now I will tell thee what at present must be thy duty and practice, until I shall come and fetch thee to my self, according as is related in the Scriptures of truth*'.[19] Mansoul's 'tenaciousness' is impressive, especially given the harsh treatment meted out by the enemy hordes in battle:

> these *Diabolonian* Doubters turned the men of *Mansoul* out of their Beds, and now I will add, they wounded them, they mauled them, yea, and almost brained many of them. Many, did I say, yea most, if not all of them.[20]

But it is the tenaciousness of the fundamentalist believer whose commitment is only ever strengthened by the experience of adversity, and who comes to accept unquestioningly Emmanuel's demand that '*thou must live upon my Word*'.[21] The authoritarianism underpinning the fundamentalist ethos becomes very evident at such points.

---

17   Ibid., p. 31.
18   See Jean-François Lyotard, *The Differend: Phrases in Dispute*, trans. Georges Van Den Abbeele (Manchester: Manchester University Press, 1988).
19   *The Holy War*, p. 248.
20   Ibid., p. 205.
21   Ibid., p. 250.

Debate in *The Holy War* is reduced to an exchange of slogans by the opposed parties: dogma rules. Opponents are, in the strictest sense, demonised. The Diabolonians are pictured as pure evil without a redeeming feature to their name, forever excluded from God's grace and the charmed circle of the true believers. Those who do not take up the offer of 'the Word' can expect no mercy, and will be granted none by an Emmanuel who will be satisfied with nothing less than total obedience to his will:

> *I also compassed thee about, and afflicted thee on every side, that I might make thee weary of thy ways, and bring down thy heart with molestation to a willingness to close with thy good and happiness. And when I had gotten a compleat conquest over thee, I turned it to thy advantage.*[22]

Dissent is effectively outlawed under such a regime, which allows no scope for deviation from its core beliefs: 'compleat conquest' makes this very clear. Even more insidiously, the textual metaphor makes us aware that this is a process of self-policing that is occurring within the individual: this particular 'Mansoul' is fundamentalizing himself. Doubt is banished and certainty comes to prevail. What we observe over the course of *The Holy War* is no less than the creation of the fundamentalist temperament; the individual moulding himself to the belief-system such that they present a united front to what is assumed to be a hostile outside world.

Finally, what are we to make of *The Life and Death of Mr Badman*? There is not even the pretence of debate in this text. Mr Badman is dead and consigned to hell before the story begins: no possibility at all remaining of redemption in his case. Wiseman and Attentive are two of the least forgiving figures in Bunyan's fiction, patently agents of God's justice rather than his mercy, and the narrative turns into an unrelieved litany of all Badman's many faults; the monitory tale of a man '*polluted, very much polluted with Original Corruption*', who recklessly plots his own damnation despite all the warnings and advice he is given by friends and family.[23] Again and

---

22 Ibid., p. 246.
23 *The Life and Death of Mr Badman*, eds James F. Forrest and Roger Sharrock (Oxford: Clarendon Press, 1988), p. 17.

again we are assured by Wiseman and Attentive that Badman had been a hopeless cause from the very beginning and that everything about his life signalled a bad end: 'an *angry, wrathfull, envious* man, a man that knew not what meekness or gentleness meant, nor did he desire to learn'.[24] The authority of 'the Word' manifestly has been denied in this instance, and the character must face the dire consequences that follow on from his foolish decision to live as he pleases.

The narrative amounts to a remorseless piece of character assassination by Wiseman and Attentive, who are only too happy to pass sentence and then dance on this unfortunate individual's grave. In true fundamentalist fashion, it is a case of 'us' and 'them', and Badman is clearly 'not one of us': as such, he merits absolutely no sympathy at all, being reduced almost to the status of a non-person. The reprobate do not count in this world-view, except as a stark reminder of the ever-present threat of God's wrath being visited upon the sinful. (Just to keep us all aware of how vulnerable we are in the latter regard, the narrative also contains the lurid tale, taken from Clarke's *Looking-glass for Sinners,* of the couple 'committing Adultery in *London* [...] struck dead with fire from Heaven, in the very Act'.[25] 'The Word' must be obeyed, or else.) It is dogmatism of the most extreme kind, and there is an unpleasant smugness to Wiseman and Attentive's judgement of their compatriot: 'He died that he might die, he went from Life to Death, and then from Death to Death, from Death Natural to Death Eternal'.[26] End of story, end of debate: there is nothing that can be said after this early declaration that can alter the unfortunate Badman's fate – nor would his fundamentalist-minded judges wish to do so.

Whereas *The Pilgrim's Progress* and *The Holy War* showed us the process by which fundamentalism took hold in the individual, *Badman* gives us the finished product in Wiseman and Attentive, secure in their self-righteousness and implacable foes of those who refuse to toe their party-line. Bunyan's fiction up to Part Two of *The Pilgrim's Progress* certainly suggests that most of humankind are

24 Ibid., p. 129.
25 Ibid., p. 56.
26 Ibid., p. 14.

guilty of the latter failing: as the author's prefatory remarks to *Badman* warn us, 'Mr Badman *has left many of his Relations behind him; yea, the very World is overspread with his Kindred.* [...] The butt therefore, that at this time I shoot at, is wide'.[27] True believers can only feel vindicated in their self-righteousness by such a state of affairs. If Part Two takes a more kindly view of human weakness (with even Mr Feeble-mind and Mr Despondency being granted salvation), then I can only reiterate the point made earlier, that this is not the Bunyan that later generations, particularly later generations of radicals, appropriate to their cause. It is the Bunyan whose hero Christian goes through the harrowing experiences of the Valley of the Shadow of Death, Doubting Castle and imprisonment by Giant Despair, to come out all the stronger in his belief, all the more determined to continue his struggles, that inspires.

A Problematical Legacy?

So, is Bunyan definable as a fundamentalist? That is, as someone intolerant, repressive, authoritarian, and biblically literalist? I would argue that in many ways he is, an amalgam of Christian and Wiseman (the most hard-line of *Badman*'s interlocutors) in this respect, but that we have to be careful to put this in historical context. It was Bunyan who was the victim of repression after all, not the political-religious establishment that outlawed nonconformity, and we might assume a certain element of wish-fulfilment on the author's part in the consignment of such as Ignorance to hell on their collective behalf. The severity of the times could not but encourage a fundamentalist mindset in beleaguered nonconformists. Bunyan was not alone in being fundamentalist in his outlook either: it was shared by many in what was, after all, still a deeply religious society in which the Bible carried an immense weight of authority and biblical literalism was practically the default position for believers (think of Filmer's construction of a

27 Ibid., p. 1.

line of divine right extending from Adam through the biblical kings to the current English monarchy, as a case in point).[28] Latitudinarianism can appear a much more positive phenomenon than Bunyan sympathisers traditionally tend to regard it under the circumstances. It represents a move away from the dogmatic temperament that marked so much nonconformism ('enthusiasm', in other words), and it points towards a more secular society in which intensity of belief is not necessarily to be seen as an admirable characteristic.

Yet intensity of belief finds other ways to express itself: through politics, for example. Political radicals can come to be just as fundamentalist in outlook as their religious counterparts, and it is on that basis that some strange alliances can be forged. It is more than somewhat strange that Marxists, for whom religion is one of the most oppressive forces in human history, the 'opiate of the masses' and all that, often can find a kindred spirit in Bunyan. What speaks to them, it would seem, is that intensity of belief, 'the spirit of the men and women who had lived and died for Protestantism' in West's admiring words, as well as Bunyan's patent integrity in the face of political tyranny,[29] the refusal to back down from authority or to negotiate with it and thus become complicit in its domination over one's society. That latter characteristic is seen to particular advantage in Bunyan's own trial and imprisonment, of course, where adhering to one's beliefs in the face of the might of the Stuart state, as symbolized by the forbidding Bedford Justices, is an act of considerable personal heroism. Bunyan steadfastly refuses to back down under cross-examination as to his lay-preaching intentions: 'I told him, as to this matter, I was at a point with him: For if I was out of prison to day, I would preach the Gospel again to-morrow, by the help of God'.[30] The implicit assumption of many Marxists is that if Bunyan were alive today he would be fighting on the side of the oppressed, an overtly

---

28　See Sir Robert Filmer, *Patriarcha*, in *Patriarcha and Other Writings*, ed. Johann P. Somerville (Cambridge: Cambridge University Press, 1991).
29　West, *The Mountain in the Sunlight*, p. 152.
30　Bunyan, *A Relation of My Imprisonment*, in *Grace Abounding to the Chief of Sinners*, ed. Roger Sharrock (Oxford: Clarendon Press, 1962), pp. 105–31 (p. 118).

political rebel rather than a religious zealot. Perhaps; but he might just as easily be defending the values of groups like the Christian Coalition in America. For that latter constituency, the world is still overspread with Badman's kindred and relations, who will be duly punished by a vengeful God at the appropriate time. Bunyan certainly can be drawn on by fundamentalist Christians today, and is (the Rev. Ian Paisley is a notable fan); and they are hardly a source of support for the Marxist project, however it might be construed.

Nevertheless, Marxists are still capable of turning Bunyan into a working-class hero, and I would suggest that it is precisely his fundamentalist side that appeals to them. In *Fundamentalist World* I define Marxism as a form of political fundamentalism – right down to its possession of sacred texts such as *The Communist Manifesto* and *Capital*. Those texts proclaim the historical necessity of the forthcoming dictatorship of the proletariat, and, I argue, 'the notion that one is being carried along by historical necessity can soon take on a fundamentalist character'.[31] So it *is* perhaps a case of fundamentalists speaking unto fellow fundamentalists: a recognition of a similar mentality to one's own, the mentality that knows it is on the side of the truth and is unwilling to compromise its belief in any way – the 'tenaciousness' praised by Hill. While this can be an admirable characteristic in someone in Bunyan's situation in a turbulent historical period (and I am certainly not going to defend the Restoration regime as a bastion of liberal and pluralist thought), it is less so now in the aftermath of Marxism's historical record in the twentieth century – never mind Christian fundamentalism's sinister activities in America in recent years. There we can find aggressively-run campaigns against abortion and sexual difference, and the championship of the teaching of creationism in schools (something that has even crept into Britain of late, much to the dismay of liberals and the left[32]). The good side of

31   Sim, *Fundamentalist World*, p. 54. For an analysis of the role played by necessity in Bunyan's fiction, see idem, '"Transworld Depravity" and "Invariant Assertions": John Bunyan's Possible Worlds', in *John Bunyan: Reading Dissenting Writing*, ed. N. H. Keeble (Bern and Oxford: Peter Lang, 2002), pp. 245-61.

32   The most notable example of this is Emmanuel College in Gateshead, the first of a burgeoning network of faith-based schools sponsored by the Vardy

Bunyan's tenaciousness is its anti-authority mindedness; the bad side, its utter conviction of rightness and refusal to accept the possibility of shades of truth – or pluralism, as most of us would describe it now. It is not always that easy to disentangle the two, however, and Bunyan's legacy is a highly complex one in that respect – perhaps more problematical after all than some of us working in the area would like to think.

Foundation. Depressingly enough, and despite loud protests from intellectual circles, this initiative has been approved by the New Labour government. Francis Wheen for one has been particularly critical, arguing that Tony Blair's support for the project 'marked a new low in contemporary British political discourse'; see his *How Mumbo-Jumbo Conquered the World: A Short History of Modern Delusions* (HarperCollins: London, 2004), p. 115.

Bibliography

Editions and translations of Bunyan cited

Bunyan's Pilgrim's Progress in Modern English, ed. John Morrison, London: Macmillan, 1896
Die Christen se Reis na die Ewigheid [*The Pilgrim's Progress*], Cape Town: N. G. Kerk-uitgewers van Suid-Afrika, n.d.
The Christian Life: An Exposition of Bunyan's Pilgrim's Progress, ed. James Black, 2 vols, London: James Nisbet, 1873
Grace Abounding to the Chief of Sinners, ed. W. R. Owens, London: Penguin, 1987
Grace Abounding to the Chief of Sinners, ed. Roger Sharrock, Oxford: Clarendon Press, 1962
Grace Abounding with Other Spiritual Autobiographies, ed. John Stachniewski and Anita Pacheco, Oxford: Oxford University Press, 1998
The Holy War, ed. Roger Sharrock and James F. Forrest, Oxford: Clarendon Press, 1980
Illustrations of the Pilgrim's Progress: Accompanied with Extracts from the Work, and Descriptions of the Plates, by Bernard Barton. And a Biographical Sketch of the Life & Writings of Bunyan, by Josiah Conder, London: Fisher, Son & Co.; Paris: Quai des Grands Augustins, [1836]
John Bunyan's 'The Pilgrim's Progress', London: Rivington, 1826
Leeto la mokreste [*The Pilgrim's Progress*], trans. Adolphe Mabille and Filemone Rapetloane, 1896; rep. Morija: Morija Sesuto Book Depot, 1988
The Life and Death of Mr. Badman, eds James. F. Forrest and Roger Sharrock, Oxford: Clarendon Press, 1988
The Pilgrim's Progress. Edinburgh: Andrew Stevenson, n.d.
The Pilgrim's Progress, ed. George Burder, London, 1786

The Pilgrim's Progress, ed. Robert Southey, London: John Murray and John Major, 1830

The Pilgrim's Progress collated, for the first time, with the early editions, London: George Virtue, 1850

The Pilgrim's Progress, with explanatory notes by William Mason, London: T. Nelson and Sons, 1857

The Pilgrim's Progress, ed. Charles Kingsley, London: Longman, Green, Longman & Roberts, 1860

The Pilgrim's Progress As John Bunyan Wrote It, London: Elliot Stock, 1895

The Pilgrim's Progress, illustrated by George Wooliscroft Rhead, Frederick Rhead and Louis Rhead, London: Pearson, 1898

The Pilgrim's Progress, ed. Edmund Venables, Oxford: Clarendon Press, 1900

The Pilgrim's Progress, ed. C. H. Firth, London: Methuen, 1908

The Pilgrim's Progress, ed. W. R. Owens, Oxford: Oxford University Press, 2003

The Pilgrim's Progress, Parts One and Two, ed. J. B. Wharey, rev. Roger Sharrock, Oxford: Clarendon Press, 1928, 1960

Zamlendo wamkrisitu kwa ana [*The Pilgrim's Progress*], n. p.: Church of Scotland Mission, 1902

Uhambo lo Mhambi [*The Pilgrim's Progress*], trans. Tiyo Soga and John Henderson Soga, 1868; Lovedale: Lovedale Press, 1937

Other works cited

Ackroyd, Peter, *English Music*, London: Hamish Hamilton, 1992

Althusser, Louis, 'Ideology and Ideological State Apparatuses', in *Lenin and Philosophy*, trans. B. Brewster, London: New Left Books, 1971

Altick, Richard D., *The English Common Reader 1800–1900: A Social History of the Mass Reading Public*, Chicago: University of Chicago Press, 1957

Altman, Rick, *Film/Genre*, London: British Film Institute, 1999
Anderson, Patricia, *The Printed Image and the Transformation of Popular Culture 1790–1860*, Oxford: Clarendon Press, 1991
Arnold-Foster, Frances, *Heralds of the Cross or the Fulfilling of the Command: Chapters on Missionary Work*, London: Hatchards, 1885
Auden, W. H., *The English Auden*, ed. Edward Mendelson, London: Faber and Faber, 1977
Badder, David, 'Powell and Pressburger: The War Years', *Sight and Sound*, 48 (1978/79), 8–12
Bain, J. A. Kerr, ed., *The People of the Pilgrimage: An Expository Study of 'The Pilgrim's Progress' as a Book of Character*, 2 vols, Edinburgh and London: Nacmiven and Wallace and Hodder and Stoughton, 1887
Baird, John D. and Charles Ryskamp, eds, *The Poems of William Cowper*, 3 vols, Oxford: Clarendon Press, 1980–95
Bebbington, D. W., *Evangelicalism in Modern Britain: A History from the 1730s to the 1980s*, London: Unwin Hyman, 1989
——, *The Nonconformist Conscience: Chapel and Politics 1870–1912*, Boston: Allen & Unwin, 1982
Beckett, Samuel, *Molloy* (1955) in *The Beckett Trilogy*, London: Picador, 1979
Bennett, Tony, *Outside Literature*, London: Routledge, 1990
Bentley, G. E., 'Flaxman's Drawings for *Pilgrim's Progress*', in *Woman in the Eighteenth Century and Other Essays*, eds Paul Fritz and Richard Morton, Toronto: Samuel Stevens Hakkert & Co., 1976
—— ed., *William Blake's Writings*, 3 vols, Oxford: Oxford University Press, 1978
——, *The Stranger from Paradise: A Biography of William Blake*, New Haven, CT and London: Yale University Press, 2001
Birrell, Augustine, 'John Bunyan Today', *The Bookman*, 73, no. 435 (1927), 148–9
Björk, L. A., ed., *The Literary Notebooks of Thomas Hardy*, 2 vols, London: Macmillan, 1985
Blatchford, Robert, *My Favourite Books*, London: Walter Scott, 1900

Bloom, Harold, *The Anxiety of Influence*, Oxford: Oxford University Press, 1973
Boswell, James, *The Life of Samuel Johnson, LL.D*, 2 vols, London: J. M. Dent, 1949
Brittain, Vera, *In the Steps of John Bunyan: An Excursion into Puritan England*, London: Rich and Cowan, 1950
Brown, John, *Bunyan's Home*, London: Ernest Nister, n.d.
——, *John Bunyan: His Life Times and Work*, London: Isbister, 1900; rev. ed. Frank Mott Harrison, London: Hulbert Publishing Company, 1928
Brown, Sylvia, 'Bunyan among the Eskimos: Missionary Translations of Pilgrim's Progress into Inuktitut', paper presented to The International John Bunyan Society, Fourth Triennial Conference, The Open University and De Montfort University, Bedford, 1–5 September 2004.
Brown, Terence, 'MacNeice and the Puritan Tradition', in *Louis MacNeice and his Influence*, eds K. Devine and A. J. Peacock, Gerrards Cross: Colin Smythe, 1998
Buning, Marius, Matthijs Engelberts and Onno Kosters, eds, *Beckett and Religion* Amsterdam: Rodopi, 2000
Burbidge, John, *Half-hours with Bunyan's Pilgrim's Progress*, Liverpool: J A Thompson, 1856
Camden, Vera, 'Blasphemy and the Problem of the Self in *Grace Abounding*', *Bunyan Studies*, 1:2 (1989), 5–21
Chalmers, John A, *Tiyo Soga: A Page of South African Mission Work*, Edinburgh: Andrew Elliot, 1877
Chambers, Douglas, *The Reinvention of the World: English Writing 1650–1750* (London: Arnold, 1996)
Chandler, James, *England in 1819: The Politics of Literary Culture and the Case of Romantic Historicism*, Chicago and London: Chicago University Press, 1998
Christie, Ian, *Arrows of Desire: The Films of Michael Powell and Emeric Pressburger*, London: Faber and Faber, 1994
——, *A Matter of Life and Death*, London: BFI Publishing, 2000
——, and Andrew Moor, eds, *The Cinema of Michael Powell: International Perspectives on an English Film-Maker*, London: BFI Publishing, 2005

Clark, David J. and Gerard McCoy, *The Most Fundamental Legal Right: Habeas Corpus in the Commonwealth*, Oxford: Oxford University Press, 2000
Clark, J. C. D., *English Society 1660–1832*, Cambridge: Cambridge University Press, 2000
Cockett, C. Bernard, *Bunyan's England: A Tour with the Camera in the Footsteps of the Immortal Dreamer*, Luton: Leagrave Press, 1948
——, *John Bunyan's England*, London: Homeland Association, 1928
Colley, Linda, *Britons: Forging the Nation 1707–1837*, second edn, New Haven and London: Yale University Press, 2005
Collmer, Robert G., 'Bunyan and the Marxists', *Christianity and Literature*, 28 (1978), 14–16
Colls, Robert and Philip Dodds, eds, *Englishness: Politics and Culture 1880–1920*, London: Croom Helm, 1986
——, *Identity of England*, Oxford: Oxford University Press, 2002
A Colonial Pilgrim, *Footsteps of The Pilgrim's Progress: A Key of the Allegory*, London: Premier Publishing, n.d.
Coulton, Barbara, *Louis MacNeice in the BBC*, London: Faber and Faber, 1980
Cutt, Margaret Nancy, *Ministering Angels: A Study of Nineteenth-century Evangelical Writing for Children*, Wormley: Five Owls Press, 1979
Damrosch, David, *What is World Literature?*, Princeton: Princeton University Press, 2003
Davies, Michael, *Graceful Reading: Theology and Narrative in the Works of John Bunyan*, Oxford: Oxford University Press, 2002
Dickens, Charles, *The Old Curiosity Shop*, ed. Angus Easson, Harmondsworth: Penguin Books, 1985
——, *A Christmas Carol*, ed. Michael Slater, Harmondsworth: Penguin Books, 1985
——, *Our Mutual Friend*, ed. Stephen Gill, Harmondsworth: Penguin Books, 1985
Dixon, A. C., ed., *The Fundamentals*, 1910–15; New York and London: Garland, 1988
Downie, John, ed., *Macaulay's Essay on Milton*, London: Blackie and Son, 1950

Doyle, Brian, *English and Englishness*, London: Routledge, 1989

Driver, Tom, 'Beckett by the Madeleine', in *Samuel Beckett: The Critical Heritage*, eds Raymond Federman and Lawrence Graver, London: Routledge & Kegan Paul, 1979

Duckworth, Colin, 'Beckett and the Missing Sharer', in *Beckett and Religion*, eds Marius Buning, Mattijs Engelberts and Onno Kosters, Amsterdam: Rodopi, 2000

Eliot, George, *Middlemarch*, ed. W. J. Harvey, Harmondsworth: Penguin Books, 1985

Ellis, Steve, 'Dante and Louis MacNeice: A Sequel to the *Commedia*', in *Dante's Afterlife: Reception and Response from Blake to Heaney*, ed. N. H. Havely, Basingstoke: Macmillan, 1998

Ellis, William, *Faithful unto Death: The Story of the Founding and Preservation of the Martyr Church of Madagascar*, London: John Snow, 1876

——, *History of Madagascar*, Vol. 2, London: Fisher, n.d.

——, *The Martyr Church: A Narrative of the Introduction, Progress and Triumph of Christianity in Madagascar*, London: John Snow, 1870

Federman, Raymond and Lawrence Graver, eds., *Samuel Beckett: The Critical Heritage*, London: Routledge & Kegan Paul, 1979

Filmer, Sir Robert, *Patriarcha and Other Writings*, ed. Johann P. Somerville, Cambridge: Cambridge University Press, 1991

Foster, Albert J., *Bunyan's Country: Studies in the Bedford Topography of The Pilgrim's Progress*, London: H. Virtue, 1901

Freud, Sigmund, *The Interpretation of Dreams*, 1953; Harmondsworth: Penguin, 1978

Froude, J. A., *Bunyan*, London: Macmillan, 1880

Frye, Northrop, *Anatomy of Criticism*, 1957; Princeton: Princeton University Press, 1971

——, *The Secular Scripture: A Study of the Structure of Romance*, London: Harvard University Press, 1976

Fussell, *The Great War and Modern Memory*, Oxford: Oxford University Press, 1975

Gash, Norman, *Aristocracy and People: Britain 1815–1865*, London: Edward Arnold, 1979

Gifford, Douglas, 'Scott's Fiction and the Search for Mythic Regeneration', in *Scott and His Influence*, eds J. H. Alexander and David Hewitt, Aberdeen: Association for Scottish Literary Studies, 1983

Godwin, William, *History of the Commonwealth of England*, 4 vols, London, Henry Colburn, 1824–8

Gough-Yates, Kevin, ed., *Michael Powell: In Collaboration with Emeric Pressburger*, London: National Film Theatre, 1970

——, 'Pressburger, England and Exile', *Sight and Sound*, 12 (1995), 30–5

Gow, Bonar A., *Madagascar and the Protestant Impact: The Work of British Missionaries, 1818–95*, London: Longman and Dalhousie University Press, 1979

Greaves, Richard L., 'Bunyan through the Centuries: Some Reflections', *English Studies*, 64 (1983), 113–21.

——, *Glimpses of Glory: John Bunyan and English Dissent*, Stanford: Stanford University Press, 2002

Gupta, M. G., *Mystic Symbolism in Ramayan, Mahabharat and The Pilgrim's Progress*, Agra: M G Publishers, 1993

Hancock, Maxine, 'Bunyan as Reader: The Record of *Grace Abounding*', *Bunyan Studies*, 5 (1999), 68–86

Hargreaves, Cyril and M. Greenshields, eds, *Catalogue of the Bunyan Meeting Library and Museum, Bedford*, Bedford: Bunyan Meeting House, 1955

Patricia Harkin, 'Romance and Real History: The Historical Novel as Literary Innovation', in *Scott and his Influence*, eds J. H. Alexander and David Hewitt, Aberdeen: Association for Scottish Literary Studies, 1983

Harper, Charles G., *The Bunyan Country: Landmarks of The Pilgrim's Progress*, London: Cecil Palmer, 1928

Harrison, F. M., 'Some Illustrators of *The Pilgrim's Progress*, Part One', *The Library*, 3 (1936), 241–63

Harvey, Kenneth D., 'The Best Seller that began with a Jail Sentence', *Belfast Telegraph*, 4 March 1978, p. 7

Hazlitt, William, *The Spirit of the Age*, ed. E. D. Mackerness, London: Northcote House, 1991

Herreshoff, David, 'Marxist Perspectives on Bunyan', in *Bunyan in Our Time*, ed. Robert G. Collmer, Kent OH and London: Kent State University Press, 1989

Hill, Christopher, 'Bunyan's Contemporary Reputation', in *John Bunyan and his England 1628–88*, eds Anne Laurence, W. R. Owens, and Stuart Sim, London: The Hambledon Press, 1990

——, *A Turbulent, Seditious, and Factious People: John Bunyan and his Church*, Oxford: Oxford University Press, 1988; published in USA as *A Tinker and a Poor Man: John Bunyan and his Church, 1628–1688*, New York: W. W. Norton, 1988

Hofmeyr, Isabel, *The Portable Bunyan: A Transnational History of The Pilgrim's Progress*, Princeton: Princeton University Press, 2004

——, 'Mini-missionaries: The Travelling Text as Evangelical Trope', *Yearly Review* (University of Delhi), 12 (2004), 77–93

——, 'Transnational Textualities', in Jamie Scott and Gareth Griffiths, eds, *Mixed Messages: Materiality, Textuality, Missions*, London: Palgrave MacMillan, in press

Hough, Graham, *A Preface to 'The Faerie Queene'*, London: Duckworth, 1962

Howkins, Alan, 'The Discovery of Rural England', in *Englishness: Politics and Culture 1880–1920*, eds Robert Colls and Philip Dodds, London: Croom Helm, 1986

Howsam, Leslie, *Cheap Bibles: Nineteenth-Century Publishing and the British and Foreign Bible Society*, Cambridge: Cambridge University Press, 1991

Howson, J. S., 'Lecture VI, *The Pilgrim's Progress*', in *The St. James's Lectures: Companions for the Devout Life*, London: Longmans, Green, Reader, and Dyer, 1874

Hume, David, 'Of the Standard of Taste', in *Essays Moral, Political, and Literary*, ed. Eugene F. Miller, Indianapolis: Liberty Fund, rev. edn, 1985

——, *The History of England*, 6 vols, Indianapolis: Liberty Fund, rev. edn, 1983

Irwin, John T., 'MacNeice, Auden, and the Art Ballad', *Contemporary Literature*, 11 (1970), 58–79

Ishay, Micheline R., ed., *The Human Rights Reader: Major Political Essays, Speeches, and Documents from the Bible to the Present*, London and New York: Routledge, 1997

Johnson, Barbara A., *Reading 'Piers Plowman' and 'The Pilgrim's Progress': Reception and the Protestant Reader*, Carbondale and Edwardsville, Ill.: Southern Illinois University Press, 1991

Jones, David Houston, 'Que Foutait dieu avant la creation: Disabling Sources in Beckett and Augustine', in *Beckett and Religion*, eds Marius Buning, Mattijs Engelberts and Omno Kosters, Amsterdam: Rodopi, 2000

Jung, C. J., *Analytic Psychology: Its Theory and Practice. The Tavistock Lectures, 1935*, London: Routledge & Kegan Paul, 1968

Keating, Peter, *The Haunted Study: A Social History of the English Novel 1875–1914*, London: Secker and Warburg, 1989

Keeble, N. H., '"Of Him Thousands Daily Sing and Talk": Bunyan and His Reputation', in *John Bunyan: Conventicle and Parnassus*, ed. N. H. Keeble, Oxford: Clarendon Press, 1988

Kelman, John, *The Road: A Study of John Bunyan's Pilgrim's Progress*, 2 vols, Edinburgh and London: Oliphant, Anderson and Ferrir, 1912

Kettle, Arnold, *An Introduction to the English Novel*, 2 vols, London: Hutchinson, 1965

Keynes, Flora Ada, *Gathering up the Threads: A Study in Family Biography*, Cambridge: W Heffer, 1950

King, James and Charles Ryskamp, eds, *The Letters and Prose Writings of William Cowper*, 5 vols, Oxford: Clarendon Press, 1979–86

Kingsley, Charles, *Alton Locke*, London: Chapman and Hall, 1850

——, *Yeast*, London: Parker and Son, 1851

——, *The Water-Babies*, London: Macmillan, 1863

Kingsley, F. E., ed., *Charles Kingsley: His Letters and Memories of his Life*, 2 vols, London: Henry S. King, 1877

Kitson, Peter, '"Sages and patriots that being dead do yet speak to us": Readings of the English Revolution in the Late Eighteenth Century', in *Pamphlet Wars: Prose in the English Revolution*, ed. James Holstun, London: Frank Cassell, 1992

——, '"Not a reforming patriot": Representations of Cromwell and the English Republic in the Late Eighteenth and Early Nineteenth Centuries', in *Radicalism in British Literary Culture, 1650–1830*, eds Timothy Morton and Nigel Smith, Cambridge: Cambridge University Press, 2002

Kittel, Gerhard, ed., *Theological Dictionary of the New Testament*, trans. G. W. Bromiley, 10 vols, Grand Rapids, Michigan: W. B. Eerdmans, 1964–76

Knott, Jr., John R., *The Sword of the Spirit: Puritan Responses to the Bible*, Chicago: University of Chicago Press, 1980

Kroll, Richard, 'Defoe and Early Narrative', in *The Columbia History of the British Novel*, ed. John Richetti, New York: Columbia University Press, 1994

Lazar, David, ed., *Michael Powell: Interviews*, Jackson Miss.: University Press of Mississippi, 2003

Leavis, Q. D., *Fiction and the Reading Public*, London: Chatto & Windus, 1932

Lindsay, Jack, *John Bunyan: Maker of Myths*, London: Methuen, 1937

Luxon, Thomas, *Literal Figures: Puritan Allegory and the Reformation Crisis in Representation*, Chicago and London: University of Chicago Press, 1995

Lyotard, Jean-François, *The Differend: Phrases in Dispute*, trans. Georges Van Den Abbeele, Manchester: Manchester University Press, 1988

Macaulay, Thomas Babington, review of Southey's edition of *The Pilgrim's Progress*, *The Edinburgh Review*, 54, no. 108, December 1831, pp. 450–61

——, *Critical and Historical Essays Contributed to the Edinburgh Review*, 3 vols, London: Longman, 1843

Macdonald, Kevin, *Emeric Pressburger: The Life and Death of a Screenwriter*, London: Faber and Faber, 1994

Maclean, Catherine Macdonald, *Mark Rutherford: A Biography of William Hale White*, London: Macdonald & Co., 1955

MacLennan, George, *Lucid Interval: Subjective Writing and Madness in History*, Leicester: Leicester University Press, 1992

MacNeice, John, *Carrickfergus and its Contacts*, London and Belfast: Simpkin, Marshall, Ltd., and W. Erskine Mayne, 1928

MacNeice, Louis, *I Crossed the Minch*, London: Longmans, Green and Co., 1938
——, *The Strings are False: An Unfinished Autobiography*, ed. E. R. Dodds, London: Faber and Faber, 1965
——, *Varieties of Parable*, Cambridge: Cambridge University Press, 1965
——, *Collected Poems*, ed. E. R. Dodds, London: Faber and Faber, 1979
——, *Selected Literary Criticism*, ed. Alan Heuser, Oxford: Clarendon Press, 1987
——, *Selected Plays of Louis MacNeice*, eds A. Heuser and P. McDonald, Oxford: Clarendon Press, 1993
Mallock, W. H., *Is Life Worth Living?*, London: Chatto & Windus, 1880
Manning, John, *The Emblem*, London: Reaktion, 2002
Manning, Robert, '*The Pilgrim's Progress*: A Vindication and Celebration of Vaughan Williams's Neglected Masterpiece', *Bunyan Studies*, 6 (1995/6), 70–7
Marsden, George M., *Fundamentalism and American Culture: The Shaping of Twentieth-Century Evangelism, 1870–1925*, New York and Oxford: Oxford University Press, 1980
Marshall, Peter, *William Godwin*, New Haven and London: Yale University Press, 1984
McCalman, Ian, *Radical Underworld: Prophets, Revolutionaries and Pornographers in London, 1795–1840*, Oxford: Oxford University Press, 1998
McDonald, Peter, *Louis MacNeice: The Poet in his Contexts*, Oxford: Clarendon Press, 1991
McKeon, Michael, *The Origins of the English Novel 1600–1740*, Baltimore: The Johns Hopkins University Press, 1987
McVeagh, John, *Tradefull Merchants: The Portrayal of the Capitalist in Literature*, London: Routledge and Kegan Paul, 1981
Melanchthon, Philip, *The Confession of Faith which was Submitted to His Imperial Majesty Charles V at the Diet of Augsburg in the Year 1530*, trans. G. F. Bente and W. H. T. Dau, in *Triglot Concordia: The Symbolical Books of the Evangelical-Lutheran Church*, St. Louis, Missouri: Concordia Publishing House, 1921

Mellors, Wilfrid, *Vaughan Williams and the Vision of Albion*, London: Barrie & Jenkins, 1989
Moor, Andrew, *Powell & Pressburger: A Cinema of Magic Spaces*, London and New York: I. B. Tauris, 2005
Newey, Vincent, ed., *The Pilgrim's Progress: Critical and Historical Views*, Liverpool: Liverpool University Press, 1980
——, *Cowper's Poetry: A Critical Study and Reassessment*, Liverpool: Liverpool University Press, 1982
——, 'Dorothea's Awakening: The Recall of Bunyan in *Middlemarch*', *Notes and Queries*, 229 (1984), 297–9
——, 'The Disinherited Pilgrim: *Jude the Obscure* and *The Pilgrim's Progress*', *Durham University Journal*, 75 (1987), 59–61
——, 'Mark Rutherford's Salvation and the Case of Catherine Furze', in *Mortal Pages, Literary Lives*, eds Vincent Newey and Philip Shaw, Aldershot: Scolar Press, 1996
——, *Scriptures of Charles Dickens: Novels of Ideology, Novels of the Self*, Aldershot: Ashgate, 2004
Newlyn, Lucy, *Paradise Lost and the Romantic Reader*, Oxford: Oxford University Press, 1993
Nicholes, Joseph, 'Revolutions Compared: The English Civil War as Political Touchstone in Romantic Literature', in *Revolution and English Romanticism*, eds Keith Hanley and Raman Selden, Hemel Hempstead: Harvester Wheatsheaf, 1990
Norvig, Gerda S., *Dark Figures in the Desired Country: Blake's Illustrations to 'The Pilgrim's Progress'*, Berkeley, CA: University of California Press, 1993
The Official Guide to Bunhill Fields, London: The Corporation of London, 1991
Owen, W. J. B. and Jane Worthington Smyser, eds, *The Prose Works of William Wordsworth*, 3 vols, Oxford: Clarendon Press, 1974
Owens, W. R., 'The Reception of *The Pilgrim's Progress* in England', in *Bunyan in England and Abroad*, eds M. van Os and G. J. Schutte, Amsterdam: VU University Press, 1990
Palmer D. J., *The Rise of English Studies: An Account of the Study of English Language and Literature from its Origins to the Making of the Oxford English School*, London: Oxford University Press, 1965

Parfitt, George, *Fiction of the First World War*, London: Faber and Faber, 1988

Paulin, Tom, *The Day Star of Liberty: William Hazlitt's Radical Style*, London: Faber, 1998

A Pilgrim, *Some Daily Thoughts on The Pilgrim's Progress*, London: Churchman Publishing Company, 1917

Piggin, Stuart, *Making Evangelical Missionaries 1789–1858: The Social Background, Motives and Training of British Protestant Missionaries to India*, Abingdon: Sutton Courtenay Press, 1984

Powell, Anthony, *Hearing Secret Harmonies*, 1975; London: Flamingo, 1983

Poynter, R. H., *Syllabus of Bunyan Lectures*, Bedford: Robinson, 1912

Primus, Richard, *The American Language of Rights*, Cambridge: Cambridge University Press, 1999

Propp, Vladimir, *The Morphology of the Folktale*, Austin, Tex.: University of Texas Press, 1968

Purdy, R. L. and M. Millgate, eds, *Collected Letters of Thomas Hardy*, 7 vols, Oxford: Clarendon Press, 1978–88

Qualls, Barry, *The Secular Pilgrims of Victorian Fiction*, Cambridge: Cambridge University Press, 1982

Quinlan, Maurice J., ed., *Memoir of the Early Life of William Cowper, Esq. Written by Himself*, Proceedings of the American Philosophical Society, 97 (1953), 359–82

Ralph, Arleane, '"They Do Such Musick Make": The Pilgrim's Progress and Textually Inspired Music', *Bunyan Studies*, 5 (1994), 58–67

A Relation of the Fearefull Estate of Francis Spira, in the yeare, 1548, trans. Nathaniel Bacon, London: Phil. Stephens and Christoph. Meredith, 1638

The Report of the Directors to the Fiftieth General Meeting of the Missionary Society Usually Called the London Missionary Society, London: London Missionary Society, 1844

Roe, Nicholas, *Wordsworth and Coleridge: The Radical Years*, Oxford: Clarendon Press, 1988

Rose, Jonathan, *The Intellectual Life of the British Working Classes*, New Haven: Yale University Press, 2001

Rutherford, Mark [William Hale White], *The Revolution in Tanner's Lane*, 1887; London: Hogarth Press, 1984
Ruthven, Malise, *The Divine Supermarket: Travels in Search of the Soul of America*, London: Chatto and Windus, 1989
——, *Fundamentalism: The Search for Meaning*, Oxford: Oxford University Press, 2004
Salmon, Edward G., 'What the Working Classes Read', *Nineteenth Century*, 20 (July 1886), 108–17
Salwolke, Scott, *The Films of Michael Powell and The Archers*, Lanham, Md. & London: Scarecrow Press, 1997
Salzman, Paul, *English Prose Fiction 1558–1700: A Critical History*, Oxford: Clarendon Press, 1985
Scott, Sir Walter, review of Southey's edition of *The Pilgrim's Progress*, *The Quarterly Review*, 43, no. 86 (October 1830), 469–94
——, *Old Mortality*, ed. Angus Calder, Harmondsworth: Penguin Books, 1985
Selous, Henry C., *A Portfolio of Outline Drawings, Illustrations of 'The Pilgrim's Progress', prepared for the Edition issued to the Subscribers of the Art Union of London*, London: H. M. Holloway, 1844
Sharpe, Robert J., *The Law of Habeas Corpus*, second edn, Oxford: Clarendon Press, 1989
Sharrock, Roger, ed., *The Pilgrim's Progress: A Selection of Critical Essays*, London: Macmillan, 1976
Sim, Stuart, *Negotiations with Paradox: Narrative Practice and Narrative Form in Bunyan and Defoe*, Hemel Hempstead: Harvester Wheatsheaf, 1990
—— and David Walker, *Bunyan and Authority: The Rhetoric of Dissent and the Legitimation Crisis in Seventeenth-Century England*, Bern: Peter Lang, 2000
——, '"Transworld Depravity" and "Invariant Assertions": John Bunyan's Possible Worlds', in *John Bunyan: Reading Dissenting Writing*, ed. N. H. Keeble, Bern and Oxford: Peter Lang, 2002
——, *Fundamentalist World: The New Dark Age of Dogma*, Cambridge: Icon Press, 2004

Smith, David E., 'Illustrations of American Editions of *The Pilgrim's Progress* to 1870', *Princeton University Library Chronicle*, 26 (1964), 16–26.

——, *John Bunyan in America*, Bloomington and London: Indiana University Press, 1966

Spargo, Tamsin, 'The Purloined Postcard: Waiting for Bunyan', *Textual Practice*, 8 (1994), 79–96

——, *The Writing of John Bunyan*, Aldershot: Ashgate, 1997

Spufford, Margaret, *Small Books and Pleasant Histories: Popular Fiction and its Readership in Seventeenth-Century England*, London: Methuen, 1981

Stachniewski, *The Persecutory Imagination: English Puritanism and the Literature of Religious Despair*, Oxford: Clarendon Press, 1991

Stennett, Richard, *The Fall of Public Man*, London: Faber & Faber, 1986

Stone, Lawrence, *The Family, Sex and Marriage in England 1600–1800*, Harmondsworth: Penguin Books, 1982

Sutcliffe, Peter, *The Oxford University Press: An Informal History*, Oxford: Oxford University Press, 1978

Sutherland, John, *The Life of Sir Walter Scott*, Oxford: Oxford University Press, 1995

Thompson, E. P., *The Making of the English Working Class*, 1963; rev. edn Harmondsworth: Penguin Books, 1972

——, *Witness against the Beast: William Blake and the Moral Law*, Cambridge: Cambridge University Press, 1993

Thorne, Susan, *Congregational Missions and the Making of an Imperial Culture in Nineteenth-century England*, Stanford: Stanford University Press, 1999

Tibbutt, H. G., 'The Dissenting Academies of Bedfordshire II – Bedford', *Bedfordshire Magazine*, 6: 41 (1957), 8–10.

——, *Bunyan Meeting Bedford 1650–1950*, Bedford: Trustees of Bunyan Meeting House, n.d.

Turner, James, 'Bunyan's Sense of Place', in *The Pilgrim's Progress: Critical and Historical Views*, ed. Vincent Newey, Liverpool: Liverpool University Press, 1980

Van Ghent, Dorothy, *The English Novel: Form and Function*, New York: Harper, 1961

Vance, Norman, 'Secular Apocalypse and Thomas Hardy', *History of European Ideas*, 26 (2000), 201–10

van 't Veld, Hendrick, *Beminde broeder die ik vand Op's werelts pilgrims wegen. Jan Luyken (1649–1712) als illustrator en medereiziger van John Bunyan 1628–1688*, Utrecht: Uitgeverij De Banier, 2000

——, 'Desired or Imposed? *The Pilgrim's Progress* in the Third World', Paper presented to The International John Bunyan Society, Fourth Triennial Conference, The Open University and De Montfort University, Bedford, 1–5 September 2004.

Vincent, David, *Literacy and Popular Culture, England 1750–1914*, Cambridge: Cambridge University Press, 1989

'The Voice of Africa: A Bit of Bunyan by Moses Mubitana', *Africa* 16:3 (1946), 179–82.

Waite, Terry, *Taken On Trust: Recollections from Captivity*, London: Hodder & Stoughton, 1993

Ward, Mary, *Robert Elsmere*, London: Smith Elder, 1888

——, *Marcella*, London: Smith Elder, 1894

——, *Sir George Tressady*, London: Smith Elder, 1896

Watt, Ian, *The Rise of the Novel: Studies in Defoe, Richardson and Fielding, 1957*; Harmondsworth: Penguin, 1983

West, Alick, *The Mountain in the Sunlight*, London: Lawrence and Wishart, 1958

Wheen, Francis, *How Mumbo-Jumbo Conquered the World: A Short History of Modern Delusions*, London: Harper-Collins, 2004

[White, William Hale,] *The Autobiography of Mark Rutherford, Dissenting Minister*, ed. William S. Peterson, Oxford: Oxford University Press, 1990

——, *Mark Rutherford's Deliverance*, Oxford: Oxford University Press, 1936

——, *John Bunyan, By the Author of 'Mark Rutherford'*, 1905; London: Thomas Nelson, n. d.

Wolfe, Don M., gen. ed., *The Complete Prose Works of John Milton*, 8 vols, New Haven and London: Yale University Press, 1953–82

Woolrych, Austin, *Soldiers and Statesmen: The General Council of the Army and its Debates, 1647–1648*, Oxford: Clarendon Press, 1987

Worden, Blair, *Roundhead Reputations: The English Civil Wars and the Passions of Posterity*, London: Penguin Books, 2002

Zinck, Arlette, 'Two Cree Translations of *The Pilgrim's Progress*', Paper presented to The International John Bunyan Society, Fourth Triennial Conference, The Open University and De Montfort University, Bedford, 1–5 September 2004

Index

Ackroyd, Peter, 21, 46–8
Addison, Joseph, 17, 56, 60
Alblas, Jacques B. H., 20
Althusser, Louis, 27
Altick, Richard D., 91
American Revolution, 187, 199, 205
Anglicanism, 55, 75, 78
antinomianism, 58, 60–1
Arber, Edward, 141
Arnold, Matthew, 40–1
Art Union of London, 88
Atkins, Robert, 200
Auden, W. H., 148–9
Augustanism, 165–6
Augustine, St., 70
Austen, Jane, 103, 149

Bacon, Francis, 75
Bain, Rev. J. A. Kerr, 113–15
Bamford, Samuel, 91
Baptists, 75, 128, 139, 142
Bastin, John, 88
Bebbington, D. W., 124
Barton, Bernard, 89
Beckett, Samuel, 22, 171–83 *passim*
Beddington, Jack, 193, 198–9
Bedford, 15, 39, 120–2, 129–31, 139–44, 210, 226
Bennett, Charles H., 74, 82
Bennett, Tony, 119
Bentley, G. E., 54, 83
Bewick, Thomas, 82
Bezer, John James, 18
Bible, 15, 23, 42, 48, 69, 101, 105, 107–8, 112, 116, 125, 150, 156–7, 166, 170, 221, 225–6
Birrell, Augustine, 124

Black, Rev. James, 102, 107–11, 113, 117
Blair Tony, 228
Blake, William, 53–4, 66, 147–8, 208
Blatchford, Robert, 127
Bloom, Harold, 54
Blunt, Anthony, 154
Boekholt, Johannes, 85
Bolam, Rev. Cecil E., 102
Boswell, James, 165
Bray, Warwick, 156
Breen, T. H., 205
Brittain, Vera, 209–10
Brodier, Joy, 210
Bronte, Charlotte, 71
Brown, John, 82–3, 87, 138–43
Brown, Richard Danson, 22
Brown, Sylvia, 120
Brown, Terence, 152, 162
Browning, Robert, 155
Buchan, John, 72, 189
Bunyan, John,
    The Barren Fig Tree, 40
    Book for Boys and Girls, 71
    Doctrine of the Law and Grace Unfolded, 40
    Grace Abounding, 30–1, 42, 73, 125–6, 159–61
    The Heavenly Footman, 40
    The Holy War, 52, 216, 219, 221, 223–4
    The Life and Death of Mr Badman, 20, 85, 216, 223–5
    The Pilgrim's Progress (Part One), *passim*
    The Pilgrim's Progress (Part Two), 93, 96, 175–7, 194, 216, 224–5

Index

Bunyan Meeting House, 39, 72, 120, 138–40, 142
Bunyan Museum, 139–40
Burder, George, 86, 123
Burney, Frances, 102
Bush, President George W., 217
Byron, Lord, 49, 149

Calvinism, 28–9, 40, 42, 73
Camden, Vera, 159
Campbell, Julie, 22
Cambridge University Press, 104, 112
capitalism, 27, 35, 110, 113, 214
Carlyle, Thomas, 71
Carroll, Lewis, 46–7
Carson, Edward, 152
Cash, Johnny, 148
Cassell Publishers, 112
Catholic Emancipation, 55
Catholicism, 27, 55, 70, 152, 219
Chambers, Douglas, 122
Chandler, James, 57–8
Charles I, King, 59
Charles II, King, 52, 59, 65
Chartism, 15, 18, 39, 73, 75, 107–8, 213–14
Chaucer, Geoffrey, 70, 191–2
Chesterton, G. K., 192, 208
Christian Coalition (USA), 227
Christian Socialism, 75, 77
Christie, Ian, 185, 187–8, 190–2, 194–7, 201–2, 206–8
Church of Ireland, 22, 149
Churchill, Sir Winston, 191, 201, 206
Clarendon Press, 116
Civil War (see English Revolution)
Clark, David, J., 202
Clark, Jonathan, 56, 205
Clarke, Samuel, 224
Clarkson, Lawrence, 61
Clephane, Margaret Maclean, 53
Cobbett, William, 57
Cockett, C. Bernard, 129, 139, 142–3

Cold War, 201
Coleridge, Samuel Taylor, 18, 49–51, 59, 67, 165, 167, 186
Collé-Bak, Nathalie, 21, 81
Colley, Linda, 205, 207
Collmer, Robert G., 213
Colls, Robert, 205
Comfort, Lance, 194
Commonwealth, 50
communism, 214
Conder, Claude Reignier, 86–7
Conder, Josiah, 89
Congregationalism, 139–40
conversion narrative, 32, 35
Cooper, Thomas, 39, 76, 214
Corporation Act, 55
Cotton, Dr. Nathaniel, 32
Coulton, Barbara, 155
Cowper, William, 20, 30–5
Crimean War, 76
Cromwell, Oliver, 60, 63
Cummings, E. E., 189
Cutt, Margaret Nancy, 124

Dalziel, George and Edward, 82
Damrosch, David, 119, 145
Dante Alighieri, 18, 79, 154, 166, 170
Davies, Michael, 23, 29, 62, 100–1, 126, 215
deconstruction, 20, 28
Dee, Sarah, 105
Defoe, Daniel, 20, 102
Deguilleville, Guillaume de, 74
Dent, Arthur, 70
Descartes, René, 121
Dickens, Charles, 20–1, 35–7, 72
Dissenting Academies, 128
Dixon, A. C., 218
Donne, John, 186
Douglas-Mackenzie, Mrs., 87
Doyle, Brian, 130
Dryden, John, 186

Index

Duckworth, Colin, 180–1
Durgnat, Raymond, 207–8

Eliot, George, 21–8, 38–9, 44, 72
Eliot, T. S., 148, 162
Elliott Stock (publishers), 116–17
Ellis, John, 195–7, 207
Ellis, Steve, 154
Ellis, William, 136
Engler, Balz, 200
English Revolution (Civil War), 49–50, 53, 58, 64–5
Erberry, William, 58
Erickson, Kathleen Powers, 16
evangelicalism, 15, 17, 22, 32, 51, 55, 119–45 *passim*, 152, 190, 217
existentialism, 45, 151, 155, 158, 162

Farlan, Abraham, 187, 199, 203
fascism, 155
feminism, 20
Feuerbach, Ludwig, 36
Fielding, Henry, 102, 128
Filmer, Sir Robert, 225
First World War, 58, 128, 189, 200–1
Firth, C. H., 122, 128
Flaxman, John, 83
Fleming, Victor, 192
Floyd, W., 89
Ford, John, 159
Foster, Albert J., 129
Fox, George, 63
Foxe, John, 57
Frankenheimer, John, 25
French Revolution, 50, 53–5, 185
Freud, Sigmund, 168–9
Froude, James Anthony, 74
Froude, Richard Hurrell, 74
Frye, Northrop, 73, 166, 170, 180
fundamentalism, 23, 213–28 *passim*
Fussell, Paul, 189

Gash, Norman, 56
Geer, Will, 25
Gifford, Douglas, 52
Gilpin, Joshua, 101, 103
Glorious Revolution (1688), 64, 206
Godwin, William, 66–7
Goring, Marius, 185
Gough-Yates, Kevin, 194, 207
Gow, Bonar A., 136
Great Awakening, 217
Greaves, Richard L., 20, 51, 58, 122, 189
Gupta, M. G., 144

Habeas Corpus, 202, 204–5
Habicht, Werner, 200
Hall, John, 86
Hammond, Mary, 22
Hampden, John, 65–6
Hardy, Thomas, 21, 72, 76–8
Harper, Charles G., 129
Harper, Sue, 201
Harrington, James, 50
Harrison, Frank Mott, 82, 87
Harvey, Rev. Kenneth D., 72
Haweis, Rev. R. H., 117
Hayley, William, 54
Hazlitt, William, 49–50, 54, 67, 151
Herbert, George, 162
Herreshoff, David, 213
Hill, Christopher, 16, 58, 122–3, 127, 189, 207, 213, 227
Hiller, Wendy, 192
historicism, 20
Hitler, Adolf, 200
Hobbes, Thomas, 60
Hobson, Paul, 58
Hodder and Stoughton (publishers), 113
Hofmeyr, Isabel, 19, 22, 120, 125, 213
Hogg, Alexander, 82
Holmes, William, 71
Holocaust, 210
Homeland Association, 142
Homer, 17, 73

Horne, Philip, 198
Hough, Graham, 151
House of Lords, 34
Howson, Rev. J. S., 99
Hudson, Rock, 25
Hughes, Glyn, 16
humanism, 28–9, 39, 149, 160–2
Hume, David, 17, 60–1, 64
Hunter, Kim, 185
hyperrealism, 127

Irving, Washington, 52
Irwin, John T., 147
Isherwood, Christopher, 149

James II, King, 65
Jenkins, Jerry B., 218
Jesus Christ, 30, 43, 110, 160–1, 217
Johns, David, 136
Johnson, Barbara, 100–1, 103, 105, 114, 189
Johnson, Samuel, 18, 102, 165–6
Judaism, 27
Jukes, John, 139
Jung, C. G., 23, 167, 169–70, 179–83
Junge, Alfred, 188

Karinthy, Frigyes, 198
Keating, Peter, 112
Keats, John, 186
Keeble, N. H., 20, 51–2
Keelin, Justice, 72
Kelman, John, 128
Kenyon, J. P., 204
Kettle, Arnold, 19, 121, 213
Keynes, Flora Ada, 140
Kingsley, Charles, 21, 72, 74–9, 82, 122, 128
Kipling, Rudyard, 208
Kitson, Peter, 50
Knott, John R. Jr., 47
Kroll, Richard, 121

LaHaye, Tim, 218
Latitudinarianism, 226
Lawrence, D. H., 46
Laws, Curtis Lee, 218
Le Sage, Alain René, 73
Leavis, Q. D., 91, 188
Lindsay, Jack, 213
Livesey, Roger, 186, 193
Locke, John, 204–5
London Missionary Society (LMS), 135–6
Luiken (or Luyken), Jan, 83
Lukács, Georg, 58
Lunsford, Sir Thomas, 64
Luther, Martin, 70
Luxon, Thomas, 62
Lydgate, John, 70
Lyotard, Jean-François, 222

McCalman, Ian, 56
Macaulay, Thomas Babington, 21, 49, 62–7, 94, 99–100, 127
McCoy, Gerard, 202
Macdonald, Kevin, 191, 193, 198, 206–7
McDonald, Peter, 150
Mackail, J. W., 77
McKechnie, James, 192
McKeon, Michael, 39, 121, 214
MacLennan, George, 34–5
Macmillan (publishers), 144
Macnab, Geoffrey, 190
MacNeice, Bishop John, 148, 152, 163
MacNeice, Louis, 22, 147–63
McVeagh, John, 214
Maguire, Rev. R., 112
Mallock, W. H., 38–9, 45
Manning, John, 71
Manning, Robert, 210
Marsden, George M., 217
Martin, John, 70, 94
Marvell, Andrew, 186
Marx, Karl, 72

Index

Marxism, 15, 23, 39, 72, 123, 213–14, 226–7
Mason, William, 105–7, 110, 117
Massey, Raymond, 199
Melanchthon, Philip, 70
Mellor, James, 127
Mellors, Wilfrid, 74
Melville, H., 89
Methodism, 127, 190
millenarianism, 60, 147, 213, 217–18
Milton, John, 17, 45, 50–1, 53, 64, 66, 170, 186–7
Ministry of Information, 193, 198–9
modernism, 153
modernity, 28, 31, 44, 107, 109, 158, 160, 162, 201, 209
Moor, Andrew, 190, 193, 197, 208
Morritt, John B., 52
Morton, Henry, 58–9
Moses, Henry, 88–9
Mubitana, Moses, 133–4
Murray, John, 94

Napoleon, 52
naturalism, 193
Naylor, James, 63
Nazis, 200, 205–7
Nelson, Thomas, (publishers), 105, 107, 115
neo-realism, 193
Neville, Henry, 50
New Labour, 228
New Model Army, 58, 65–6
New Testament, 112, 150
Newey, Vincent, 20–1, 31, 35, 38, 72
Newlyn, Lucy, 51, 54
Newman, Cardinal John Henry, 74
Newton, John, 31
Nicholes, Joseph, 50
Nisbet, James, 104, 109
Nishimura, Kazuko, 19
Niven, David, 185–6

nonconformism, 17, 19, 40, 54–7, 62, 65, 100–1, 123–5, 128, 141, 213–14, 225–6
Norvig, Gerda S., 83

Ogilby, John, 17
Old Testament, 112, 157
Operative Institution, 114
Orwell, George, 206
Owen, Robert, 57
Owens, W. R., 20, 90, 147
Oxford University Press, 81, 112, 116

Paine, Thomas, 57
Paisley, Rev. Ian, 227
Palmer, D. J., 128
pantheism, 44
Parfitt, George, 190
Pearson Publishers, 116–17
Piggin, Stuart, 124
Pilgrim Fathers, 27
Pitman Publishers, 116
Ponder, Nathaniel, 84–5
Pope Alexander, 180, 186
Porter, Vincent, 201
positivism, 38, 45
postcolonialism, 20
postmodernism, 20
Powell, Anthony, 91
Powell, Dilys, 207
Powell, Michael, 23, 185–211 *passim*
Poynter, Richard, 130–1
predestinarianism, 42
Presbyterianism, 55–6, 152
Pressburger, Emeric, 23, 185–211 *passim*
Primus, Richard, 209
Propp, Vladimir, 167
Protectorate, 60
Protestantism, 16, 19, 22–3, 27, 55, 70, 113–14, 125, 131–2, 137, 143, 148, 158, 160, 163, 214, 218–19, 226

psychoanalysis, 34, 168, 182
Puritanism, 25–6, 28, 35, 37, 40–2, 45, 67, 75, 109, 138, 150–2, 162–3, 188, 213

Quakers, 61
Qualls, Barry, 36, 71
Quarles, Francis, 71

Radama, King (of Madagascar), 135
RAF, 185, 204
Raleigh, Sir Walter, 70, 76, 186, 188, 194
Ralph, Arleane, 210
Ranavalona, King (of Madagascar), 135
Randolph, John, 25
Rank, J. Arthur, 190
Ranters, 61
realism, 20, 22, 119–45 *passim*, 150, 193, 195
Revolutions of 1848 (Europe), 108
Restoration, 17, 59, 62, 213, 227
Richardson, Samuel, 128
Rivington Publishers, 102, 115
Roe, Nicholas, 50–1
Rolls, Charles, 88
Romanticism, 16, 18, 31, 49–67 *passim*, 72, 85–6, 90, 123, 193
Rose, Jonathan, 72, 189
Rose, Samuel, 30
Rump Parliament, 60, 66
Rupert, Prince, 64
Rutherford, Mark (see William Hale White)
Ruthven, Malise, 216–17

Salmon, Edward G., 108
Salter, David, 185
Salzman, Paul, 121–2
Sambourne, Linley, 76
Sartre, Jean-Paul, 73
Sassoon, Siegfried, 190
Sawolke, Scott, 202

Scott, Sir Walter, 18, 21, 49–65, 67, 94
Second World War, 22–3, 58, 155, 185, 187, 200, 208–10
Selous, Henry C., 87–8
Sennett, Richard, 34–5
Shakespeare, William, 186–7, 197–8, 200
Sharpe, Robert J., 202, 204
Sharrock, Roger, 90, 167
Shaw, George Bernard, 208
Shelley, Percy Bysshe, 49, 186
Shields, Frederick J., 87
Sidney, Algernon, 50
Sim, Stuart, 23, 62, 216, 219, 227
Smiles, Samuel, 113
Smith, David E., 82, 200
Smollett, Tobias, 128
socialism, 39, 73, 75, 77, 149, 207
Soga, Tiyo, 135
Southey, Robert, 21, 49–51, 53, 55, 59, 61–7, 71, 94, 99–101, 103, 123
Spargo, Tamsin, 62, 120, 210
Spenser, Edmund, 18, 74–6, 150–1, 162, 166
Spinoza, Benedict de, 44
Spira, Francesco, 160
spiritual autobiography, 67, 127, 158
Spufford, Margaret, 91
Stachniewski, John, 28, 160
Sterne, Lawrence, 102
Stone, Lawrence, 34–5
Stothard, Thomas, 87, 93
Strobl, Gerwin, 200
Stuart, Lady Louise, 52
Sturt, John, 83
Sufism, 144
surrealism, 47, 199
Sutherland, James, 208
Sutherland, John, 55, 57
Swift, Jonathan, 102

Tennyson, Alfred Lord, 186
Test Act, 55

Index

Thackeray, William, 71
Thompson, E. P., 39, 54, 56–7, 205, 207, 214
Thorne, Susan, 124, 138
Tibbutt, H. G., 140
Toryism, 55–6, 207–8
Toynbee, Arnold, 79
Trump, David, 156
Turner, James, 121
Tyndale, William, 69

Unionism (Ulster), 152
Unitarians, 44, 78
United Nations, 209

Van Ghent, Dorothy, 121
Van 't Veld, Hendrick, 81, 120
Vance, Norman, 21, 78
Vane, Sir Henry, 63
Vaughan Williams, Ralph, 72–3, 77, 79, 210
Venables, Edmund, 116
Vincent, David, 91
Virgil, 17
Virtue, George, 104

Waite, Terry, 210
Walker, David, 21, 62, 219
Ward, Mary, 21, 72, 78–9, 112
Watt, Ian, 121
Welch, Robert, 152
Wells, H. G., 208
West, Alick, 213–14, 226
Wheen, Francis, 228
Whigs, 62–4, 66
White, Robert, 90
White, William Hale (Mark Rutherford), 19, 21, 39–46, 72
Williamson, Henry, 189
Wilson, Jean Moorcroft, 190
Winstanley, Gerard, 214
Wither, George, 71
Woolrych, Austin, 59
Worden, Blair, 50
Wordsworth, William, 44, 53, 186
Wren, Sir Christopher, 148
Wycliffe, John, 69

Yeats, W. B., 148, 152

Zinck, Arlette, 120

Religions and Discourse

Edited by James M. M. Francis

Religions and Discourse explores religious language in the major world faiths from various viewpoints, including semiotics, pragmatics and cognitive linguistics, and reflects on how it is situated within wider intellectual and cultural contexts. In particular a key issue is the role of figurative speech. Many fascinating metaphors originate in religion e.g. revelation as a 'gar-ment', apostasy as 'adultery', loving kindness as the 'circumcision of the heart'. Every religion rests its specific orientations upon symbols such as these, to name but a few. The series strives after the interdisciplinary ap-proach that brings together such diverse disciplines as religious studies, theology, sociology, philosophy, linguistics and literature, guided by an international editorial board of scholars representative of the aforemen-tioned disciplines. Though scholarly in its scope, the series also seeks to facilitate discussions pertaining to central religious issues in contemporary contexts.
The series will publish monographs and collected essays of a high scholarly standard.

Volume 1   Ralph Bisschops and James Francis (eds):
           Metaphor, Canon and Community. 307 pages. 1999.
           ISBN 3-906762-40-8 / US-ISBN 0-8204-4234-8

Volume 2   Lieven Boeve and Kurt Feyaerts (eds):
           Metaphor and God Talk. 291 pages. 1999.
           ISBN 3-906762-51-3 / US-ISBN 0-8204-4235-6

Volume 3   Jean-Pierre van Noppen: *Transforming Words.*
           248 pages. 1999. ISBN 3-906762-52-1 / US-ISBN 0-8204-4236-4

Volume 4   Robert Innes: *Discourses of the Self.*
           236 pages. 1999. ISBN 3-906762-53-X / US-ISBN 0-8204-4237-2

Volume 5   Noel Heather: *Religious Language and Critical Discourse Analysis.*
           319 pages. 2000. ISBN 3-906762-54-8 / US-ISBN 0-8204-4238-0

Volume 6   Stuart Sim and David Walker: *Bunyan and Authority.*
           239 pages. 2000. ISBN 3-906764-44-3 / US-ISBN 0-8204-4634-3

Volume 7   Simon Harrison: *Conceptions of Unity in
           Recent Ecumenical Discussion.* 282 pages. 2000.
           ISBN 3-906758-51-6 / US-ISBN 0-8204-5073-1

Volume 8   Gill Goulding: *On the Edge of Mystery.*
           256 pages. 2000. ISBN 3-906758-80-X / US-ISBN 0-8204-5087-1

Volume 9   Kune Biezeveld and Anne-Claire Mulder (eds.):
           Towards a Different Transcendence. 358 pages. 2001.
           ISBN 3-906765-66-0 / US-ISBN 0-8204-5303-X

Volume 10 George Newlands: *John and Donald Baillie: Transatlantic Theology.*
           451 pages. 2002. ISBN 3-906768-41-4 / US-ISBN 0-8204-5853-8

Volume 11 Kenneth Fleming: *Asian Christian Theologians in
           Dialogue with Buddhism.* 388 pages. 2002.
           ISBN 3-906768-42-2 / US-ISBN 0-8204-5854-6

Volume 12 N. H. Keeble (ed.): *John Bunyan: Reading Dissenting Writing.*
           277 pages. 2002. ISBN 3-906768-52-X / US-ISBN 0-8204-5864-3

Volume 13 Robert L. Platzner (ed.): *Gender, Tradition and Renewal.*
           165 pages. 2005. ISBN 3-906769-64-X / US-ISBN 0-8204-5901-1

Volume 14 Michael Ipgrave: *Trinity and Inter Faith Dialogue:
           Plenitude and Plurality.* 397 pages. 2003.
           ISBN 3-906769-77-1 / US-ISBN 0-8204-5914-3

Volume 15 Kurt Feyaerts (ed.): *The Bible through Metaphor and Translation:
           A Cognitive Semantic Perspective.* 298 pages. 2003.
           ISBN 3-906769-82-8 / US-ISBN 0-8204-5919-4

Volume 16 Andrew Britton and Peter Sedgwick: *Economic Theory and
           Christian Belief.* 310 pages. 2003.
           ISBN 3-03910-015-7 / US-ISBN 0-8204-6284-5

Volume 17 James M. M. Francis: *Adults as Children: Images of Childhood in the
           Ancient World and the New Testament.* 346 pages. 2006.
           ISBN 3-03910-020-3 / US-ISBN 0-8204-6289-6

Volume 18 David Jasper and George Newlands (eds):
           *Believing in the Text: Essays from the Centre for the Study of
           Literature, Theology and the Arts, University of Glasgow*
           248 pages. 2004. ISBN 3-03910-076-9 / US-ISBN 0-8204-6892-4

Volume 19 Leonardo De Chirico: *Evangelical Theological Perspectives on
           post-Vatican II Roman Catholicism*. 337 pages. 2003.
           ISBN 3-03910-145-5 / US-ISBN 0-8204-6955-6

Volume 20 Heather Ingman: *Women's Spirituality in the Twentieth Century:
           An Exploration through Fiction*. 232 pages. 2004.
           ISBN 3-03910-149-8 / US-ISBN 0-8204-6959-9

Volume 21 Ian R. Boyd: *Dogmatics among the Ruins: German Expressionism and
           the Enlightenment as Contexts for Karl Barth's Theological Development*.
           349 pages. 2004. ISBN 3-03910-147-1 / US-ISBN 0-8204-6957-2

Volume 22 Anne Dunan-Page: *Grace Overwhelming: John Bunyan, The Pilgrim's
           Progress and the Extremes of the Baptist Mind*. 355 pages. 2006.
           ISBN 3-03910-055-6 / US-ISBN 0-8204-6296-9

Volume 23 Malcolm Brown: *After the Market: Economics, Moral Agreement and
           the Churches' Mission*. 321 pages. 2004.
           ISBN 3-03910-154-4 / US-ISBN 0-8204-6964-5

Volume 24 Vivienne Blackburn: *Dietrich Bonhoeffer and Simone Weil:
           A Study in Christian Responsiveness*. 272 pages. 2004.
           ISBN 3-03910-253-2 / US-ISBN 0-8204-7182-8

Volume 25 Thomas G. Grenham: *The Unknown God: Religious and Theological
           Interculturation*. 320 pages. 2005.
           ISBN 3-03910-261-3 / US-ISBN 0-8204-7190-9

Volumes 26 & 27 Forthcoming.

Volume 28 James Barnett (ed.): *A Theology for Europe: The Churches and
           the European Institutions*. 294 pages. 2005.
           ISBN 3-03910-505-1 / US-ISBN 0-8204-7511-4

Volume 29 Thomas Hoebel: *Laity and Participation: A Theology of Being
           the Church*. 401 pages. 2006.
           ISBN 3-03910-503-5 / US-ISBN 0-8204-7509-2

Volume 30   Frances Shaw: *Discernment of Revelation in the Gospel of Matthew.*
370 pages. 2007.
ISBN 3-03910-564-7 / US-ISBN 0-8204-7591-2

Volumes 31 & 32 Forthcoming.

Volume 33   W. R. Owens and Stuart Sim (eds): *Reception, Appropriation, Recollection: Bunyan's Pilgrim's Progress.* 253 pages. 2007.
ISBN 3-03910-720-8 / US-ISBN 0-8204-7983-7